Poor Cottages
& Proud Palaces

The days that transient time has shut away in superseded calendars.

Horace, *Odes*, Book IV, 13.

Poor Cottages & Proud Palaces

The Life and Work of the Reverend Thomas Sockett of Petworth

1777~1859

Sheila Haines & Leigh Lawson

The Hastings Press

British Library Cataloguing in Publication Data:
A catalogue record for this book is available from the British Library

ISBN 978-1-904109-16-7

Published 2007
The Hastings Press
PO Box 96 Hastings TN34 1GQ
hastings.press@virgin.net
www.hastingspress.co.uk

Set in Garamond
Printed by TJ International, Padstow, England

Cover illustration: Petworth, Sussex, with the canal and Lord Egremont's seat c1792, by Hendrik de Cort. Photographed by Philip J Brittan.
Cover design by Richard Lawson.

THOMAS SOCKETT

ACKNOWLEDGEMENTS

After the publication in the year 2000 of two books, *Assisting Emigration to Upper Canada* and *English Immigrant Voices*, on the history of the Petworth Emigration Scheme it seemed appropriate to look at the man responsible for the scheme's conception and implementation, the rector of Petworth, Thomas Sockett. This project owes its conception and completion above all to the Jackman Foundation of Toronto and we wish to acknowledge the generous financial assistance and encouragement given by the Foundation and especially that of the Reverend Edward J.R. Jackman.

We also wish to warmly acknowledge our debt to Lord Egremont who kindly gave us permission to use a wealth of material from the Petworth House archives. Alison McCann, the archivist in charge of the collection, gave us much knowledgeable advice and transported quantities of documents between Petworth House and the West Sussex Record Office on our behalf. Nancy and Gary Wilson uncovered a treasure trove of material in the Archives of Ontario and generously shared it with us.

Our thanks are also due to Charlotte Kershaw of Strutt and Parker, Lewes; and Malcolm Lill for arranging access to Sheffield Park House; and to Canon Derek and Mrs. Whitehead for showing us the library where Sockett would have worked with Lord Sheffield. Carole Muir kindly welcomed us and Canadian visitors to the Old Rectory, Petworth. We are indebted to Brian Rich for information on real tennis at Petworth and in London. We thank Alexandra Nightingale for her translations of the Latin and Greek in Sockett's text. The late Joe Haines transcribed Sockett's shorthand.

Other people whom we would like to thank personally are Philip Brittan, Barbara Brydone Calder, Wendy Cameron, Tony Crapnell, Elinor Gallant, the late Richard Grimsdale, Adrian Hancock, Peter Jerrome, Lester Jones, Richard Lawson, Kim Leslie, the late Cecil Longhurst, Tim McCann, Joan McKillop, Pat Osborn of Suffield Baptist Church in Olney, Julian Pooley, Rosie Ritchie, Allan Sewell, Clare Sockett, Peter Taylor, W. & D. Thompson.

The following institutions, museums, record offices and societies have given us help in our research and supplied material for the text and illustrations. Archives of Ontario, British and Foreign Society Archives, the British Library, Buckinghamshire Record Office, Bridgman Art Library, Cornwall Record Office, Courtauld Institute of Art, Cowper and Newton Museum at Olney, East London Family History Society,

East Sussex Record Office, the English Folk Dance and Song Society, Trustees of the Goodwood Collection, Guildhall Library Prints and Maps, Hampshire Record Office, Hertfordshire Record Office, Lambeth Palace Library, Lincolnshire Archives, Mitford Archives, National Archives at Kew (formerly the Public Record Office), National Trust, Probate Registry of Her Majesty's Court Service, Royal Pavilion Libraries and Museums at Brighton, Shropshire Archives, Stationers' Company Records, Surrey History Centre, University of Sussex Library, St George's Church at West Grinstead (transcript of memorial inscriptions), West Sussex Record Office, City of Westminster Archives Centre.

We appreciate the painstaking care and attention given to the text by our two editors; Mary McDougall Maude in Canada and Helena Wojtczak in the United Kingdom. Any continuing imperfections are entirely due to our intransigence.

The cover was designed by Richard Lawson, from a photograph taken by Philip Brittan of an original sepia and pencil drawing of 1792. The layout of the book was undertaken by Helena Wojtczak, our publisher, whom we thank for her patience and diplomacy at times of indecision and perversity.

Sheila Haines and Leigh Lawson, Sussex, 2007

ABOUT THE AUTHORS

SHEILA HAINES, MA PHD, was born in Crowborough, Sussex, and lives in Brighton. As a mature student she took a BA at the University of Sussex followed by postgraduate studies in English and History and a Certificate in Education. Sheila taught history for many years for the Centre for Continuing Education, University of Sussex. She edited *No Trifling Matter* (University of Sussex, 1990) an account of the voyage of the Petworth ship *British Tar*, written by members of her Worthing Adult Education study group. In 1990 she began research for Wordforce and the Jackman Foundation, Toronto, into the history of the Petworth Emigration Scheme; two books were published in Canada in 2000: *Assisting Emigration* and *English Immigrant Voices*. Since *No Trifling Matter* Sheila has had a continuing interest in the organiser of the Petworth scheme, the rector Thomas Sockett. She has lectured extensively and written many articles on emigration.

LEIGH LAWSON was born in Littlehampton, grew up in Horsham and now lives in Worthing. On leaving school, she studied textiles and theatre design at West Sussex College of Design and worked in theatre wardrobe for seven years. She was a contributor to *No Trifling Matter* and assisted greatly with the genealogical research in the UK for the database of emigrants, an important part of the Petworth books. She organised the Anglo–Canadian launch of these books at Petworth House in 2000. She has compiled an updated list of post-1837 emigrants on the Petworth Emigration website. At the request of the Hon. H. N. R. Jackman of Toronto, Leigh has written a genealogical history, *The Jackman Family in West Sussex 1565–1836*. Sheila and Leigh are partners in Kinship, which specialises in genealogical research in Sussex.

A NOTE ON CURRENCY

Prior to 1971, the UK's currency consisted of pounds (£), shillings (s) and pence (d). £1.8s.4d, for example, means one pound, eight shillings and four pence. There were twelve pence in a shilling and twenty shillings in a pound. A guinea was twenty-one shillings, or £1.1s.

CONTENTS

Introduction: A Plain Country Clergyman?

'The career of a plain country clergyman however long and useful his life may have been, is yet so uniform and his sphere of action so circumscribed so as to afford but few occurrences of striking effect as incidents in a biography', wrote the author of Sockett's obituary in the *Sussex Agricultural Express* for 26th March 1859.

As the Reverend Thomas Sockett died in 1859, Anthony Trollope began to write *Framley Parsonage*, the fourth of his Barchester novels, bestsellers with a sphere of action circumscribed by the nuances and minutiae of life in country parsonages and cathedral closes. In Trollope's hands, however, an account of everyday life among the clergy was of striking effect and certainly not plain nor dull to his many devoted readers. The reporter for the *Sussex Agricultural Express* did not try his hand at aping Trollope but was evidently daunted by his task and cobbled together a memoir of Sockett largely justified by the fact that Sockett had been rector of Petworth and Duncton for forty-three years. Yet an account of his life offered material enough for an enlightening biography, even one squeezed into a column in a local newspaper. Whoever gave the reporter his facts had many of them wrong or distorted, and the memoir is largely an account of the men of note who had been, in part, responsible for Sockett's career, rather than an account of the man himself.

Thomas Sockett's life had been neither uniform nor circumscribed, for he progressed geographically, socially and intellectually slow-by-slow from the East End of London to the Earl of Egremont's estate, Petworth House, in West Sussex. Born in 1777, the son of an impoverished — and eventually bankrupt — bookseller and stationer in Smithfield, he was taken as a boy to his mother's country in Buckinghamshire to live in a small cottage near William Cowper, the poet. Through an unexpected call for his skill as manipulator of an electrical shock machine, Tom, aged fifteen, made the acquaintance, through Cowper, of William Hayley and went, in 1792, to West Sussex as his secretary and as tutor-companion to Hayley's son, Thomas Alphonso. By 1794 Sockett was in East Sussex, at Sheffield Place, helping Lord Sheffield to put together Edward Gibbon's *Memoirs* and then, at the age of nineteen, by Hayley's recommendation, he moved into Petworth House as tutor to the three sons of the Earl of Egremont and Elizabeth Ilive. Between 1805 and 1807 he kept an illuminating journal of his life; he was by this time a friend of the Nicols of Pall Mall, booksellers to King George III, and of John Walter, the owner of *The Times*. He played tennis and hunted with the itinerant aristocratic French émigrés visiting Petworth and dined at neighbouring big houses.

When his sons no longer needed a tutor, the Earl of Egremont paid for Sockett to take a degree at Oxford University and gave him the livings of Duncton and Petworth in Sussex and North Scarle in Lincolnshire. He remained rector of these three parishes from 1816 until his death. For over sixty years, he worked first as an aide to the Earl and later to George Wyndham, his erstwhile pupil. He mixed with men and women of note in Petworth and London, yet found time to be a friend and support to his parishioners, not harassing them with visions of hell-fire but sitting by their fireside to enquire if they were getting enough meat pudding. He fought the stringencies of the new Poor Law of 1834 on their behalf and, to try to ameliorate their lot, settled some two thousand English emigrants in Canada through the Petworth Emigration Committee (henceforth, PEC). On the strength of the success of his emigration scheme he gave evidence to three government Select Committees.

There were experiences of which a casual reporter would not be told. Sockett knew the dire reality of the bailiffs calling, an experience that was to mark him for life. The mistake in the newspaper obituary over Sockett's birthplace may have been deliberate; 'one of the Midland counties' sounding vaguer and perhaps more desirable than the East End of London, although Sockett himself clearly entered in the 1851 Petworth census that he was born in the parish of St Botolph's, Middlesex, London.

Of Sockett as priest we know relatively little. There are seemingly no copies of his sermons in existence and little of his preaching or teaching. He was at Oxford long before the Tractarians came on the scene, and found in himself no calling to his father's Nonconformist enthusiasm. His comments to the Petworth Scientific and Literary Institution spoke of God as a remote albeit marvellous creator of a beautiful and intricate world and are largely the only expression we have of his faith, yet this remote and marvellous God draws near when Sockett admitted he would have found it incredibly hard to say 'Thy will be done' when his younger son, Henry, was sick unto death.[1] Such a cry may have been wrenched from him at the loss of his young wife, Sarah, and his children, little Sarah Ellen, Charlotte Agnes, and Frances.

In the year that Sockett died, Charles Darwin published *On the Origin of Species by Means of Natural Selection*. Darwin gave many churchmen a painful time, but probably would not have unduly agitated Sockett, who was always interested in new scientific and technological ideas. His arrival in Sussex was the result of his boyish ability with an electrical shock machine and he was to be interested in the development and application of electricity and magnetism until he was an old man, and was glad to see the coming of the railways in his time.

Sockett was to say: 'It is a sweetener of the bitters of this life when one has a chance of doing anything for a friend',[2] and he was to experience many sweet things in his progress through life, but there were also bitter things that he was, as a human being, called upon to cope with and endure.

Sockett Family Tree

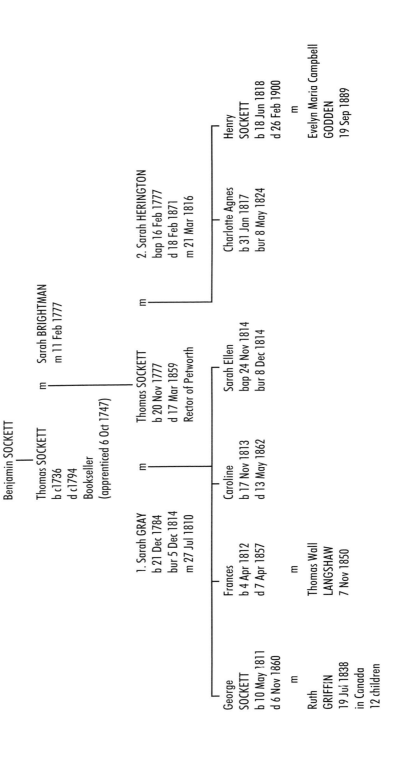

Benjamin SOCKETT

Thomas SOCKETT
b c1736
d c1794
Bookseller
(apprenticed 6 Oct 1747)

m

Sarah BRIGHTMAN
m 11 Feb 1777

Thomas SOCKETT
b 20 Nov 1777
d 17 Mar 1859
Rector of Petworth

1. Sarah GRAY
b 21 Dec 1784
bur 5 Dec 1814
m 27 Jul 1810

m

2. Sarah HERINGTON
bap 16 Feb 1777
d 18 Feb 1871
m 21 Mar 1816

m

George
SOCKETT
b 10 May 1811
d 6 Nov 1860

m

Ruth
GRIFFIN
19 Jul 1838
in Canada
12 children

Frances
b 4 Apr 1812
d 7 Apr 1857

m

Thomas Wall
LANGSHAW
7 Nov 1850

Caroline
b 17 Nov 1813
d 13 May 1862

Sarah Ellen
bap 24 Nov 1814
bur 8 Dec 1814

Charlotte Agnes
b 31 Jan 1817
bur 8 May 1824

Henry
SOCKETT
b 18 Jun 1818
d 26 Feb 1900

m

Evelyn Maria Campbell
GODDEN
19 Sep 1889

IN THE BEGINNING: SMITHFIELD, 1777

In the beginning Thomas was a town child, born in the city of London within the sound of the bells of St Mary-le-Bow and within walking distance of the River Thames and the docks. His birth on 20th November 1777 took place at 110 Aldersgate Street, a building now lost under the present-day Barbican Underground Station.[3] The family moved briefly to 4 Chiswell Street and then, when Tom was two, moved again to settle in nearby Cloth Fair, off Smithfield Square, where his father, Thomas Sockett, had a shop as a bookseller and stationer.[*]

Tom's parents, Thomas Sockett and Sarah Brightman, were married on 11th February 1777 at Newport Pagnell in Buckinghamshire.[†] Although they were Dissenters, by law they had to be married in the Church of England, but two witnesses at their wedding were William and Hannah Bull. William Bull was minister of Newport Independent Church. Tom was born nine months later.[‡] Sarah was the daughter of Henry and Dorcas Brightman of Olney, Buckinghamshire, and was about thirty-seven when she married and gave birth to Tom. There is no record of any brothers or sisters. It may have been a difficult birth, for Sarah seems to have been unwell after Tom's arrival, and her husband made her one of the newest health contrivances — an electrical shock machine. Tom was later to be described as 'an interesting youth ... who had been afflicted with great illness in his childhood'[4] and on one occasion was said to have a 'wry-neck'.[5] This may have been so, but he was later to play tennis very well, hunt, and enjoy building and sailing boats and does not seem to have been physically handicapped to any appreciable or noticeable extent.

The animals young Tom would have seen as a city child were the thousands being herded to Smithfield market for slaughter for the London meat market. The sounds of doomed cattle, pigs and sheep being driven along St John's Street and Cowcross Street and the cries of the drovers and butchers would have filled the air. Under foot was the blood and muck — in winter slippery and treacherous, in summer fly-ridden and foetid — a scene of seething life and death, as, in its own

---

[*] D. F. McKenzie, ed., *Stationers' Company Apprentices*, 3, 1701–1800 (Oxford Bibliographical Society, 1978). Sockett senior had been apprenticed by Benjamin Sockett, his father, to the stationer John Bailey of Coleman Street, just off London Wall.

[†] Newport Pagnell, Bucks, Marriage Register, Thos. Sockit, of the parish of St Michael, Queen hith [Queenhithe], and Sally Brightman of this Parish, spinster, were married in this Church by Licence this eleventh day of Febry in the year One Thousand Seven Hundred and Seventy Seven by me Robt. Watson Vicar.

[‡] Family Bible given by Thomas Sockett to his son, George Sockett.

way, was the ancient St Bartholomew's Hospital on the other side of Smithfield Square.

However, on 3rd September each year, Smithfield was transformed into St Bartholomew's Fair. No livestock, carriages, or coaches were allowed through the square, now thronged with crowds come to see the many sideshows. Tom, not yet a year old in 1778, was too young to appreciate the serpents that danced on silken ropes, but a year later he may have enjoyed 'Mr Hall's fine exhibition of stuffed animals and birds' or the menageries of 'wild beasts'. If there was money to spare, he could later have bought gingerbread, 'very fine with dutch gold on their different shaped ware', cheap toys, oysters and fruit. There were also Flockton's renowned wooden puppets. His Newfoundland dog fought the good fight against one devilish puppet and, having won, ran off with it.[6]

Have you seen

THE BEAUTIFUL DOLPHIN

The Performing Pig & the Mermaid?

If not, pray do! as the exhibition contains more variety than any other in England. Those ladies and gentlemen who may be pleased to honour it with a visit will be truly gratified.

TOBY,

The Swinish Philosopher, and Ladies' Fortune Teller.

That beautiful animal appears to be endowed with the natural sense of the human being. He is in colour the most beautiful of his race; in symmetry the most perfect; in temper the most docile; and far exceeds any thing yet seen for his intelligent performances. He is beyond all conception: he has a perfect knowledge of the alphabet, understands arithmetic, and will spell and cast accounts, tell the points of the globe, the dicebox, the hour by any person's watch, &c.

2. Advert for the Beautiful Dolphin et al.

The every-day market sheep pens were transformed by greenery, tables and chairs, and given fancy names — Fair Rosamund's Bower, the Imperial Hotel and the Brighton Pavilion. In these leafy bowers, sturdy women cooked sausages and other delicacies over charcoal braziers. Charles Lamb describes how boy chimney sweeps were treated every year 'in these little temporary parlours' to a 'feast of sausages with bread and ale'.[7]

The Sockett family was possibly another kind of presence at the fair. William Hone described, among the throng, a man selling Bible prints and cheap pamphlets with wood-cut illustrations and on another occasion an agent of a religious society, who 'was anxiously busy at the fair distributing a bill entitled "are you ready to die"'.[8] If Tom's mother and father deplored the riotous behaviour of the crowds, they may well have seen them as souls to be plucked from the burning, or at least plucked from the doctrines of the Roman Catholic Church and the sterile practices of the Church of England. There would have been other sellers of cheap literature at a penny a sheet; old fairy stories and rhymes for children; for adults descriptions of murders and the dying words of the hanged man with crude wood-cuts; books for fortune telling and the interpretation of dreams. As Tom grew up, the popular appeal and cheapness of such literature was taken up and used by varying sectors of the Christian church. The largely Dissenting and Evangelical Religious Tract Society, the Anglican Society for Promoting Christian Knowledge, the Quakers and other evangelizing societies increasingly used such literature in the first half of the nineteenth century to inform and reform an increasingly numerous and barely literate working population.

Thomas Sockett senior sold this kind of material among other books and stationery, although the material he stocked cost threepence or sixpence rather than a penny. Some of the pamphlets were copies of sermons, '*The Nature and Importance of Walking by Faith: Sermon*

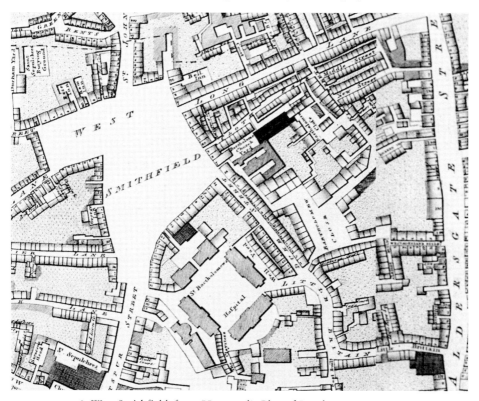

3. West Smithfield, from Horwood's Plan of London, 1792–1799.

delivered at the Annual Association of the Baptist Ministers and Churches, met at Nottingham, June 2nd, 1784..., by Andrew Fuller..., sold by ... T. Sockett, in Cloth Fair, West Smithfield, London'.[9] Sockett's bookshop was hard by the ancient church of St Bartholomew the Great, then a ruined shadow of its former self. Young Tom may have wandered through its gloomy depths, stopping to watch the blacksmith at work in the bricked-up north end and the letter-foundry in the Lady Chapel. He was not taken there to be baptised, nor to St Botolph's, his parish church, for his father and Sarah did not subscribe to infant baptism. They may have gone on Sundays to John Tower's nearby Independent or Congregational chapel in Bartholomew Close or to hear Mr Towle at his chapel at London Wall.[10]

One minister obviously dear to Sockett senior's heart was Henry Blaine. He had Blaine's 1783 pamphlet of thirty-four pages, entitled *A Plain Conversation between Poor John and Will the Thatcher. Designed for the Instruction of Plain Country Christians*, printed at his own expense in 1784 and offered it for sale at 3d. per copy or 20s. a hundred. This tract aimed, in stilted fashion, to be reader-friendly, consisting of a dialogue between two men meeting on their way home from work. Poor John, who has a firm grasp of the truth, confounds Will, the thatcher, who is a hazy member of the Church of England and dubious about the men who have recently been preaching in barns and the open air in his neighbourhood. John argues that poor men are often nearer to Christ: the New Testament does not tell of lord bishops, long robes, holy days, godfathers in church and above all infant baptism. He attacks the Church of England clergy:

> We have many younger sons of noble families who must be provided for, according to their birth, and church divinity is both genteel and profitable, and they who are too faint-hearted for the field, or too dull for the law, may wear a mitre with renown.

There was no need, John maintained, to go 'through a course of academical studies, turn over large volumes of school divinity, or consult men deeply read in science', while their parishioners were left to cold church services 'once a fortnight, or a month, performed with the hasty impatience of a young gentleman of small fortune devoted to the drudgery of curacy, who is forced to ride post every Sunday to three, four or five parishes, for a maintenance'. Humble folk were nearer to God and needed only to be able to read one chapter of the New Testament 'without any hard names', and salvation was 'as plain as God himself can make it'.[11]

Such enthusiasm, or ardent zeal, on Sockett senior's part may have later haunted his son but did not deflect him on his path in life. The bailiffs' arrival may have severely shaken his beliefs. Certainly, by the time he was well in his twenties, he reflected on 'that cheerful religious enthusiasm which comforted my poor father in all his afflictions'[12] but regretted that he personally did not have it. Thomas senior did not do well in his bookselling business, and the family frequently moved. In 1786, Sockett senior's address was given as the Ratcliffe Highway. One would certainly need to sell a great many pamphlets or sermons at a few pence each to make a living. Thomas Sockett was to be declared bankrupt, and in 1787 young Tom, aged ten, and his father and mother retreated fifty-five miles up the Great North Road to Weston Underwood in Buckinghamshire, his mother's countryside.

The Brightman family had lived in the area around Olney for generations. They were reasonably prosperous farmers and tradesmen with both Dissenting and Anglican links, and it was the Brightmans who provided a measure of practical and financial support in this period of Tom's life. Sarah had a sister, Elizabeth, and a brother, Henry, both still alive, who owned considerable property in Olney, Weston Underwood, and nearby Yardley Hastings.[13] Elizabeth was a Baptist; Henry was churchwarden in Weston Underwood parish church.[14] When the Sockett family arrived in 1787, they occupied a cottage, rented from Thomas Higgins, in the village of Weston Underwood, two miles west of Olney.[15] The cottage was small, having a land tax of 4s.0d. a year. A Mr Brightman, possibly Henry, paid £7.1s.1d. in the same village. It may have been small but it was desirable; one of the neighbours was William Cowper, the poet, who had fled from Olney to Weston Underwood in 1786 and lived nearby in Weston Lodge. Cowper wrote to his cousin, Hesketh: 'Mr. Socket lives in the small house to which you had once conceived a liking'.[16] The Socketts made a little money by taking in lodgers, one of whom was Mr Canniford, a prospective new parish vicar. In Olney he was greeted with delight after preaching but once, and 'hailed as the Sun by the Greenlanders after half a year of lamplight'[17] but was ultimately unsuccessful. Cowper took an instant dislike to him.

For Tom, the change from the city of London to rural Weston Underwood must have been an acute experience. Now the cattle and sheep spent at least part of their time grazing in the field and the pig in the orchard. The rowdy pleasures of St Bartholomew's Fair were far away, doubtless to William Cowper's great relief when he wrote: 'We dwell in a neat and comfortable abode in one of the prettiest villages in the kingdom'.[18] Nevertheless, the village was largely cut off in winter

Brightman Family Tree

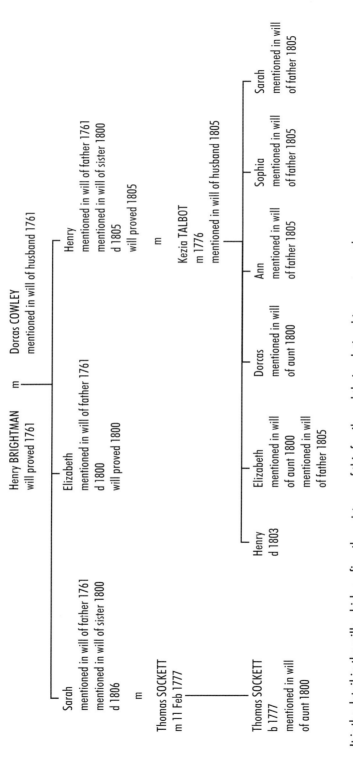

Henry BRIGHTMAN
will proved 1761

m

Dorcas COWLEY
mentioned in will of husband 1761

Sarah
mentioned in will of father 1761
mentioned in will of sister 1800
d 1806

m

Thomas SOCKETT
m 11 Feb 1777

Elizabeth
mentioned in will of father 1761
d 1800
will proved 1800

Henry
mentioned in will of father 1761
mentioned in will of sister 1800
d 1805
will proved 1805

m

Kezia TALBOT
m 1776
mentioned in will of husband 1805

Thomas SOCKETT
b 1777
mentioned in will
of aunt 1800

Henry
d 1803

Elizabeth
mentioned in will
of aunt 1800
mentioned in will
of father 1805

Dorcas
mentioned in will
of aunt 1800

Ann
mentioned in will
of father 1805

Sophia
mentioned in will
of father 1805

Sarah
mentioned in will
of father 1805

It is the detail in the wills which confirm the existence of this family and their relationships one to another.
They do not appear in parish baptismal registers being Non-Conformist.

by the terrible roads. These were taken in hand while Tom was there and may have offered some interest; noxious ponds were drained, roads were gravelled, and the turnpike from Olney to Weston Underwood greatly improved.[19] There was some excitement in April 1789 when the Throckmortons — the *only* family in the village so far as Cowper was aware — illuminated the front of their house, 'threw up many rockets, gave a large Bonfire and Beer to the people'[20] to celebrate the recovery of George III from his illness. Minor excitements were two turkeys fighting to the death in the orchard, the local hunt, and the arrival of the wagon which, given reasonable roads, could do the journey from the Windmill, St John Street, London, to Olney in a day.

Cowper was greatly preoccupied with his translations of Homer, and any village children whom Tom may have known were not noticed by Cowper in his letters. He certainly had little approval for the urchins of Olney, whom he felt stood in dire need of a good Sunday school; coupled with fear of the local women, especially those from Silver End, who were free in the use of their tongues and their nails.[21] Weston suffered, now and then, from drunken parties passing through the village late at night on their way home to Olney, breaking windows and knocking on doors.[22]

4. Weston Lodge, William Cowper's house at Weston Underwood, 1822. The Sockett family rented one of the nearby cottages.

The experience of being in desperate financial straits was traumatic for Tom and affected him for the rest of his life. Nevertheless, his experience of his family's poverty, his need for work, and his dependence on his own efforts and other people's goodwill, developed his sympathy for the plight of the poor that marked many of his actions in later life. He had one positive asset — a good education. His obituary said he had received 'the best education that the means and resources of the neighbourhood afforded'.[23] His education probably began in London although he does not appear, for example, on the lists of nearby Charterhouse. He may have gone to one of the often excellent Dissenting schools, or been largely taught by his father. Later, in Weston Underwood, he may have walked to Olney to be a pupil of Samuel Teedon, Cowper's impoverished schoolmaster friend, or gone to the acclaimed Congregational Newport Pagnell Academy, set up by William Bull and Samuel Greatheed, but this school was some distance away and, although it offered a good all-round education, it was intended to train boys for the Congregational ministry. Tom may have realised he did not wish to be a Congregational minister and anxiously looked elsewhere for help.

Indeed, it was here in Weston Underwood in 1792, when he was coming fifteen, that Tom met William Hayley, who provided the crucial turning-point in his life. Hayley — a poet of some note then if not now, — had come to Weston Underwood from Eartham, West Sussex, to visit Cowper — a poet whose reputation has survived. Hayley was working on a life of Milton and Cowper on a commentary on Milton's work. Hayley felt that cooperation between the two men would be fruitful. He was said to be a charming man. He cultivated the great and the good, but was a kind and staunch friend and took a number of less fortunate protégés under his wing. Lame and physically handicapped from childhood, his own experience fostered his concern for those in need of emotional and practical support. Such concern spurred his interest in young Tom.

One of Hayley's charitable missions was the provision of medical care for his dependents and neighbours, a desirable service in the small village of Eartham, where the nearest doctor was seven miles away in Chichester. His medical skill was called for during his visit to Cowper when Cowper's elderly companion and friend, Mary Unwin, had a second severe stroke. Hayley recommended the then increasingly fashionable electrical shock treatment. It speaks for the popularity of such treatment that Hayley and Cowper hoped to find a machine in the tiny village of Weston Underwood, and indeed Tom's mother had the one her husband had made for her. The practice of electrical shock treatment had been around for some time. John Wesley was using it in 1756:

> Tuesday, November 9 [London]. Having procured an apparatus on purpose, I ordered several persons to be electrified, who were ill of various disorders; some of whom found immediate, some a gradual cure. From this time I appointed, first some hours in every week, and afterward an hour in every day, wherein any that desired it, might try the virtue of this surprising medicine ...[24]

Hayley had used his apparatus in 1777 on his wife, Eliza, as a 'sovereign cure' for her 'royal fingers'[25] and had been using it regularly on his neighbours in Eartham. Sockett's machine had not been taken away by the bailiffs; perhaps, as Cowper said, 'not knowing why I presume and much less who would want it'.[26] It consisted of a glass cylinder against which a leather cushion and a flap of silk gave off an electrical charge when rotated by a crank handle. A machine of some size, and Tom would need to carry it carefully and with some effort around to Cowper's house. It was perhaps significant that it was the fourteen-year-old boy who was au fait with its use.

5. The electrostatic machine.

Tom asked Hayley if he could find him a post as a clerk in the city, for he did not wish to be a burden to his parents (and he may have wanted to return to London). If Hayley had done as he asked, instead of taking him back to Eartham, then Tom's future life would have been very different. In 1792, apart from his possible physical handicap and his financial distress, it was his youth, his good eyesight, and ability to write a good hand that recommended Tom as a likely lad to Hayley.[27] He was kind to his protégés but he was also prudent and pragmatic. Tom offered skills as a companion, a tutor, and a secretary. Hayley was in financial straits too, and the boy could be taken in as a kindness — with his keep provided but little or no money. Hayley wanted a companion for his son, Thomas Alphonso, now aged eleven, who was educated at home by his father. Previous attempts to provide Thomas Alphonso with a companion had come to nothing. Tom Sockett, who was three years older, would not only be a companion but also a tutor, for he was said to be 'deep in arithmetic'[28] and also had some Latin and French. In return, he could acquire some Greek from both Hayleys, father and son.

If Tom had been educated at a Dissenting school or academy he would have learned arithmetic and science, subjects that were almost entirely absent from the classics-based curriculum of a Church of England school or college. His ability to write a good hand would also have been encouraged as a desirable skill for a boy destined for trade or the office, careers to which the Dissenter often aspired but the upper middle-class and aristocratic family spurned. Such families did not value good handwriting; their secretaries and clerks provided this. Tom could also see, and Hayley could make good use of a secretary for his own eyesight had been bad since he had the fever as a child. Inflamed and infected eyes were endemic in the eighteenth century and were exacerbated by poor artificial light. It was, therefore, with a mixture of humanitarian and pragmatic motives that Hayley proposed to the Sockett family that he take young Tom home with him to Sussex.

LITTLE TOM AND TOM THE GREATER: EARTHAM, 1792

They went first, however, to London to stay with George Romney, the fashionable portrait painter, at his house in Cavendish Square. Hayley was energetically embarking on a lengthy campaign to squeeze a pension out of the government for Cowper and had on this occasion a frustrating interview with Cowper's erstwhile friend, Lord Thurlow, the Lord Chancellor. Hayley had been friends with Romney, another of his protégés, since the mid 1770s when he decided the painter was 'in need of the council of a frank and faithful monitor to encourage him and pay attention to his health'.[29] Romney paid annual autumn visits for some fifteen years to Eartham, where there was a painting room set aside for him, and he was to visit Sussex again in the ensuing autumn.

By 10th June Tom and Hayley came home to the horses, dogs, cats, and servants at Eartham.[30] To Cowper, who came to visit two months later from the 'snug concealment of Weston Underwood',[31] the village appeared to be surrounded by 'wild hills that aspire to be mountains, cover'd with vast unfrequented woods and here and there affording a peep between their summits at the distant ocean'.[32] This may have been the first time that Tom had seen the sea, and the village may have seemed remote and wild to him too after a childhood spent in Smithfield and relatively civilised Buckinghamshire.

6. Hayley's house at Eartham, 1792.

7. William Hayley, by George Romney.

In 1801 the parishioners numbered 114. Hayley's father had bought the land and house in 1743 as a summer residence. After his father's death, William went to live permanently at Eartham, enlarging the house by adding a library and billiards room, planting the gardens, and building a greenhouse and a covered, hundred-foot riding room in the grounds screened on three sides by foliage, with a broad, gravel walk on the south with extensive views of the sea. Here Hayley could exercise himself and his horses in wet weather. He was a keen horseman and was reported to ride with his umbrella up — in bad weather as protection and in good weather as a parasol to guard his eyes from the sun'.[33] When Tom arrived in 1792, Romney had a new painting room built at the end of this riding room, with a good north light and a fireplace.

The household young Tom Sockett joined was unconventional. Thomas Alphonso Hayley was the son of Mary Cockerell, Hayley's housekeeper, although his wife Eliza, living away in Derby, was always referred to as Mama by Thomas and his father. Mark Anthony Lower in his *Worthies of Sussex* (1865) says that Thomas was told he was an adopted child.[34] He had certainly taken Hayley's name, although it must have been fairly common knowledge locally that Mary was Tom's mother, as he was baptised on 5th November 1780 at nearby Walberton as the child of Mary Cockerell.* Thomas Alphonso gives no indication in his letters of being aware of his real mother, but he was fond of Mary and, when he went away to school after 1793, his letters home contain affectionate messages for 'my dear friend'.[35] Mary Cockerell was placed in a difficult and ambivalent position but perhaps she was pleased enough to have Tom in good care, with good prospects, and under her motherly eye to endure the falsity of her position. When Hayley sold the house at Eartham in 1803, he left Mary Cockerell her cottage, some farm buildings and a field.[36]

The regime at Eartham was austere. Cowper remarked that Hayley, when a guest at Weston Underwood, lived largely on water and mustard. Johnson — a not entirely unbiased commentator — spoke bitterly of 'the stale bread, sour beer and almost raw beef' dished up by the 'skin-flint housekeeper'[37] that he and Cowper and Mary Unwin endured at Eartham in August 1792. This opinion of Mary Cockerell as housekeeper was ameliorated, however, by the acclaimed sausages, hog puddings and apples, and a reputed ointment for chilblains, that she later sent to London when Thomas Alphonso was there in 1797. She may well have appeared as a skinflint for, as Hayley admitted, his finances were not 'in a very flourishing state' in 1792.[38]

* Walberton Parish Register, WRSO, PAR 202/1/1/3.

Hayley believed in fresh air and exercise. An early riser, he took a dish of coffee at 4:00 a.m. before walking in his garden in summer and winter. One guest reported that, when the ground was covered with snow, Hayley outside thoughtfully repeatedly threw up the sash of his friend's sleeping room on the ground floor to give him the benefit of the morning air'.[39] Cowper and Mary Unwin certainly seem to have shivered a good deal during their stay and found Eartham of 'a melancholy cast',[40] particularly when the weather turned wet and windy in September. The fireplace installed in Romney's new painting room was a great indulgence from Hayley to his friend.

The two boys probably did not notice the cold and austerity as much as the invalid Cowpers, but even they had their limits for they shuddered at the thought of the cold shower bath installed in a tower in the hall by December 1792 and used by Hayley every morning.[41] Tom may have enjoyed sea-bathing rather more, for Hayley had a cottage at Felpham and was keen on swimming for himself, the boys and Romney. The two Toms also had fresh air and exercise together in the north woods with Thomas Alphonso's pony, Bruno, riding and jumping him over the fallen trees. Possibly Tom learned to ride here at Eartham although he may already have done so at Weston Underwood. There were also lessons with Hayley, who would not let his son go to public school where he himself had been so very unhappy. The little boy was taught at home and was reputed to have learned Latin when he was four and started Greek at five. Hayley said that the two boys were good friends from the beginning. Tom seems to have been homesick in the early days, for letters come and go as often as possible between himself and his parents. Tom was said on occasion to be 'a little grieved' at his mother's and father's silence.[42] His parents were intermittently in Weston Underwood and London where Sockett senior was setting up a shop in the Ratcliffe Highway for selling lace; presumably aided by one of the Brightman relations involved in the Olney lace trade. Sarah was anxious about her son and visited Cowper soon after Tom's departure:

> Mrs. Sockett call'd on me yesterday and sat with me about a quarter of an hour. She sends her love to her son and expresses herself completely happy in his situation. I assur'd her she had all the reason in the world to be so and she believed me.[43]

Cowper and Mary Unwin were a link with home when they arrived at Eartham early in August after a three-day coach journey. Cowper endured the journey with the help of nightly doses of laudanum at the inns en route, and the party, including John Johnson,* Sam the servant with his wife, and the spaniel, Beau, arrived late in the evening of 3rd August, Cowper in a state of collapse by the final stage of the journey from Petworth over the tremendous height of Duncton Hill looming in the moonlight.

They brought messages and letters for Tom from his parents. The electrical machine came too, or perhaps they used Hayley's own, for the treatment on Mary Unwin went on daily, and on fine days the two Toms, like 'two griffins',[44] pulled her around the garden in a little carriage. As well as the Cowper party there were other visitors to Eartham during that summer — in spite of Hayley's financial situation — including Romney from London; Charlotte Smith, the novelist, from Brighton;[45] and the poet James Hurdis from Bishopstone. There were visits to Petworth House — the friendly palace† — and the seashore.

The house was a scene of artistic and cultural activity. After an early breakfast — early for Cowper but late for Hayley — the two men worked in the library on their projected studies of Milton; any warmth from the fugitive sun kept at bay by Venetian blinds installed to protect Hayley's sore eyes. Romney worked in his painting house on crayon portraits of Cowper and Charlotte Smith. Charlotte worked on the opening chapters of her latest novel, *The Old Manor House*, writing twenty pages every morning and reading the latest instalments to the assembled party in the evening. She was indebted to Hayley and Cowper for their help in the publication of her first work, *Elegiac Sonnets*, in 1784 and for Hayley's encouragement of her ensuing literary and financial success. She and Hayley had grown up in the same neighbourhood. After her arranged marriage at the age of fifteen to Benjamin Smith, she had twelve children and endured financial trouble and distress from her husband's extravagance before the couple separated and Charlotte came back to Sussex.[46]

How much did this cultural atmosphere rub off on the two young Toms? They had both grown up in a world of books and might well have enjoyed the readings from the opening chapters of *The Old Manor House*. The scene was obviously set in the nearby countryside and there were lively accounts of two boys fishing for minnows, hunting cats and shooting one of the guinea hens. Charlotte had sons of her own and may well have been drawing on her own experience, but perhaps she was observing the two boys around her, and the description of the lumber room that housed the leaping bar for the horses, cricket gear,

---

* Johnson was Cowper's first cousin once removed on his mother's side.

† Hayley frequently uses the term 'friendly palace' as a description of Petworth House; see William Hayley, *Memoirs*, 480

8. George Romney 1784. Self portrait.

and the gamekeeper's nets and rods, may well have been drawn from a recognisable room at Eartham.

The two Toms may have enjoyed her description of the frissons of the haunted chapel, the ghostly cellars and secret stairway, but when the beautiful, if tear-sodden, Monimia began to dominate the scene they may have gone away to play 'coits' or billiards. Charlotte's attitude to the boys may have been indulgent, or it might have been one of exhausted apathy after her experiences with her own sons. Both boys were on friendly terms with Cowper and, after his visit to Eartham, he asked to be remembered to 'my best of Critics little Tom and to Tom the greater'.[47]

For Tom, on his first long time away from home, the unconventional ambience of the household may have felt comfortable. He did not find himself in a morally or socially straight-laced society. Hayley, Romney and Charlotte were all separated from their respective spouses, and Cowper and Mary Unwin were not a conventional couple. None of the group, apart from Hurdis, had orthodox Church of England allegiances, but Hayley pointed out that, although he was continually absent from church, he did read the church service every Sunday to the domestics detained at home.[48] Tom's Dissenting background would have been perfectly acceptable to Cowper's and Mrs Unwin's evangelical beliefs. Romney's family background, like Tom's, was trade.

Nevertheless, Tom was only a companion-cum-servant, dependent for his bread — and perhaps some butter — and perpetually answerable to other people's wishes and plans. Hayley asked Cowper to make it plain to Tom's father, on his return to Weston Underwood, 'against a notion that his son's establishment' with him would be permanent. Cowper himself was fond of Tom, assuring him in his letters that he was not forgotten, but it was the little man, Thomas Alphonso, who received a present from Cowper of a 'smart pocket-book with scissars [sic], pencil etc'.[49]

The house party broke up in September 1792. Romney went home to London with his usual plethora of portraits and sketches; many of them destined to be unfinished. Charlotte Smith went back to Brighton, and on Monday, September 17th, Cowper and Mary Unwin set off for Weston Underwood. It was a pouring wet morning and Hayley, Thomas Alphonso, and Tom went through the north woods to give the party a last farewell on their road to Kingston.

During the forthcoming year, as well as the routine of lessons and exercise, Tom took a more and more defined role as secretary to Hayley, who continued his campaign for Cowper's proposed pension with

Wyndham Family Tree

George O'Brien WYNDHAM
3rd Earl of Egremont
b 1751
d 1837

m

Elizabeth ILIVE
b c1769
d 1822
m 1801

George
b 1787
d 1869
1st Lord Leconfield

m

Mary
BLUNT
m 1815

Frances
b 1789
d 1848

m

Charles Merrik
BURRELL
m 1808

Henry
b 1790
d 1860

m

Elizabeth
SOMERSET
m 1812

Edward
b 1792
d 1792

William
b 1793
d 1794

Charlotte
b 1795
d 1870

m

John
KING
m 1823

Charles
b 1796
d 1866

m

Elizabeth
SCOTT
daughter of
6th Lord Polwarth
m 1835

Elizabeth
b c1802
d 1803

lengthy letters to Lord Thurlow, Earl Spencer, and the Prime Minister, William Pitt. There were also excursions to lectures in Chichester, and a visit from Edward Gibbon, the historian, en route to Petworth House. He was a constant visitor to Sussex, for his father had lived just over the Hampshire border in Buriton. Gibbon was on visiting terms with the Earl of Egremont at Petworth, and had first visited Hayley at Eartham in 1781 after the publication of the second and third volumes of *The Decline and Fall of the Roman Empire*. Hayley wrote a sonnet in Gibbon's honour:

> An English sparrow, pert and free,
> Who chirps beneath his native tree,
> Hearing the Roman eagle's near,
> And feeling more respect than fear,
> Thus, with united love and awe,
> Invites him to his shed of straw. *

It was during this time that Tom himself would have first gone to Petworth, the town and house that were later to be his home for over sixty years. There was constant coming and going between Eartham and the 'friendly palace' at Petworth. Years later, Sockett was to speak with feeling of the people of the town: 'men whom I have known from their boyhood, who were boys with myself; men whose habits I know, into whose cottages I frequently walk, and at the side of whose fire I often sit'.[50] Many of these cottages in 1792 were rough and ready in the extreme. A visitor to Petworth House from London thirty years later was to speak scathingly of the

> most uncouth and unsightly of villages, named Petworth, consisting of dwellings (houses the inhabitants probably call them) ... the largest looking like prisons for the confinement of malefactors the smallest like sheds for the shelter of animals ... all closely and confusedly huddled together ...[51]

He found the boors and clowns of Petworth rude and uncouth; nevertheless, this critical visitor found Petworth Park and Petworth House a scene of enchantment and beauty, and young Tom visiting in 1792 was doubtless similarly impressed as he rode into the stable yard and

---

* See Gibbon's notes to chapters VII and VIII of his *Memoirs*: '[Hayley] afterwards thanked me in verse for my second and third volumes, and in the summer of 1781, the Roman eagle (a proud title) accepted the invitation of the English sparrow, who chirped in the groves of Eartham'.

saw the park and pleasure grounds, which had been laid out by Capability Brown in the 1750s, and the long façade of the great house, rebuilt in the late seventeenth century.

It was indeed a friendly palace for the park was open to all, and the doors of the house stood open to countless visitors, including Hayley, his family, and friends. The family Tom found at Petworth in 1792 was extensive. The Earl of Egremont was forty-one. He had inherited Petworth House when he was twelve, along with estates in Sussex, Wiltshire, Somerset, Yorkshire and Cumberland, and Irish estates later, in 1774. Elizabeth Ilive, the mother-to-be of eight of the Earl's children was twenty-four. George, their eldest son, was five years old. His life was to be bound up with Tom Sockett's, first as his pupil, and later, as heir to Petworth, as his master; although doubtless as the two boys aged five and fifteen regarded each other they would have been amazed to hear it. In the nursery there was Frances, the eldest daughter, aged three, and Henry, aged two. The latest little boy, Edward, was born and died in 1792. During Tom's stay at Eartham, there would be three more children, William, born in 1793, Charlotte, born in 1795, and Charles, born in 1796. William died in February 1794. He was William Hayley's godson, and Elizabeth Ilive and the other children were said to have stayed with Hayley at Eartham until after the baby's funeral.[52] Tom may have found the number of children around Petworth House bewildering for there were more of the Earl's children with other mothers. The Earl was reputed to have had a considerable number of illegitimate children, including four or five by Elizabeth Fox of Brighton.

In the autumn of 1793, Thomas Alphonso went away to school, his father wishing him to have 'some intercourse with various young persons of elegant manners'.[53] Tom Sockett apparently did not fill this criterion nor did the little children at Petworth. Mr Ward's Academy at Mickleover included quantities of dancing and elocution in its curriculum, and 'Mama' provided a home from home in nearby Derby. What happened to Tom Sockett? Hayley was away from Eartham for much of the winter of 1793/94. Thomas Alphonso wrote to his father in November 1793: 'I am glad to hear that you have such a good prospect of a place for your late secretary',[54] and again from Derby: 'I shall be much obliged to you for Socket's direction which when I know I will write to him'.[55] It is possible that he went to be a temporary assistant secretary to Samuel Rose, Cowper's godson and a young up-and-coming lawyer in London. Rose was made responsible by Cowper for giving Tom money to buy a new electrical machine, on the assumption that Rose knew where Tom was, and they arrived together at Sheffield Park in the summer of 1794 to work on the Gibbon manuscript. After Rose's premature death in 1804, Mrs Rose and Sockett maintained a correspondence; she wrote to Sockett after his mother died in 1806.

Or it may have been at this point that Sockett first encountered the Nicols. George Nicol, the Pall Mall bookseller and publisher, was engaged in 1793 and 1794 with printing and publishing Hayley's *Life of Milton*, and perhaps Tom was taken on as a temporary printer's assistant. He knew Hayley's handwriting and had helped him write the manuscript. George Nicol had problems with the book, not so much with the text but with Hayley's commentary. Much of it, Nicol said, was 'written in a strong spirit of republicanism'[56] and, as bookseller to the King, he was reluctant to print it. In the end he compromised. Two versions were printed — one purged of its troublesome context and the other largely untouched.

9 Sheffield Place

SHEFFIELD PARK, 1794: SCRIBBLE, SCRIBBLE, SCRIBBLE

In the summer of 1794 Tom was seconded to help Lord Sheffield, of Sheffield Park, some thirty miles across the county in East Sussex, write a memoir of Edward Gibbon, Lord Sheffield's friend and the acclaimed author of *The Decline and Fall of the Roman Empire*.* The Gibbon, as he was affectionately referred to by Sheffield, had died in London in January 1794. He was interred in Fletching parish church, at the gates to the Sheffield estate, and had bequeathed some personal papers to Lord Sheffield with leave to publish them.

Tom would have had a difficult ride across the county on the notoriously muddy roads — as he was to recall himself, it was out of the question at the end of the eighteenth century 'to pass with wheels' in the Sussex Weald[57] — before he came to the park gates and reported to William Virgo and his wife at the lodge. Sheffield Place was bought in 1769 by John Baker Holroyd; he was created Baron Sheffield in 1780 and became Earl Sheffield in 1816. Sheffield Park consisted of 5,000 or 6,000 acres of grassland, lakes, extensive timber, and gardens of some hundred acres. Lord Sheffield was a prominent farmer and landowner. Arthur Young, the agriculturist and journalist, included Sheffield Park as well as Petworth on his visiting list when he was out in the field gathering material for his *Annals of Agriculture*. The first Lady Sheffield, Abigail Way, had died the year before Tom arrived, leaving two daughters, Maria Josepha and Louise.

Maria, back in Sussex after a stay in London, records Tom's arrival in disparaging terms: 'the wry necked secretary is an acquisition lately made, and intended for Country use'. The fact that he was only sixteen was a comfort, for being so young he was put to live with the servants: 'it would have been very unpleasant to have a Person in that Situation one of us'.[58]

Catherine Maynard, the housekeeper, held sway in the servants' hall. Her daughter, Marina, was aptly named as she had been born, amidst some excitement, on 6th November 1791 on board the packet-boat between Calais and Dover as Lord Sheffield and his family returned from a trip to visit Gibbon in Lausanne. Lady Sheffield assisted at

---

* In his introduction to his abridged version of *The Decline and Fall …* (Harmondsworth: Penguin Classic, 1985), Dero Saunders quotes a possibly apocryphal story to the effect that, when Gibbon presented the second volume of his history to the Duke of Gloucester, the duke exclaimed good-naturedly: 'Another damned thick, square book! Always scribble, scribble, scribble! Eh, Mr Gibbon?'

the birth and Maria contributed her flannel petticoat and 'served as a pillow'.* [59]

As Tom arrived at Sheffield Park, Marina, now three years old, was recovering from whooping cough. Other servants were recovering from mass vaccination for smallpox, a procedure widely promoted by local landowners for the protection of their servants and tenants as well as their own children. There had been an epidemic of smallpox in the area; 2,500 people had been vaccinated in nearby Lewes. Mr Barr, the Sheffield Park physician, charged half a guinea a piece to vaccinate, among others, Will Virgo and the Virgo children;† Dick and another stable boy; Nanny, the kitchen maid; Mary Fleming;‡ Mr Lupton's little girl; the little Porters; and the gardener's baby, one month old. The servants were confined to the farmhouse, as a pest-house, whilst the vaccination took its course and were probably vaccinated one from another, a procedure recommended by Jenner to the Earl of Egremont, for Jenner considered vaccine soon lost its specific effects 'when dried and exposed to the air'. [60] If Tom was not vaccinated as a child in London, he may have been included in the mass vaccination organised early in 1788 by the overseer of the parish of Weston Underwood. 'No circumstance whatever was permitted to exempt the Inhabitants of Weston', wrote Cowper. 'The old as well as the young, and the pregnant as well as they who had only themselves within them, have all been inoculated'. [61]

Conditions in the servants' hall at Sheffield Park were far less austere than those at Eartham, and the food under the superintendence of Mrs Harrison, the cook, was more abundant and satisfying for a growing boy. Tom was probably far happier eating 'boyld beef, shoulder of mutton and pigg's offal', from the Sheffield Park farm, around the servants' table than partaking of 'ribbs of pork', turkeys, geese and pheasants at My Lord's table with the scornful Maria Josepha. [62] Doubtless helpings of the latter dishes did unofficially come the way of the servants — and there were vegetables and fruit from the garden. Maria reported

---

* Catherine Maynard was maid to Lady Sheffield during this trip to the continent. Did she not realise she was pregnant when the party set off in June 1791? In any event her pregnancy may have accounted for her being extremely sick on the thirty-seven-hour journey over the Channel from Brighton to Dieppe. Perhaps she expected to be home earlier than she was, although she nearly made it. The baby was baptised at Fletching on 10th December 1791, the daughter of John and Catherine Maynard, with a note as to the circumstance of her birth on the *British Fair*, Capt. Samson, Commander, on its way from Calais, 6th November.

† Possibly Mary Virgo, baptised in 1792, and her brother Edward, baptised in 1793 at Fletching. East Sussex Record Office (ESRO), PAR 329, Baptisms 1655–1796.

‡ Possibly Mary Fleming, baptised in 1776 in Uckfield. ESRO, PAR 496 Baptisms 1747–1812.

that the fruit trees and grapes promised exceedingly well that summer. Mrs Harrison's skills were tried in 1795 when she had to make bread with one-third potatoes in the mixture, as a response to the dire rise in the price of wheat, for no imported grain was coming into the English Channel ports as a result of the French blockade.

The servants would have been very well aware of the threat of a French invasion over the nearby Channel. French troops were massing on the coasts of Brittany and Normandy, and there were British army camps at nearby Brighton, Bexhill and Hastings and on Ashdown Forest. Sheffield Park had seen, for the past two years, many French émigrés arriving on the coast in a dire state and receiving a welcome and temporary refuge at the Great House. Nevertheless, all seemed fairly serene at Fletching: 'I hope no unpleasant reports from abroad will happen during the summer to disturb our Pleasure in the Country', wrote Maria Josepha.[63]

Life amongst the family of servants had its vicarious excitements. During the hot weather in July, Lord Sheffield, Maria and their visitors were almost drowned when boating on the nearby River Ouse. The end of the boat caught on an iron lock gate and threatened to fill up with water and sink. Some of the party jumped safely on to dry land; some had to be hauled up the side of the lock by William Vine. Tom was apparently not of the party, but all the details were later relayed to the servants by the coachman, who said 'he had never been so frightened in his Life', adding he had expected to see all the family 'knocked up, at once'.[64]

During the summer of 1794 great alterations were underway in the house. Sheffield was busy reorganising his rooms and putting up new bookcases for his law books and those to come from Gibbon's library. During the heat of that summer, the upstairs family lived in the cool breezes of the north hall. Tom spent much of his time between the servants' hall and the library, a socially ambivalent position he was to occupy for much of his life. He must have spent laborious hours with Sheffield, sorting Gibbon's papers and writing by hand the preliminary manuscript of the *Memoirs*.

Sheffield had complained in 1792 over the weakness of his eyes,[65] and Tom was now employed at £20 a year. For all her disparagement, Maria was glad for him to take over the duties she and her aunt found very tiresome. During this year Tom may have learned and perfected the shorthand that stood him in good stead later in his life. Shorthand was one means by which he preserved some privacy of thought and opinion in his often dependent and ambivalent status. The shorthand he used, with some abbreviations of his own, was that developed by Samuel Taylor in 1786 and used all over Europe, later forming the basis of Pitman's popular system.

10. Maria Josepha Holroyd, painted by Edridge
in 1795, with Sheffield Place in the background.

During the autumn, Hayley came on a visit from Eartham to discuss the organisation and publication of Gibbon's papers. There were six manuscripts of memoirs that Sheffield had to draw upon but little material for the last twenty years of Gibbon's life, a gap that was to be filled by some of his correspondence. Much of the material was in French, and it was fortunate that Tom had some knowledge of the language. Hayley suggested that much material needed to be lopped for the proposed publication and he took away a 'cargo of Gibbonian MSS',[66] to be brought back in January 1795, when he returned, with Thomas Alphonso, to partake of wedding cake and congratulate Sheffield on his marriage, on the previous snowy Boxing Day, to his second wife, Lady Lucy Pelham of Stanmer. The servants took part in the marriage celebrations, dancing to the fiddle in the laundry; perhaps Tom danced too and had a happy time.

The hot summer of 1794 was now forgotten in the rigours of a very cold winter. *The Gentleman's Magazine* for February 1795 reported temperatures below freezing indoors, and people skating through the streets,[67] but Tom's fingers were perhaps kept warm enough to write since barges now came, via the newly developed Ouse navigation (unless that too was frozen) to Sheffield Bridge, supplying all the rooms in the house with coal for the recently installed fireplaces and stoves.

Maria had labelled Tom as 'intended for country use', but he was in London in 1794 for we know his father died that year and Tom arranged his interment in a private burying ground near the Ratcliffe Highway in Whitechapel. He was to care for his mother for the next twelve years. She had been left £250 by her father in 1761,[68] but this money may have been swallowed up in her husband's financial distress unless the Brightmans had kept a tight legal hold on it on Sarah's behalf. If not, Sarah would have had little to live on. Possibly she had a trade of her own, but she was in her mid-fifties. Tom was certainly at the Sheffields' London residence, in Portland Place, in the early months of 1795. Thomas Alphonso, now living in London as a pupil of Flaxman, the sculptor, made several visits to see Tom, drinking tea with him in February, finding the whole family ill with bad colds a week later, and going with him to the theatre in March at Lord Sheffield's instigation.

As is often the way with all incipient books and hopeful authors, Sheffield's memoir was said to be coming to a conclusion in May 1795; was reported to be going on 'swimmingly' in July, when publication was hoped for in September; but 'printers are people who want much spurring'.[69] Indeed the first edition did not appear until 1796. The introduction to this first edition was dated August 1795 and the work was seemingly largely finished by then, for Tom had gone back to Eartham in June. Hayley noted that Tom's 'noble late master' had parted with him in a liberal manner, and it is to be hoped Tom did return with money in his pocket for he had no formal recognition of his work in the introduction to the book,[70] nor informal recognition from Hayley himself, when he wrote in glowing terms in April 1796 of 'Our Lord Hercules Sheffield reposing after his work'.[71] In spite of his year spent among the Gibbon manuscripts, Tom did not venture to read the six volumes of *The Decline and Fall of the Roman Empire* until twelve years later when, bedridden after a hunting accident, he described it as 'a Book I have not yet read but which I think with the fair prospect of confinement I have now before me I may perhaps get thro'.[72]

Hayley would have been glad to see Tom back earlier in May for he now had another protégé in his household: little George Wyndham, the eldest son of the Earl of Egremont and Elizabeth Ilive. George, aged eight, had been sent away to school — quite possibly to Midhurst[73] — where he had been very unhappy and seriously ill. His hair was shaven off as treatment for fever, and he was nursed back to health at home where he bitterly resisted any idea of returning to school. Hayley, having had much the same experience, took pity on George and offered to have him as his pupil. The Earl and Elizabeth Ilive had been impressed with the attainments of Thomas Alphonso and agreed to put George into Hayley's care. How much Tom was involved with George's education at this point is questionable, but Tom was intelligent, had been well taught and had an enquiring mind. He was said to have a natural facility and interest in languages and science. At this early stage, he was well able to teach the rudiments of Greek and Latin — the essentials of a gentleman's education — for he had been taught Latin himself at school and had studied Greek with Thomas Alphonso. He was well versed in mathematics and French. Later he was to do what many teachers do — keep one step ahead of his pupils.

One hopes George was happy at Eartham for there was strain and distress in the house when Thomas Alphonso became increasingly ill and travelled between Eartham and London, having consultations with doctors in London and Mr Guy, the surgeon, in Chichester. The letters between Hayley and his son at this period zigzag between hope and disappointment over Thomas Alphonso's health, the emotions made the more poignant as he was showing considerable promise during his apprenticeship with Flaxman.[74] In February 1795 Thomas Alphonso was enduring vile headaches. In 1796 he was home with fever and breathing problems after varying reports that the trouble was with his chest and lungs. In 1797 he was finally diagnosed as having Pott's disease, that is, tuberculosis of the spine.* By 1798 he was increasingly confined to a wheelchair as he lost the use of his lower limbs. In 1799 he was being dosed with opium and could scarcely hold a pencil.[75]

Thomas Alphonso was in need of increasing care and attention, and by 1797 Hayley decided he must send George home to Petworth. George burst into tears at the news, fearing a return to the dreaded school. Hayley searched anxiously for someone to take over as tutor to George and his brother, seven-year-old Henry. After several fruitless suggestions, he then put forward nineteen-year-old Tom Sockett. He gave Tom a good reference, stressing the:

> great advantage which George has derived from the industry and intelligence of Mr Sockett. He is a young man, who to a strong understanding adds a grateful heart, and whom I zealously recommend to the favour of your Lordship, not only on his own account but on that of his younger fellow student.[76]

He also congratulated himself: 'I trust, I have secured the prosperity of a very industrious, deserving and grateful orphan for life'.[77] Indeed he had.

---

* The disease was named after the English surgeon, Sir Percival Pott (1713–1788).

11. Elizabeth Ilive, Countess of Egremont.

The Friendly Palace: The Tutor, 1797

Tom now became Mr Sockett, the tutor, as he moved into his quarters on the upper floor of Petworth House. As well as his pupils George and Henry, there were Frances aged eight, Mary aged six, Charlotte aged two, and baby Charles.

Sockett's principal task was reading Latin and Greek with the boys. From his Journal for 1805–1807 we learn what texts he used: Aeschines' *Orations*, Demosthenes' *Olynthiacs* and *di Corona*, Euripides' *Orestes* and *Hecuba*, Horace's *Satires* and Sallust's *Bellum Catalinae*. As the boys grew older, they also had French and German masters. The pattern of the day for Sockett was, loosely, lessons for the boys in the morning; recreation in the afternoon — tennis, riding, and hunting; dinner around four o'clock; and his own reading in the evening.

The girls had a governess but Sockett may have taken part in teaching them to read and write, for along with periodic bills for Mr Sockett from James Goldring, the local stationer and printer, in 1804 there was an account for stationery 'to teach the young ladies to write'.[78] In 1805 there was a bill for a very large slate and six slate pencils — and a toothbrush for Mr Sockett.[79] Goldring also supplied copybooks, a pence-table, and a box of ivory letters.[80] George had broadsword lessons in 1797, and he and Henry had dancing lessons in 1799 with the little girls.[81]

Their mother bought them books: *Barbauld's Lessons* in 1798, including one lesson book in French, and later editions in 1803.[82] Anna Laetitia Barbauld's *Lessons for Children* were best sellers at the end of the eighteenth and well into the nineteenth century. Produced in parts as reading books for children aged two and up, they combined lessons in reading with instructive and interesting stories. The children also acquired *Lilliput*, which had been published in 1802; a collection of ten little volumes of stories in a small cabinet; dissected maps of Europe, England, Asia, America and Africa, as well as maps of England and Europe.

Life was not all earnest for there was a skittle alley, and a 'managery' with rabbits, guinea pigs, a parrot and other birds. The estate carpenters made a playhouse with miniature furniture, a chair for the 'great doll', a swing in the pleasure ground, a cart and a garden rake for Master George, and mended a rocking horse for Charles.[83] Goldring supplied toy animals, a fishing rod, and three dolls at one shilling and two shillings each.[84] A much grander leather doll for one guinea came from Charles Wigley of Charing Cross with toy soldiers and a toy watch for two shillings. Henry had a horn for five shillings,[85] and there were considerable bills for drawing paper and colours for painting — not all for the children. The painter, Joseph Farington, wrote in his diary:

> Mrs. Wyndham, who lives with Lord Egremont called on me to see my pictures. I told her I had none finished by me but hoped in a few months to have several to shew her. She professed to have a great delight in painting and devotes much of her time to it. Mr. André, the Surgeon, she said lives with them and had mentioned me as had Philips. She had a fine little Boy* with her abt. 2 years old *very like Lord Egremont* ... She invited me to Petworth and said Ld Egremont wd be glad to see me there. She seldom comes to town, not oftener than once a year, but thinks she shall come in the Spring to see the Orleans collection which I mentioned to her — she appears to be abt. 36 years old.[86]

The children had four-bladed penknives; Frances Wyndham had hers re-ground for four pence in December 1798 by Thomas Winpenny — she probably used it for trimming her quill pen. In the same month, Winpenny supplied George and Henry with skates for use on the frozen lake with four pairs for 'the ladies', at half a guinea each.[87] The winter of 1798–99 was extremely cold. James Woodforde, at his rectory in Norfolk, wrote in his journal for 28th December,

> Frost last night & this Morning & all the Day intense — it froze in every part of the House even in the Kitchen. Milk and Cream tho' kept in the Kitchen all froze. Meat like blocks of Wood ... So Severe Weather I think I never felt before.[88]

Conditions must have been the same, if not worse, in the echoing rooms and corridors of Petworth House. There were, however, quantities of ice to be cut from the lake for the ice house.

As well as educating the children, Sockett educated himself, as his Journal reveals. George Frederick Handel Arnold, his godson and pupil in later years, said: 'his untiring love for the classics in general, and for Horace in particular, was truly remarkable. The New Testament he always preferred to hear in the Greek original'.[89] His small, leather-bound Greek testament, published in Amsterdam in 1698, is still to be found on the shelves in the Old Library at Petworth. Apart from loving Horace's work, Sockett possibly felt an affinity with this man from a

---

* The little boy would be Charles.

humble background, well educated at some trouble by his father, who came under the patronage of the wealthy Roman knight, Maecenas. Horace owed much of his economic security, and recognition as a poet, to Maecenas whom he loved but treated with due respect.

Sockett now had the run of the Earl's libraries. Lining the walls was a wealth of material, not only the expected classics, but also books on philosophy, medicine, gardening and botany, cookery, chemistry, law, and eighteenth-century novels. In 1799 and 1800, the Earl spent almost £100 on books and book-binding from Nicol alone. Petworth House also provided copies of national and local newspapers and literary periodicals. In 1799 and 1800 Nicol bound for the Earl volumes of Arthur Young's *Annals of Agriculture*; *Philosophic Transactions*; *Transactions of the Society of Art*; *The Gallery of Fashion issued by Nicolas Heideloff*,[90] *The Costume of China, No 5*; and the two parts of *Bubble and Squeak, 'A Gallimaufry of British Beef with the Chopped Cabbage of Gallic Philosophy and Radical Reform, by the author of Topsy Turvy'*. [91]

On Boxing Day 1821, William Cobbett wrote to the Earl asking why he wasn't taking his *Political Register*, stressing that all sectors of the agricultural interest should stick together in the face of stockjobbers, etc.[92] The Earl had let his subscription slip, for the *Register* had appeared in the Petworth accounts for 1803–4.[93] His reply is not known, but both the *Register* and Cobbett's *English Grammar* appeared in Elizabeth's, now Countess of Egremont's, 1822 account for newspapers and books.[94]

The Earl of Egremont had bought electrical machines in 1779 and 1780, and when Sockett arrived there was a laboratory and a circle of people interested in scientific and philosophic ideas, among whom was Elizabeth Ilive. In 1798, for example, the group acquired mathematical instruments,[95] a Lunar Globe and a 'selenographic instrument' for studying the surface of the moon.[96] Arthur Young was a member of this group. He visited sporadically and corresponded regularly with the Earl and Elizabeth on agricultural research and development, and he bought Elizabeth materials and books for the laboratory. Elizabeth won a silver medal in 1796 from the Society for the Encouragement of Arts, Manufacture and Commerce. Young was forthright in his criticism of the Earl for refusing to allow Elizabeth's name to appear over an article to be published in an edition of the *Annals of Agriculture* in 1797, commenting that what did age, sex, or beauty of the writer matter 'provided he or she writes good sense'.[97] Young regularly sent warm regards to Elizabeth and spoke of her excellent disposition and good sense.[98]

Other members of the philosophic group included Benjamin Arnold, the music master at Petworth House; Sockett himself, who played the flute,[99] and William André, the surgeon, who provided a surgery and dispensary for the House and town.*

Elizabeth Ilive was buying scientific apparatus from 1797 onwards at the time Sockett appeared on the scene. Perhaps they encouraged each other's interest in scientific topics and practical experiments in the laboratory — they were both young and in somewhat ambivalent social situations. If the Earl and Elizabeth decided that the boys were to be educated at home, then perhaps their education was to include contemporary science and scientific ideas for, as well as apparatus, scientific books were increasingly added to the Earl's library after 1798.[100] There was a model telegraph in the grounds, a camera obscura, and a room for silkworms.[101] Nevertheless, there is no record in Sockett's Journal of science being formally taught to the boys.

In July 1801 Elizabeth at last married the Earl, but Lady Elizabeth Wyndham, the only legitimate baby of their relationship, died early in 1803 and was buried at Petworth on 9th February. There is seemingly no existing record of the date of her birth and baptism, but after her death her wet nurse, Ann Wild, submitted a bill for £21 'for acting as wet nurse to his Lordship's last (decd) [baby], (a daughter)',[102] suggesting the baby had needed a nurse for about a year at say ten shillings a week. If this is so, Elizabeth was pregnant when she married. After little Elizabeth died, Lady Egremont left Petworth not to return. Situations that seemed romantic and exciting at seventeen may have seemed far less so to Elizabeth when she was in her thirties and had given birth to eight children, three of whom had died, an experience exacerbated by the presence of other mistresses and other children at Petworth. She spent the next twenty years at various addresses in London, settling finally at 4 Waterloo Place.

Nevertheless, in spite of this change in the household, and the death in 1800 of Thomas Alphonso Hayley, Sockett's erstwhile friend and pupil, life must have seemed expansive and good geographically and mentally in the wide spaces of Petworth House, in the grounds and on the lake, for the young man in his early twenties. In 1800 he inherited

---

* The Wyndham children were dosed regularly on unspecified draughts and there was syrup of poppies for their mother. After André committed suicide at the end of 1807, at the age of sixty-four, by cutting a vein and letting himself bleed to death (Joseph Farington, *Diary*, VIII: 3171–72, December 1807) his monumental inscription in Petworth's new burial-ground noted his onslaught on smallpox, adding that he was 'A man of the most blameless conduct and most inoffensive manners. To his professional skill, hundreds have been indebted for health and life'. James Dallaway, *The Parochial Topography of the Rape of Arundel in the Western Division of the County of Sussex*, 1832, vol II: 339

some money from his aunt Elizabeth Brightman, sharing the proceeds of her estate in Olney with two cousins.* This inheritance provided an hitherto unknown degree of security and independence, and he had a regular salary from the Earl. André, the surgeon, received £100 a year, and Sockett's salary may have exceeded this for surgeons did not figure highly in professional or social circles.† Although his position as tutor was analogous to the ambivalent situation of a governess, he did not now eat in the kitchen with the servants but dressed for dinner with the family, mingled with the many notable and mundane guests at Petworth House, and had friends in the neighbourhood. From 1805 to 1807 he described his life and spoke for himself in his Journal.

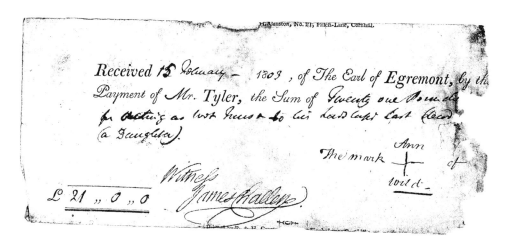

12. Payment to Ann Wild, wet nurse to Lady Elizabeth Wyndham.

---

* His aunt Elizabeth, his mother's sister, had died in May 1800 and was buried in the Baptist Chapel burying-ground in Olney. She left one half of her property to her nieces, Elizabeth and Dorcas Brightman, and the other half to Thomas, her nephew, 'son of my sister', Sarah Sockett. PRO, PROB 11/1341.

† The Duke of Rutland's tutor received £300 a year in the 1790s, but Sockett being young and tutor to a lowlier Earl's sons would not have received as much as this. See F.M.L. Thompson, *English Landed Society in the Nineteenth Century*, (Routledge and Kegan Paul, 1963), 84.

Monday 30 Quite recovered — read Horace
with Henry in the morning — drew
a little — played at tennis after
luncheon — read Charles V in
the evening —

Tuesday 1st Oct. Read Demosthenes ΠΕΡΙ
Στέφανς with H J Lord E went to
town wrote to Nicol & sent 1st vol
of Ainsworth to be bound — wrote also
to my Mother read Euripides after.
lessons & afterwards played at tennis
read Euripides in the evening — I

[line of shorthand]
[line of shorthand]
[line of shorthand]

Wednesday 2nd Went a hunting at 8
& returned at 5 of course
not much done —

Thursday 3d

Friday 4

Sat 5 Went in a boat to Wiggonholt
& brought back 4 plants of Butomus

13. Section of Thomas Sockett's Journal from Monday 30th September to Saturday 5th
October 1805, with an example of his shorthand. This page is transcribed on pages 64 and 66.

THE FRIENDLY PALACE: MR SOCKETT'S JOURNAL, 1805

Sockett's Journal is that of a young man of twenty-eight.[103] There is no evidence that he kept any other journal besides this; his rueful acknowledgement that there are great gaps in this one and his doubts if he will ever manage to keep it properly suggest a state of mind which will strike a chord with many would-be keepers of journals.

What spurred him into beginning in September 1805? He had the prospect of interesting things to record. A trip to the Isle of Wight was planned for that month, and the national hero, Lord Nelson, was expected at Portsmouth. Travel journals were in vogue, and Sockett describes in approved contemporary fashion visits to gentlemen's houses, including the splendours of the cultivated views and parklands at Stansted, and others on the Isle of Wight, coupled with a visit to Portsmouth dockyard, where there were then, as there are now, trophies of national pride and stirring action to be seen.

After their precipitate return to Petworth — Sockett is cross with Miss Wyndham for cutting the trip short — the Journal reverts to a day-by-day account of his life as tutor at the Great House. Here there are no lively snapshots of people or events, such as that tiny but memorable account of the sailor at Portsmouth running to see 'that old b---r Nelson' once more. There are no physical descriptions of the Petworth family, we are not told what George or Henry looked like, and no records of conversations. Sockett has no need to describe them for himself; he knows these people very well, but sadly we do not hear what the French émigrés looked like, what they wore, or what they said, although Sockett sits with them in the drawing room, goes hunting with them on the Downs, and evidently talks to them, if only to improve his French.

His silence on such things may reflect his male temperament; we hear at length what he does but not what he thinks or feels. This reticence may also reflect carefulness born of years spent in other people's houses. In a house such as Petworth, with visitors, children, and servants milling around, it was not circumspect to write things that might be read by uninvited eyes. He is a lone, silent observer and will not put his thoughts and comments on these people into writing. One would like to know what he said to his friends, Carleton the footman, Mr Guy the surgeon in Chichester, Nicol the bookseller in London. On occasion Greek or shorthand come in useful as a private written medium.

Only when he feels himself on his own ground does he feel free to pass judgements and criticisms. He can play tennis and play it well, and on the tennis court can pass qualified opinion on Monsieur and the Duc de Berri as players and opponents. He is on his own ground with his personal sorrows, the death of his mother and his hunting accident, both of which are described in detail and with emotional involvement. It is significant that one of his overwhelming emotions at his mother's illness and death is the realisation he is now really alone; his mother does not recognise him, he was not there when she died; who will care about him as she did?

The keeping of a journal was recommended as spiritual and intellectual discipline wherein one should record weaknesses and failings, and chart hoped-for changes and improvements in one's behaviour. Sockett reprimands himself over his propensity to fall asleep; it weakens his constitution and wastes valuable time. He justifies the evening hours spent in the drawing-room and billiards room with the émigrés — it improves his French. He notes how he has spent his day and improved himself by useful toil; he puts his time to good use with serious reading when confined to bed. When he is ill he hopes he will bear with resignation 'whatever it may please Providence to inflict upon me'.[104] He sets himself to follow the example set by his late father and mother: 'farewell my parents may my life and conduct whether long or short be pure & upright as yours was'.[105]

At an immediate level the details of what the tutor at Petworth House was doing are interesting and informative. We learn what he is reading and teaching, his interest in books and contemporary literary journals and in botany. He is a silent observer but he moves among local, national, and international society with apparent ease and seems at home at Petworth, in the house, in the park, on the lake. He dines with the Mitfords at the neighbouring big house. This is not the awkward boy of Sheffield Park. Such ease of manner and everyday behaviour is probably a tribute to the atmosphere at Petworth as much as to Sockett himself, yet from his writing we get little sense of unease or sycophancy; he grumbles at Henry when he is displeased; he is straightforward in his description of Charles as slow and heavy. Certainly he is fulsome at the end of his journal in praise of the Earl of Egremont but he has good reason to be so. It is interesting that his initial reaction to the offer of the living of Petworth is that it will give him a liberal and independent establishment — it will free him from living in other people's houses; he will at last have a home of his own, and a good income not immediately dependent on other people's goodwill.

His final words describing George as a noble youth and a potential credit to the family may seem overdone flattery, but it should be remembered that he has had charge of George and his education for the past ten years and this is, in one sense, a tribute to what he, as tutor, has done.

14. Stansted House, seat of the Revd. Lewis Way.

Drawn and engraved by I. Higham for *Excursions Through Sussex*; published in August 1820 by Longman & Co. Paternoster Row.

1805

Sept 12 (Thursday) Went to Chichester with L^d E and all the family
— from C we went on to Stanstead (late the residence & property of
Mr Barwell but since his death purchased by a Mr Way — They would
not let us see the ~~house~~ inside of the house — it is a handsome square
building flanked by a couple of wings at right angles to it containing
the kitchen office &c which are connected with the house by an open
colonnade — the front of the house looks down a remarkably fine
avenue ~~of~~ running thro what is called Stanstead Forest & which is I
suppose two miles long — the view of the house from the end of it is
very fine & much improved by the down that appears rising behind it
in the distance — From Stansted we went on to ~~Portsmouth~~ Havant
thro what is called … & from Havant to Portsmouth where we arrived
to a late dinner — we put up at the George but could not get any beds
in the house which was very full owing ~~to~~ partly to the arrival of people
from India & partly to there being several people there belonging to L^d
Nelson who was hourly expected.*

*13 Friday — L^d E hired a sailing boat & we set off for Spithead with
an intention of going on board the Victory but when we came near her
they were getting under way for St Helens [Isle of Wight] and of course
we could not go on board however we lay to & saw her anchors got up
and accompanied her part of the way to St Helens when we hauled our
wind & made for Ride which as the wind was directly contrary we did
not reach without 2 or 3 tacks After taking some refreshment at Ride
we set off to walk towards St Helens we saw the house & Grounds of
a Mr Simeon — the view of the sea an[d] opposite from the grounds
is wonderfully beautiful over a rich fore ground of trees which break
the line of the water in a way that produces the most pleasing effect
imaginable.*

George and Henry were now in the army, but Charles, now nine years old, may have been part on this occasion of 'all the family', which included Miss Wyndham, Frances, age sixteen, the eldest daughter of the Earl of Egremont and Elizabeth Ilive; Frances's younger sister, Charlotte; and a third little girl, Mary, the daughter of the Earl and Eliza Fox. There were also a number of servants — in the eighteenth century often included in the word 'family' — including Carleton, a footman.

It is surprising that an illustrious visitor such as the Earl of Egremont was turned away from the door of Stansted, especially as the Earl had hired the house to live in while work was going on at Petworth between 1775 and 1776; or perhaps because he had. It was common practice for eighteenth century tourists to visit stately homes to be shown around by the housekeeper, or, if illustrious enough, by the owner. Nevertheless, Richard Barwell, the recently deceased owner of Stansted, had a bad reputation for hospitality. He 'made it his study, as it should seem, to render himself obnoxious to persons of all ranks, shutting up gates and paths through the park ... men, women and children hissed and hooted at him as he passed'.[106]

The George, a seventeenth-century hotel in the High Street in Portsmouth, was destroyed by bombs in the 1940s. It had been renowned as the hotel used by many naval heroes. Lord Nelson, who was expected, left his house at Merton, Surrey, late in the evening as the Egremont party arrived.[107] There had indeed been an influx of people from India who had taken the opportunity to off-land at Portsmouth as a convoy of over thirty ships from India had gone up the Channel in the past week; travelling together as protection from the attentions of the French navy.

*The house commands a most complete prospect of Spit head &
Portsmouth with the whole of the entrance of the harbour — We then
went on to <u>the Priory</u> the Seat of Judge Grose from whose Grounds the
view is very beautiful but not to be compared I think to that from Mr
Simeon's as it totally wants that variety which ~~so much~~ adds so many
charms to the latter — the line of the trees ~~is too~~ over which you look
from the house & lawn is too formal & the prospect of the Sea tho very
extensive has a sameness in it which tires — the Judge however has the
pleasure of completely commanding the Road of St Helens & we could
now see very distinctly the Victory which had brought up there & was
(as it was said) only waiting Ld Nelson arrival on board to put to Sea
— We returned to Ride along the Shore which is much the pleasantest
road — what strikes a stranger most on this side of the Island is I
think the appearance of large timber trees & shrubs of all descriptions
~~flourishing~~ growing in a most luxuriant manner down to the high water
mark — In returning along the shore we saw a Salt-work & I picked
the following Plants —*

*We got on board again about 7 & sailed for Portsmouth but as the wind
had died away considerably with the Sun we were much longer in
getting there than we had expected to be, & it was quite dark & rather
cold before we got on shore — Miss W had been qualmy in the boat &
Mlle Lord & the two ~~children~~ little girls had been sick so that they were
all heartily glad to get on shore — but when we got there Miss W could
eat no dinner because she had been told in the morng that an Officer
just arrived from ~~the~~ India was lying dead in the house & she fancied
that all the people of the Inn would be touching him and then handling
the victuals — I was sorry to see that a young Lady so very amiable as
she is should give way to so absurd a weakness — how is she ever to get
thro' the world? surely tho' mildness & gentleness of manners is a great
recommendation to any person yet ~~firm~~ a certain degree of firmness
is not less so — when mildness and gentleness are carried beyond a
certain point they degenerate into real weakness.*

Sir Nash Grose, a judge of the King's Bench, had bought St Helen's Priory, the site of an eleventh century Cluniac priory, in 1799. Sockett was a man of his time in his cultivated appreciation of landscape and the importance of the view as a work of art. The walk along the sands to Ryde at low tide is indeed very pleasant. The Isle of Wight had a number of sites for extracting salt from sea water before they fell into disuse during the nineteenth century. We shall never know what plants Sockett picked along the shore.

The lengthy and uncomfortable journey on the way back to Portsmouth highlights the vagaries of the crossing before the advent of the steamship not dependent on wind nor tide. Sockett was obviously irritated by Miss Wyndham's concerns about the dead sailor. In fairness, it might be claimed that it was the qualmy crossing that upset her appetite rather than adolescent fancies. Sockett is perhaps speaking from his own experience in his criticism of too much gentleness and mildness as a means of making one's way in life. As one who moved on the fringes of the lives of the great and noteworthy, he had possibly found that a degree of firmness was needed to ensure that one was not entirely at other people's beck and call. Perhaps he remembered his father as being too gentle and lacking in firmness. It would be interesting to know if Sockett voiced his opinions before Miss Wyndham or prudently kept them for the privacy of his Journal.

Nelson had arrived in Portsmouth at 6:00 a.m. after his overnight journey. This was the last time he was on English soil. He was to die at the Battle of Trafalgar on 21st October. He wrote:

Saturday, September 14th 1805,

At six o'clock arrived at Portsmouth, and having arranged all my business, embarked at the Bathing Machines with Mr Rose and Mr Canning at two; got on board the Victory at St Helens, who dined with me; preparing for sea.[108]

Saturday 14 Carleton informed me this morning when he came to call us (about 7) that Lord Nelson had been arrived above an hour — I got up & dressed myself immediately & went to the Inn where I found so great a crowd in the gateway that it was not without some exertion that I could gain admittance — just as I got to the foot of the stairs I met L^d N full dressed with 3 or 4 stars on his breast he seemed very anxious to get on board — soon after L^d N went out into the street to call on somebody when he was followed by a number of people who crowded after him in all directions eager to the greatest degree to gain a sight of him — I was amused by the eagerness of a common Sailor I met who was running with all his might and who on being asked by another if he had seen <u>him</u> replied no but D——n the old B——r I <u>should</u> like to see him once more — & away he posted full speed — this I suppose to be the utmost expression of nautical affection — L^d N left Portsmouth about one to go on board the Victory & it is said he is to sail immediately —

On meeting at breakfast this morng it appeared that Miss W was already completely tired of the expedition & wanted to return so it was determined that we should go in a boat up the harbour see the dockyard & return home accordingly we embarked & went about 3 miles up the harbour went on board the Brunswick the Ship which was so much shatter'd in Ld How's Action & on board of which Capt [Harvey] received the wounds of which he died soon after he came on shore — we met with the Carpenter on board who ~~was~~ acted in that capacity during the Action he was a very civil intilligent man & pointed out to us the direction that several of the shot took — he shewed us the place where one had entered which had killed & wounded 16 men at one gun & two at another — a french 74 was at one time so close to them (having hooked one of her anchors into one of the Brunswick's Ports) that the[y] could not open their lower deck ports & were obliged to fire thro them the frenchman after some time got loose & soon after sunk — We also went on board the two Spanish Frigates that were taken at the commencement of hostilities with Spain — one of them is much torn by the shot — the other struck without making any resistance.

William Carleton, the footman and Sockett's friend, who accompanied this visit to Portsmouth, appears in the household accounts for 1802 as William Peacock, alias Carleton.[109] Perhaps his real name was Peacock, or perhaps the Earl — as was sometimes the practice — liked his footmen to be called Carleton. In 1803 Carleton received a salary of £18.8s.0d. For this trip to Portsmouth he claimed 2s.0d. for his expenses to Portsmouth, 2s.0d. at Portsmouth and 2s.0d. from Portsmouth.[110] He had acquired, on the Earl's account, a new hat costing 17s.0d. in October 1804, a suit of clothes costing 14s.0d. in March 1805, and at the same time some breeches, a 'jackett', waistcoat, and coat mended, for which the bill was 2s.[111] There were regular bills for mending breeches — perhaps an occupational hazard for footmen. The hat sounds very splendid if it cost more than a suit of clothes, and almost as much as Carleton's yearly salary.

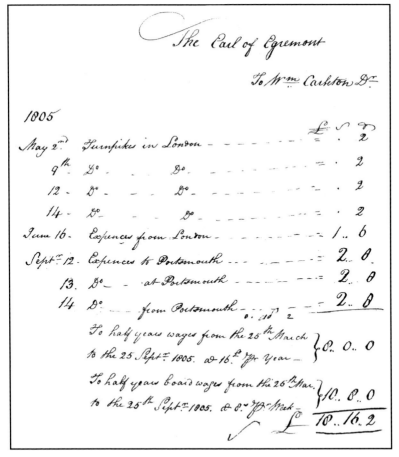

15. William Carleton's account with the Earl, including the trip to Portsmouth, 1805.

On our return from this sail up the Harbour we went to the Dock Yard where we saw the steam engine & the machinery which is worked by it for making blocks for the use of the Navy — ~~they are~~ this machinery has been invented & adapted to the steam Engine by a Frenchman named Brunelle we could not learn his history but they say he has lived much in America — we did not see the machines at work but they seem very competent for producing the effect required they are most of them worked on the same principle as a lathe by means of barrels going along the top of the building which are turned by the steam engine in the same way that I have seen for the spinning of cotton —

We left Portsmouth about 1/2 past 2 I set off first to order dinner at Chichester & tho I was but 2 hours going yet they came so fast after me with the carriages that I had barely time to execute my commission before they arrived — while the dinner was dressing I called on my old Friend Mr Guy the Surgeon & had 1/2 an hours chat with him — after dinner we came home where I arrived about 1/2 past 8 and the rest of the party about 9.

Marc Isambard Brunel lived for six years in America, having fled from the French Revolution in July 1793. He became an American citizen and a professional engineer, and among other projects developed plans of his machinery for block making. He arrived in England in 1799, at the age of thirty, with the hope of interesting the Admiralty in his plans, and to get married. He was introduced to Henry Maudslay, the master craftsman, who, from Brunel's drawings, produced models of the block machines. A seventy-four-gun ship needed 1,400 blocks for tackle, and a quick and cheaper method of production was of great interest to the Admiralty. Maudslay was instructed to produce blocks that Brunel was to install at Portsmouth. Samuel Smiles says that production of the blocks by the new machinery was not begun until 1808, which may account for the fact that the Egremont party did not see it working. Smiles said of it in 1863:

> the machinery was of the most beautiful manufacture and finish ... The framing was of cast-iron, while the parts exposed to violent and rapid action were all of the best hardened steel... there were various Sawing Machines ... Boring Machines, and the Mortising Machine, of beautiful construction, for cutting the sheave holes, furnished with numerous chisels ... the total number of machines employed in the various operations of making a ship's block by the new method was forty four; and after being regularly employed in Portsmouth Dockyard for upwards of fifty years, they are still as perfect in their action as on the day they were erected.

He claimed that, when the plant was in production, ten men could now do the work of 110.[112] In 1805 Brunel and his wife, Sophia, were living at nearby Portsea. Marc Isambard and his son, Isambard Kingdom, born the next year in 1806, were to achieve fame as civil and railway engineers and doubtless by the time he was an old man Sockett would have learned a great deal more about their history too.

Sunday 15 I answered a letter which I had rec^d from my Mother late last night in which she informed me that she had been very unwell & is much troubled with deafness — she informed me too that Mrs B had not sent her the money nor taken any notice of my letter to her on the subject (of the 22^d Aug^t) in consequence of which I called on D[unster] & asked his advice as to what ought to be done in case we should find it necessary to proceed legally — he could no[t] give me much because he was unacquainted with the securities my Mother has for the money & I could not inform him — I wrote to Mr Hill to beg he would inform me if he knows whether they are embarassed — After I had written these letters I felt myself very dull & heavy & went to sleep till it was time to dress for Dinner — there were no Strangers at Dinner only Major Biddulph & 2 of his officers Hart and Capt Willis —

Sockett's mother obviously had a financial claim on the Brightmans. This was perhaps the money left her in the 1761 will of her father, Henry Brightman. He left £250 to his daughters, Sarah and Elizabeth, on the day of their respective marriages subject to the approval of their mother.[113] Possibly this money was paid after Sarah's marriage in 1777, not in a lump sum but in small regular amounts, particularly if Thomas Sockett was regarded as financially unstable, or to prevent the money falling into his creditors' hands. It might be money from Sarah's sister, Elizabeth's, will of 1800,[114] but Sarah was to inherit only if one of the beneficiaries, Elizabeth and Dorcas, daughters of her brother Henry, or her own son, Tom, had died; and there is no evidence of this. Henry, Sarah's brother, had died in June 1805. He does not leave any money to his sister, but if he had been handling money on her behalf the residue might fall due to her. This may be the money Mrs Sockett had been expecting but had not arrived. [See the Journal entry for 14th April 1806.]

The Reverend Charles Dunster MA was rector of Petworth from 1783 to 1816 and of Oddingley and Naunton Beauchamp in Worcestershire. Dunster was a notable scholar and poet. In 1812 he produced *Psalms and Hymns selected and adapted for the Use of a Parochial Church; by a Country Clergyman*, evidence of the use and value of hymns being increasingly accepted by the Church of England under Evangelical and Methodist influence.[115] When he died in 1816, many of his books were auctioned over a period of four days by Sotheby. Described in Sotheby's catalogue as his 'entire remaining library',* the catalogue was fifty-five pages long, and, as well as an impressive collection of serious volumes, there were also five volumes of *Evening Amusements* by W. Frend. Sockett obviously valued Dunster's advice and appreciated his literary accomplishments and collections. [See also the entries for 21st and 24th September.]

---

* 'A Catalogue of the entire remaining library of the Rev. Charles Dunster, M.A. deceased ... For sale by Mr Sotheby, 145 Strand, 11 November 1816 and 3 following days. Price 6d'.

Monday 16 Sent my L[ett]re to Mr Hill and finished one to Nicol that I had begun ab^t a fortnight ago & sent it with an order for Drury Lane which L^d E had given me for him — Read some of the 4 vol of Roscoe's Leo X — I was hindered part of the morning by waiting for a Gentleman & his wife whom Mr Hayley had written a note to me about desiring I would be civil to him as he was passing thro Petworth. I accordingly called on him at the Inn last night and told him I should be happy to shew him the pleasure grounds which he expressed a wish to see or any thing else in my power & he had appointed to call this morning about 1/2 past 10 I arranged my ...

[The top of the next page is missing for about 8 lines]

16. Drury Lane Theatre, 1804.

Nicol had a wide choice of plays; it was common practice to have a double bill at each performance. Richard Brinsley Sheridan, the author of *The School for Scandal*, had reopened Drury Lane Theatre in 1794, after the earlier building had been destroyed by fire. Lord Egremont had his own box; in 1804 it was number 4D.[116] The plays at Drury Lane in the second half of September were:

17th	*The Honey-moon — The Spoiled Child*
19th	*The Wonder! — No Song for Supper*
21st	*King Henry the Fourth — The Lying Valet*
24th	*Romeo and Juliet — Matrimony*
26th	*King Henry the Fourth — The Citizen*
28th	*The School for Scandal — The Anatomist*[117]

William Roscoe (1753–1831), a Liverpool attorney, published *The Life of Lorenzo de Medici* in 1795. He retired in 1796 and the first edition of *The Life and Pontificate of Leo X* was published in 1805, so Sockett was reading it fresh off the press. (As a contrast to his historical publications Roscoe wrote in 1806 *The Butterfly's Ball and The Grasshopper's Feast*. Written for his youngest son, it became a favourite children's book.[118])

Tuesday 17 Finished the 1ˢᵗ Olynthiac of Demosthenes with Henry in the morning — drew a little & read some of Leo X till 2 O'Clock when I went to play at tennis with Henry — after I had dressed read Leo X till dinner was ready — the part I have read to day treats of the state of the Arts during the Pontificates of Julius 11 & Leo X & contains very good Accounts of Michael Agnolo [Angelo] Rafaello & other contemporary Artists — read Leo X after dinner till bed time and finished the work excepting the Appendix — the life of Leo terminates at a most interesting and eventful period which I must renew my acquaintance with by persuing some ~~of~~ history that will serve as a continuation of Roscoe I think of reviewing Robertson's Charles V —

Wednesday 18 Lord E gave the boys a holiday & I did not get up till 9 — wrote a letter to Colˡ Lyon abᵗ ammunitiⁿ — had our ammunition brought to the front of the house & aired read some of the Appendix to Leo X after Luncheon sat down to read more but went to sleep — I sleep too much — it wastes the time and enervates my constitution I <u>must</u> resist the propensity — received a Letter from my Mother — she is better — has not heard from Mrs B — in the evening skimmed over Roscoe's Appendix to his last vol & finished the work with which I have been much pleased & from which I have gained much information tho I think the ~~choice of~~ confining the work within the limits of the Life of Leo is rather a detriment to it of which indeed Mr Roscoe seems to have been aware as he has in several instances been obliged to bring down his sketches of individual biography to a much later period — Lᵈ E & Miss W went to Town — Read 300 lines of the beginning of the Hecuba of Euripides.

Thursday 19 Began the 3ᵈ Olynthiac with Henry — read some of the Hecuba played at Tennis a little while first with Mitford then with Henry afterwards went into the Paddocks to get Sedum Telephium to dry but it was all out of flower — as I returned went on board the Nile & sailed a little while till dressing time — after dinner began Charles V Rain with thunder in the evening —

William Robertson wrote three volumes of *The History of the Reign of the Emperor Charles V*, the first published in 1749.

The *Nile* was presumably named in honour of Nelson's victory of Aboukir Bay in August 1798. There was also the *Nelson*, taken out of the pond and broken up in 1807.[119] Sockett spent a considerable amount of time messing about in boats on the lake and pond, as well as on the River Rother at Coultershall Mill.* [120] Egremont owned a number of boats including a brig, the *Egremont*, owned jointly with Jeremy Scarwell, a coal dealer of Littlehampton, at the end of the eighteenth century.[121] In 1800 Egremont ordered a skiff, from Searle and Honey 'Boate builders' of West Bridge, Surrey. This boat with 'boat hooks, carte and wagon and attendance' for delivery cost £19.8s.6d.[122] In 1802 he took delivery of two pleasure sailing boats from Richard Roberts. One was a small 'Peter' boat — a decked fishing boat — and the other a 'very handsome built half Deck Sailing Pleasure Boat of English Oak'. With their 'appurtances' they cost £116.0s.6d., including 10s. 'for the expenses for assistance getting the Boats into Carts'.[123] A bill from J. Crookenden for £5.2s.6d. was for a small boat, ordered by Sockett, and delivered to Coultershaw Mill.[124] He presumably used this boat to go to Wiggonholt in October 1805. The family also enjoyed considerable river trips. In the spring of April 1802, the 'great boat' was taken from Coultershaw Mill to Pulborough and from thence with 'My Lord and Company' down the Arun to Arundel; later in the month, Mrs Wyndham and company went from Coultershaw to Houghton.[125]

Sedum Telephium is a member of the stonecrop family with pink, red, or white flowers that bloom from July to September. [126]

---

* The mill burned down in 1923.

Friday 20 Began the Bellum Catalinarium with Henry — drew a little, & fixed some plants read Hecuba — read Charles V in the Evening — (Wind S.W fair)

Saturday 21ˢᵗ Read part of the 3ᵈ Olynthiac with Henry & afterwards nearly finished it by myself — played at Tennis after 3 with Carleton — after dinner visited Mr Dunster & had some conversation with him about the collection of old Plays &c

Sunday 22 Finished the Olynthiac by myself — looked over the pamphlets & loose books in Lᵈ E's room & brought many of them away — Sent a Requisition to Col Lyon for rifle — ammunⁿ in answer to a Letter I recᵈ from him this morning — went on with the Hecuba — Read Sallust with Henry in the evening Lᵈ E and Miss W returned and Mr C Wyndham came —

Monday 23 Henry & C[harles] finished their lessons early & went a hunting — read Hecuba wrote to my Mother and enclosed 1/2 of a 5£ Note (No 8529) & a B P Bill (882) for £10 — Finished the Hecuba — x

Tuesday 24 Read Demosthenes with H in the Morning, fastened plants Mr Dunster called & brought me 3̶ 4 numbers of the Censura Literaria — recᵈ a letter from Mr Hill — Rode out at 3 & dined at Pits Hill —

Wednesday 25 Read Horace with Henry 'Quae virtus et quanta boni sit vivere parvo' [What and how great a virtue it is, my friends, to live frugally], very idle and languid, drew a little & began the Orestes of Euripides — went in the pleasure ground to look for Fungi — found Asplinium dilatatum which I brought home & dried — Mr Wyndham gone.

In his library Dunster had several volumes of old plays, including six volumes of *English plays, being a Selection from the early Dramatic Writers*, published in 1814–1815, and three volumes of *Ancient British Drama*, published in 1810.

The yeomanry was revived in the early 1790s with the threat of the French Revolution and war with France. A local volunteer force of gentlemen and farmers was on call in 'case of invasion or internal commotion'. The Petworth Troop of Yeoman Cavalry was raised in 1795 with the Earl of Egremont as Commander-in-Chief and its headquarters at Petworth House. The Earl's obituary in January 1838 said:

> when it was deemed necessary to arm against the threatened aggression of France, he came forward with alacrity; and his nervous, soul-stirring eloquence, at the public meetings of this period are not yet forgotten. At that crisis his Lordship raised and placed himself at the head of, one of those bodies of British volunteers, in whose imposing force and attitude the Nation probably found its safety at the hour of need ...[127]

Thirty-five men volunteered in the first year; by 1798 there were fifty-two including Sockett. Half of the troop came from Petworth itself; the other half from nineteen other parishes in the Arundel Rape. John Taylor was the troop's sergeant, Colonel Lyon the local inspecting field officer. The government allowed £6.16s.6d. per volunteer for clothing, equipment, and keep of a horse, which the man provided himself. The Earl supplemented these basic items from his own pocket, buying cloaks, feathers, helmets, arms, etc., for his troop from firms in London, and leather goods from tradesmen in Petworth. There was dissension in the county over the uniform. Some citizens thought a smart uniform gave a psychological boost, making volunteers feel like real soldiers thereby encouraging recruitment, especially among the young men. Others felt there was no need for such foppery and expense, the volunteers should largely clothe themselves from their own wardrobes, with some modest marker such as red cuffs to establish their status.

In spite of all the initial activity by national and local government, it was fortunate there was no invasion; the Duke of Richmond, for one, was privately very pessimistic about the ability of an ill-trained, ill-armed volunteer force to keep an invading French army at bay, and he was dismayed at government plans for evacuating everything moveable in the county and laying waste to all that remained; including, presumably, his own estate of Goodwood House as well as Petworth House. With the renewal of war in 1803 came renewed activity. A consignment of

Right Honble Earl of Egremont

To Richd Roberts

		£
1801	To a Peter Boat built Sailing Pleasure Boat of English Oak with a Well, handsomely finished and compleatly Painted, with Mast Gaff & Paddles —	32 -- --
	To a Mainsail and Foxes' Blocks & Rigg Complt —	9 .. 7 .. --
	To an Anchor Cable and Pennant —	1 .. 10 .. --
1802	To four Hatches as pr Order, double Thicknesses —	4 .. 10 .. --
	To a very handsome built half Deck Sailing Pleasure Boat of English Oak — Square stern with Mast Gaff Paddles, Boathook, Main Sail Foresail and Iron Ballast —	63 -- --
	To four Hatches fitted to Do double Thicknesses —	4 .. 10 .. --
	To Anchor & Cable, sundry Spare Blocks & Pennant —	2 .. 13 .. 6
	To Expences for assistance getting Boats into Carts —	-- .. 10 .. --
		£ 116 -- -- 6

17. Richard Roberts's account with Earl of Egremont for boats, 1801–02.

arms came down to Petworth, via Sparshott's wagon, from the Ordnance department in the Tower of London, a two-day journey. A load of cartridges and flints came separately. Sockett was responsible for a flurry of activity in 1804 and 1805 with orders to local tradesmen for saddlery, powder and shot, camp kettles, cutlery, blankets, the repair of arms, and a new cavalry jacket for his Lordship.

Nevertheless, in spite of the anxiety and activity there were complaints that suitable men to become officers were slow to come forward in Sussex, and there was an appeal to men who had enlisted among the lower classes as privates to take on the responsibilities of officers. There were practical inducements to service in the yeomanry in the shape of exemption from taxes on horses, hair powder and road tolls. These inducements were lost if the volunteer resigned, as he could do with due notice but if he was called into active service, any non-attendance might result in a military court martial.[128]

The *Censura Literaria, Containing Titles, Abstracts, and Opinions of Old English Books, With Original Disquisitions, Articles of Biography, and Other Literary Antiquities* by Sir Samuel Egerton-Brydges Bt, was published in ten volumes between 1805 and 1809 by Longmans & Co, London.

Pitshill, a house built in the neo-classical style in the nearby parish of Tillington, was the home of the Mitford family. The second son, Charles, born in 1785, was Sockett's friend and tennis opponent. There were also five daughters, Frances, Emma, Charlotte Georgina, Augusta and Caroline.[129] Sockett would have a good dinner, perhaps that is why he felt languid and idle the next day. Dinner was usually served at three or four o'clock — later at Petworth where there were usually only two courses — but if this was service à la française, as was usual at the early part of the nineteenth century, a great variety of dishes would be put on the table at the same time.

The housekeeping accounts for 1805 at Pitshill show that bills for the year July 1804–July 1805 amounted to £270.17s.9d. In the autumn of 1805, apart from the usual grocers', bakers' and butchers' bills there were purchases of dozens of fowl — mainly ducks and chickens — at about 1s.6d. each; hundreds of eggs; shrimps, oysters and fish; fifteen pounds of butter; nine gallons of damsons at 1s. a gallon; three dozen quinces for 3s., and fifteen pounds of morello cherries at 9d. a pound, these latter fruits presumably for preserving, and quantities of walnuts for walnut catsup. All these goods came from local sources, although on one occasion in 1806 fish was brought from Worthing by the coachman.[130]

18. East Lodge, the Egremont Brighton house. W. A. Delamotte, 1853.

19. Pitshill.

Thursday 26 Read Demosthenes with H went a hunting — Mr Wyndham returned having only been to Brighton Lady King & her Son came read some of Ch V in the Evening —

Friday 27 Very unwell with a complaint in the bowels which attacked me in the middle of the night — read Horace with H & afterwards some Euripides by myself —

Saturday 28 Still unwell — disturbed much in the night — read with Henry part of Demosth di Corona which is inserted in the Collectanea majora & afterwards finished it by myself read several articles in the MR & some of Euripides — did not go down to dinner — better in the Evening — read Ch V—

Sunday 29 Read Euripides in the morning — went to Chapel — afterwds rode to the farm much better than yesterday.

Monday 30 Quite recovered — read Horace with Henry in the morning — drew a little played at tennis after luncheon — read Charles V in the evening —

Tuesday 1st Octr Read Demosthenes [here Sockett used Greek script for the title, which was a speech on the Crown, i.e. kingship] *with Hy — Lord E went to town wrote to Nicol & sent 1st vol of Ainsworth to be bound — wrote also to my Mother read Euripides after lessons & afterwards played at tennis, read Euripides in the evening —*

[In shorthand]
Had some very serious converse with Henry on certain aspects of his behaviour which I do not approve of, was much pleased by the manner in which he seemed to take what I said. Hope it will have a beneficial effect upon him —
[see page 38 for the original shorthand entry]

Wednesday 2nd Went a hunting at 8 & returned at 5 of course not much done —
Thursday 3d
Friday 4

The Brighton house, East Lodge, now demolished, was on the east side of Upper Rock Gardens in Kemp town. The Earl of Egremont frequently visited the seaside resort, the centre of much local and London social life, and was a friend of the Prince of Wales at the Royal Pavilion. Egremont went to Brighton and Lewes races and was well known in Brighton for his philanthropy. He was a founding subscriber to the Royal Sussex Hospital; where his portrait hangs to this day and a ward is named after him. There is also a Brighton and Hove bus named after him in the twenty-first century.

Lady King's son, John King, was later to marry Charlotte Wyndham.

The MR was the *Monthly Review*, founded in 1749 by Ralph Griffiths, and published until 1845. It was a rival to the Tory *Critical Review*, published from 1756 to 1817. Samuel Johnson, asked by King George for his opinion of the two periodicals, retorted; 'the *Monthly Review* was done with most care, the *Critical* upon the best principles adding that the authours [sic] of the *Monthly Review* were enemies to the Church. This the King said he was sorry to hear'.[131]

What Henry had done on this occasion we do not know but Sockett was always ambivalent in his relationship with Henry. Years later, in 1839, he wrote of him: 'I brought up Henry Wyndham from a child. I loved him as if he had been my own. I exalted in his glorious military career, and I love him now — but I have always deeply grieved for his unconquerable temper, and his proneness to be misled by others, against his own better feelings'.[132] Henry joined the Duke of Wellington in Portugal in 1811, suitably equipped with his uniform and £3 worth of portable soup. As General Henry Wyndham, he was to be handsomely described in later years as:

> a gentleman who through the whole of the Peninsular war had headed a dashing regiment (cheers) — who all but took the King of Spain — (renewed cheering) — who had at the battle of Vittoria shewed himself a brave man, an heroic leader — (continued cheers) — who on one occasion was chosen, on account of his mildness, his moral courage, and his military prowess, to quell the insubordination of one of the regiments which had become disordered and to bring them back to discipline (Cheers).[133]

Robert Ainsworth's *Compendius Dictionary of the Latin Tongue*, in two volumes, was first published in 1746 and ran to many editions between 1746 and 1796. It seemingly had good use in the Petworth House schoolroom if one volume needed to be rebound.

Sat 5   Went in a boat to Wiggonholt & brought back 4 plants of Butomey [Butomus] which I planted in the Pond — ret^d at 9.
Sunday 6 In consequence of the Inspection having been fixed for old Mich day & the farmers having all represented on Saturday how inconvenient & almost impossible it would be for them to attend a circumstance I was not aware of till Taylor came & mentioned it to me while dressing in the morning as soon as I had breakfasted I set off to Chichester saw Col^l Lyon & got the day postponed — got back at 5.

Monday 7 — Tuesday 8 The Quarter Sessions.
Wednesday 9 — went a hunting on the Downs.
Thursday 10 Played at Tennis with Mitford — beat him.
Friday 11 — Went hunting about 1 on the Commons.
Sat^y 12

Sunday 13 I have not been particular in my account of the last 5 or 6 days as I had neglected to fill them up at the time but tho I have been a good deal from home yet I have not been quite idle. I have finished the Orestes read the introd. to Æschines ag^t Clesippa and arranged a number of my plants —

This evening arrived to dinner the D de Bourbon, Comte de Vaudreuil, Comte de Rouillie, Comtesse de Rouillie daughter of the D de B.

Monday 14 Read with H part of Taylor's Preface to Æschines Oration agt Ctes Mr Biddulph lent me Dix's Method of drawing Maps which I looked over —played at Tennis with Carleton he beat me 4 ~~games~~ sets out of 6 hardly played — arrived to dinner L^d and Lady Piercival and M de Quesne a Gentleman attending the D de Bourbon Comtess the Vaudreil

Tuesday 15 Read the Introd to Æsch with Henry — Tropp met at 2 1/2. I drew in the mroning having begun to copy a drawing lent me by Miss Mitford — arrived to dinner the D de Berry, M de Polygnac & M de Menars

Wednesday 16 Read Bellum Catalinarium with H went a hunting at 12. The D de Bourbon M de Rouillie M de Quesnoit and M^{dam} Rouillie were out. M^{dme} rode the Majors Horse who was also there — did not read in the evening for they dine so late & I staid down stairs seeing them play at Billiards.

Wiggonholt, a small village, lies seven miles southeast of Petworth by land, and more by water. Sockett presumably went on the Rother from Coultershaw bridge to Stopham and then on the Arun. He would then have had a walk over the fields to Wiggonholt Church — if he went that far.

Butomus umbellatus grows in shallow, fresh water in the south of England and bears pink flowers in July and August. Old Michaelmas Day was 11th October, a quarter day when tenant farmers' rents became due.

The French émigrés were visitors to Petworth House on several occasions during their peregrinations around the aristocratic houses of Great Britain. 'Monsieur', Charles Phillipe, Comte d'Artois, was the eldest brother of Louis XVIII, now in exile on the continent. Artois was living in South Audley Street, London, on a British government pension of £500 a month. The Duc de Berri, his son, also in London, had a pension of £300 a month. The Comte de Vaudreuil had attended Artois from the time of his early days as an émigré in Edinburgh. The Duc de Bourbon was the son of Prince de Condé. The Duc de Berri was a connoisseur and collector of art — when he could afford it — and doubtless admired the pictures at Petworth.[134]

In the summer of 1801 the firm of Solomon Erwood, 'Billiard Table Maker of Holborn', sent a man down to Petworth to repair and put in order the billiard table at a cost of £20.14s.6d.[135]

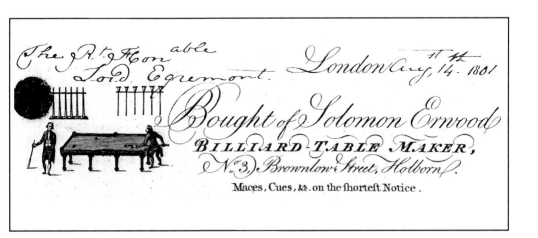

20. Headed notepaper of Solomon Erwood.

Thursday 17 ~~At 9~~ Read Æschines with H before breakfast at 9 played at Tennis with the D de Berry — I had expected to find him a good player but was disappointed I could give him 30 but he says he has lately begun to learn — read Æschines afterwards & at 1/2 past 2 played at Tennis with Carleton beat him 3 sets out of 4 (both played badly)

Friday 18 Read Bell. Catalin. in the Morning with H afterwards went a hunting The two French Countesses M le Menars, M de Polgniac, L^d E, L^d P and the Major were out — staid down stairs in the Evening — Wrote to Mr J Talbot.

Saturday 19 Read Æsch[ines] with H — Mr J Johnson called on me about 2 & staid till 3 when I played at Tennis with Carleton. We both played much better than usual & I beat him 3 sets out of 4 — The Duke de Berry, MM de Menars and Polygniac & Ld Percival went to day — Capt & Mrs Herbert and a Miss Loveday came to dinner I am ashamed to say that again I did nothing in the evening — I have lost every evening this week tho' indeed they have not been entirely lost as I have had opportunity of hearing a good deal of french & of speaking it.

Sunday 20 Read the service at Chapel in German & the old Test Lesson — Lady Percival & the remainder of the Fr. went away Capt Willis at Dinner Ellis and Hale —

Monday 21 Read ~~Æsch~~ Horace in the Morng with Hy — hunted, Genl Crosbie and Mrs C ~~came~~ with the Nappers & wives to dinner.

~~Tuesday 22 Troop out At 12 inspected by Coll Lyon — Genl Crosbie [?] the ground~~

Tuesday 22 Read Æsch: in the morn^g with H^y Troop & Vol^rs out at 12 to be rev^d by Gen: Crosbie The Officers dined Party in the house same as yesterday rec^d a letter from Nicol

Wednesday 23^d Read Sallust with H^y & began protracting a Map of Europe.

21. Charles Mitford, 1785–1831 as an Eton boy, with his college in the background.

22. The Comte d'Artois.

1806 Jany 22nd

Here is an immense blank in my Journal tho I know not if it is any great loss but I will endeavour to fill up what has passed from memory & do propose (shall I keep my purpose?) to be more regular in future. A few days after my regular account ceases Nicol came to see me & we went on as usual attending to our studies in the evenings & morning & hunting in the middle of the day two or three times a week — we continued reading Sallust Æschynes &c & Henry began Blackstones Commentaries. & About the middle of Novr Nicol went away I went with him as far as Guildford where we had appointed to meet Bedford — we found him there accordingly & had a comfortable dinner & spent the evening very pleasantly together, we breakfasted there the next morning & afterwards walked about the place till ab^t 1 when we separated they steering for Town & I for Petworth —

On Monday the [blank] of Nov I met with a fall with the horse I was on into a ditch & he rolled side ways upon me so as to bruise very much my ~~left~~ *right testicle & after riding home in great pain I was obliged to go to bed where I lay for a fortnight & then gradually mending had flattered myself that I was entirely recovered when two or three days ago the swelling resumed & to day Mr André examined it & expresses great apprehensions of Hydrocele — a comfortable prospect! but I hope I shall bear with patience whatever it may please providence to inflict upon me*

During my confinement I read Robertson Ch V and Watsons Phil 2^d & 3^d & advanced considerably ~~with my~~ *in German. Just before Xmas some of the French Princes came here [ie?] Monsieur, The D de Berry, D de Bourbon attended by the Comte de Vaudrieul, M de Polygnac & M de P. I played one morning at Tennis* ~~with~~ *against Monsieur and The D de Berry —*

M has been a particular good player & still plays very well much better than I can, but by playing most of my balls to the D de B I contrived de leur faire tete ['an even contest']. There has been another house full of Company besides but I cannot recollect half of them, therefore I shall not attempt it —

A hydrocele might well give Sockett reason for anxiety; Gibbon suffered greatly from one for much of his life and it was the cause of his death in 1794. There is a graphic account of his last days in the *Memoir* that Lord Sheffield had written with Sockett's help. Nevertheless, in spite of his weakness and anxiety Sockett recovered enough to play tennis against Monsieur and the Duc de Berri, and to astutely use his knowledge of the weakness of the Duc to hold his own.

23. The Duc de Berri.

The last Book I have read is Mem: de Marmontel from which I have enjoyed much amusement the part from the beginning of the Revolution is more particularly interesting — what a picture of madness and folly in all parties! I have begun [?] Gibbons Roman Empire a Book I have not yet read but which I think with the fair prospect of confinement I have now before me I may perhaps get thro' —

Sat 25 I have passed the best part of every day in bed since the 22ⁿᵈ & I think the inflamatory symptoms are some what abated by dint of bleeding physicing and dieting. I have amused myself with reading Marmontel's Contes Moreaux & Hudibras & with learning German.

April 13 Another immense chasm in my Journal & indeed I do not think I shall ever bring myself to keep it regularly — Various & afflicting ~~events have~~ circumstances have harrased me much since the last date — I ~~have been~~ was obliged to go to Town soon afterwards to a Surgeon who declared my case to be a Hydrocele of the tunica vaginalis — after staying a week in London I returned and about a month afterwards again went up when the Surgeon let out the water & told me that it was possible it might not collect again but that it most probably would & so it has & I expect it will be necessary to have a regular operation performed — but this has not been the worst of my troubles — soon after returning from Town the second time I received a letter from Miss Thomas informing me that my poor Mother had had a parletic stroke which had deprived her of the use of one side and rendered her speech almost unintelligible I was therefore obliged again to ask Lᵈ E for leave of absence which he with his usual kindness most readily granted & I hastened immediately to see my afflicted parent —

I found her as had been described & ~~when~~ till I had been with her a day could not convince her of my being her son — that child on whom she doted was now as a stranger to her — but much to my comfort & satisfaction she did at last recognise me & expressed pleasure at my presence tho' not so strongly as she had done on former occasions I staid with her a week; at the end of which period she seemed somewhat better, & it was the opinion of the Physician & Apothecary that she would still continue some time —

It was perhaps this reminder of Gibbon that led Sockett, at last, to consider reading *The Decline and Fall.* He was a scholar of his time in his attention to German language and literature, the late-eighteenth century anti-Classical movement and the pre-cursor of the Romantics.

Hudibras, a satire in the genre of Don Quixote, was set in England, and a best seller from the first part in 1663 until well into the nineteenth century. Sockett was to quote — or rather misquote as most people did — probably the most well known phrase from *Hudibras* — 'For those that fly, may fight again, Which he can never do that's slain' — to his friend James Brydone in 1834.

Having seen every thing done for her that could be done & being perfectly satisfied with the care & attention paid her by Miss Thomas & two other Ladies in the house, who tho but recent acquaintances, were as kind to her as if she had been their own nearest and dearest relation I returned to Petworth in the Night of Sunday the [blank] ~~time~~ & arrived time enough to get a little sleep and be ready for business on the Monday Morning (for I had lost so much time that I wished to make it up as fast as I could) —

When I left my Mother I had hopes that the family would be in London in about a fortnight & that I should then have an opportunity of watching over her health — but alas! I was to see her no more! having received one good account after my return a second came on Saturday the 30th of March a fortnight after I had left Bethnal Green which seemed to say that I must look for the worst — I returned to Town on the Sunday where I arrived abt 8 & going to a Tavern in the City sent a Porter with a Note to enquire how things were at B.G. he returned with the inform^n that my dear Mother had escaped from all her sufferings at 1/2 past 6 that very evening I then was much grieved that I had not hastened up on the Saturday or in the night but was afterwards ~~reconciled~~ more satisfied as I found that the dear object of my care had not known any person or spoken for two days & to have found her in that state would have been a torture to me almost beyond my powers to sustain ~~so that~~ long as I had expected this event yet when it actually arrived it hurt me much more that [than] I had expected it would — there is something peculiarly oppressive at least to my mind in being left in the world without one individual who has a tender and affectionate care for ~~your~~ one's welfare — tho' that I hope is not entirely my case for I have I think one friend on whom I could rely & who to a tenderness and affection never exceeded joins a ~~manliness~~ degree of manly good sense not often equalled — ~~with regard~~

The death of his mother was a great emotional blow. Tom was her only child and the bond between mother and son was great. To whom is he referring as the one friend who shows tenderness and affection never exceeded? Possibly Nicol, hardly the Earl; perhaps Sockett is referring obliquely here to Sarah Gray, whom he probably met at the Nicols' house, and whom he was to marry in 1810. Coupling her tenderness and affection with a degree of manly good sense may well be an intended compliment linking her feminine qualities with a degree of ascribed male virtue that served to enhance her overall value. Frances Wyndham could, in Sockett's opinion, well do with a modicum of manly good sense.

I can most truly apply to both my parents those ~~words~~ *beautiful
expressions of Horace concerning his Father — purus et insons (Ut
me collaudem) si vivo, et carus amicis, Causa fuit pater his* [If I praise
myself and live a pure and guiltless life, loved by my friends, my father
was the cause of this] *now they are both gone — and how soon I may
follow them Heav'n only knows I do not believe myself made for long
life nor am I sure that I wish for it did I possess that cheerful religious
enthusiasm which comforted my poor father in all his afflictions I am
sure I should not — my poor Mother was buried on Saturday the 5ᵗʰ
of Apʳ in a private burying ground in the New Road Whitechapel near*
~~*where*~~ *the place where my father was laid 12 years ago — I intend
to erect a modest grave stone to both their memories — farewell my
parents may my life & conduct whether long or short be pure and
upright as yours was!*

*April 14 I went with Nicol to the Cross Keys Sᵗ Johns Sᵗ to meet a Mr
Morgan from Olney who paid me 104£ being the balance of the acᶜᵗ
between Mr Talbot Exʳ to Mr Brightman & myself for the money due
from Mr Brightmans Estate to my Mother he having before remitted me
£100 — Henry & Charles arrived in Town on Friday last (the 11ᵗʰ) I
had engaged a German & a French Master for Henry who both came
on* ~~*Saturday Morning for the*~~ *Friday morng by appointᵐᵗ as I expected
Henry in Town on Thursday.*

*17 Lord Egremont came to Town to dinner. The French & German
Masters have been every morning & Henry has given the greatest
part of his time to those two languages only reading a little Homer &
Horace daily just to keep him from forgetting his Greek & Latin — recᵈ
a Letter from George — Saw a double match at Tennis between Monsʳ
& Barcellon & Sir John Shelley & Lᵈ Fred: Beauclerk —*

*21st Wrote a Letter to Mr Hayley & a note to Miss T saying I would be
there thursday or friday continue labouring away at French & German.*

23 Went to Dʳ Smith's Lecture at the Institution —

The private burying-ground in the New Road, Whitechapel may be that shown in the New Road between Chapman Street and Lower Chapman Street.[136] If so it had become a United Methodist Free Chapel by 1873 and has now been lost to an extensive twentieth century housing estate. The 'modest grave-stone' has sadly disappeared along with the burying-ground. Many such private burying-grounds disappeared with the redevelopment in the nineteenth and twentieth centuries of that area of Whitechapel.[137] Sockett was unduly pessimistic in his prognostications of an early death; he lived to be eighty-two.

The Cross Keys, a coaching inn in St John Street, would have been familiar to him from his childhood in nearby Aldersgate. St John Street had 'numerous inns at which travellers were lodged and entertained and from whence the waggons etc., conveyed travellers to the several towns on the Great North Road'.[138] The visitor Sockett and Nicol went to meet was possibly John Morgan, a lace and thread merchant of Olney.

The Royal Institution, founded in 1799, obtained its Royal Charter in 1800. Its purpose was the facilitating of mechanical inventions, the promotion of their use, and the teaching of science and its applications by means of lectures and experiments. Humphrey Davy and Michael Faraday were members of the Royal Institution, and Faraday gave one of a series of Christmas lectures that are still held to this day.

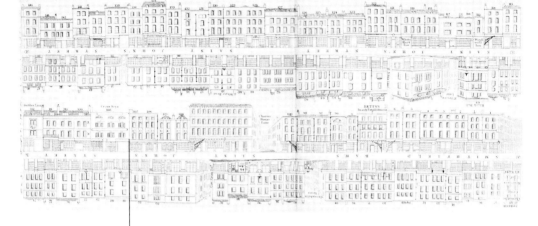

24. John Tallis's *London Street Views* part 37, showing St John's Street, Smithfield c1838.

Below, a magnified detail showing the Cross Keys Inn.

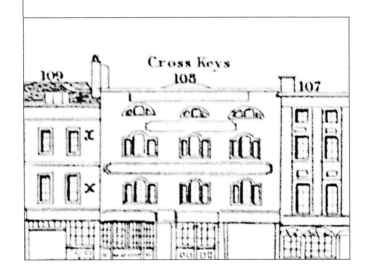

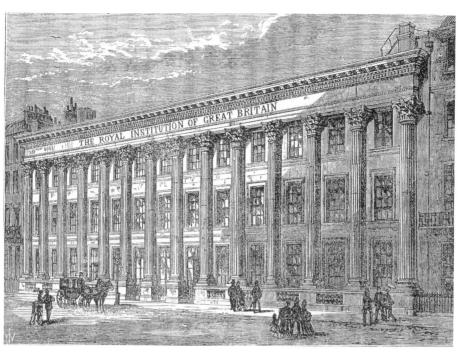

25. The Royal Institution of Great Britain, founded 1799.

26. The Old Tennis Court, James Street.

24 Went to Bethnal Green to dinner & when I settled every thing with Miss Thomas & called at Mr Sadlers & paid him (£19..18) rec^d a letter from Mr Hayley —

~~28~~ 30 — Wrote to Mr Hayley.

May 1st Nothing material since my last date — saw a match at Tennis between Barcellon & Cox — the latter gave B 3 bisques — B: won the two first sets which decided the match it being for the best of 3 sets — it was well contested rec^d a Letter from Mrs Rose —

3^d Rained all day — did not go out till after dinner — have got a German Don Quixote —

7th Lent Mr Phillips £200 for which I rec^d his note payable on demand with interest — paid Mucklow £14. 17. for balls &c for Ld Egremont — Obs part of the 200 I paid Mr Phillips was by a draft on Nicol for £25 — the rest was in bank notes

19th Went with Charles to see St Pauls

Augt 17 Here is another long break in my Journal however I will make a slight sketch of what has happened to me & what I have done since the last date

~~I remained in London till~~ Towards the end of June Lord E one day after dinner we being alone proposed to me to go into orders & at the same time in the Kindest & most liberal manner offered to give me the living of Petworth — I was much gratified by the proposal in every point of view — The offer of a liberal independant establishment is pleasing but infinitely more so to my feelings is the idea that my conduct has been such as to give satisfaction than which I think there cannot be a more convincing proof that L^d E wishing to settle me close to his own door — were he not satisfied with my past conduct & confident of my future good behaviour he would find some other mode of remuneration —

'Real tennis' was enthusiastically played by Sockett. He played with Henry, Carleton, Mitford, and the French aristocrats visiting Petworth in 1805 and 1806. Sockett was pleased when he beat the latter but gave due credit to Monsieur, Comte d'Artois, who was forty-nine years old. There had been a tennis court at Petworth House since the early seventeenth century; the court that Sockett played in had been resited to adjoin the east side of the house in 1797. In June 1798 Egremont paid H. Knott £10.15s.0d for four new 'rackquets', three 'rackquets' to be restrung, balls and catgut.[139] In April and May 1806 Sockett went to see tennis matches in London at the famous James Street court in the Haymarket. Barcellon and Cox were both considered to be of world champion standard. Mucklow, from whom Sockett bought tennis balls, was the keeper at the James Street court.[140]

The living of Petworth Church, Lord Egremont's gift, was typical of that made by rich patrons to the erstwhile tutors of their children. As Disraeli was later to note rather tartly while writing of the 1830s, 'a priest is scarcely deemed in our days a fit successor to the authors of the gospels, if he be not the editor of a Greek play; and he who follows St Paul must now at least have been private tutor of some young nobleman who has taken a good degree'.[141] Charles Dunster possibly suggested the idea to Egremont, regarding Sockett as a very suitable successor to himself for they shared the same interests, and Dunster may have known of the Sockett clergy in Gloucester.

Having the idea of going into the Church I thought it would be advisable to enter at one of the Universities & to take a degree or not as might afterwards best suit my convenience accordingly on the 12 of July when L^d E & the family left town for Petworth I went to Oxford accompanied by Walter who very kindly went with [me] to assist me in case I should find no one there whom I knew. I found Penrose there who was very civil & after some consideration recommended Exeter College for me to enter at we accordingly waited on the Rector the next morning (Sunday) ~~who was very kind & promised to assist me all~~ *to whom I explained my situation & that I wished to get a degree with as short an attendance as possible — he was very kind & promised that I should be accommodated as much as possible — & on the monday he went with me himself to the Vice Chancillor & I was* <u>matriculated</u>

On the Sunday Evening I met with Johnson (whom I thought absent from Oxford) at the Chapel of New College — we drank tea with him & he dined with us at New College the next day —

On the monday Night ab^t 12 Walter & myself left Oxford in a Chaise in Company with a friend of Johnsons whom we had accidentally met at the Inn I ~~left~~ *parted from Walter at Hounslow set off in a Chaise & overtook the Petworth Coach whilst the Passengers were breakfasting at Esher — I arrived at Petworth about 1/2 past two on the tuesday having passed L^d E on the road but having been up all night, I was fast asleep & did not see him —*

Since my return here nothing particular has happened — the Company who have been here since the return of the family from Town ~~have been~~ *are the Comte de Vandreul his Wife her sister & Mother — two or three people before Brighton races & two or three since Mr Datins [?] & Mr Clarke are now here & have been about 3 weeks — Henry* ~~having~~ *being in the Guards we do not see much of him & my care is now solely confined to Charles whom I hope to make a good Scholar but he is somewhat slow & heavy & does not advance so fast as I had hoped & expected Wrote today a note to Mr Hayley which I gave to Mr Clarke who goes there tomorrow —*

Sockett apparently assumed he had not been baptised in the Church of England and as his parents were no longer alive he could not ask them. His mother's death may have emotionally freed her son to relinquish family Dissenting loyalties and to pursue a career in the Church of England, for it would seem to be a career and not a great spiritual calling on his part. Consequently, on 24th August 1806, Sockett went to East Horsley, Surrey, to be baptised by the rector, the Reverend John Austin, according to the instructions of the Archbishop of Canterbury. East Horsley was a parish in a Peculiar of the See of Canterbury. Austin was a contemporary of Sockett and was to be rector of Pulborough to the east of Petworth during Sockett's time. Was it Sockett himself who scratched out the entry recording his baptism or a later censor of his Journal?

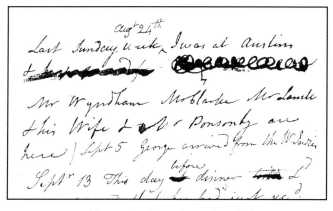

27. Thomas Sockett's journal, with the
entry recording his baptism blacked out.

John Walter, who accompanied him on the matriculation visit to Oxford, had evidently become an acquaintance and friend in London. The son of the founder of *The Times*, he was one year older than Sockett. He had taken one year at Trinity College, Oxford, himself in 1795 with the intention of entering the Church but left, aged nineteen, to work with his father in the management of *The Times*. He was an influential friend for Sockett and was responsible in 1837 for calling him to give evidence to the Select Committee on the Poor Law Amendment Act. The 'civil' John Penrose was the Bampton Lecturer for 1808.

The matriculation ceremony required a candidate to have a sufficient knowledge of Greek and Latin and to subscribe to the thirty-nine articles of the Church of England, for the primary purpose of Oxford's curriculum was to prepare candidates for ministry in

Sept 1ˢᵗ I ~~continue myself~~ I have been constantly employed in reading the greek testament & other books that are connected with divinity — Lord E told me about a week ago that he would see the Bᵖ soon & ask him to ordain me —

Last Sunday week, Aug 24ᵗʰ I was at Austins & ...

[the next line is heavily scored out — the first half of the line should read '& baptised for' ... the second half is illegible]

... Mr Wyndham Mr Clarke Mr Lambe & his Wife & Mr Ponsonby are here.

Sept 5 George arrived from the W Indies

Septʳ 13 This day before dinner ~~time~~ Ld mentioned that he had just recd information of the death of Lᵈ Thurlow It is curious that Lᵈ E had recd a letter by the post that very morning from Lᵈ Thurlow, not indeed written by himself but by his direction saying that he was better & would come to Petworth in a few days.

Octʳ 12 Left Petworth with Lᵈ Egremont for London on my road to Oxford

1807 March 8 (Oxford)
I should have mentioned above that Lᵈ E waited on the Bᵖ at Chichester aᵇᵗ the beginning of Septʳ & asked him to ordain me which he refused saying he could not do it unless I had taken a degree in consequence of which refusal Lᵈ E determin'd that I should keep my terms at Oxford as fast as possible & permitted me to take Charles with me — I arrived at Oxford on the 14ᵗʰ Octʳ & left it the 11ᵗʰ Novʳ — We went thro' to Petworth in one day & staid there till Febʸ 16 (1807) when we returnᵈ to Oxford ~~where~~ —
I cannot in this part of my Journal omit mentioning tho I know not how to express my feelings as I would wish of the kindness Lᵈ E has shewn towards me with respect to my keeping terms at Oxford — he permits me to ~~take~~ have Charles with me, & a Servant & bears every expence in the most delicate & liberal manner — he is a Patron

George has been with us at Oxford near a fortnight of this term — the more I see of him the more I admire him — he is a noble youth & if he lives will be a credit to his name and family —

the Church of England. Dissenters were not admitted and indeed fraternisation with Dissenters was formally penalised. Egremont's plan to have Sockett ordained without a degree was not outrageous; George Crabbe, the poet, was thus ordained, first as deacon and then as priest, by the Bishop of Norwich in 1781. Nevertheless, the Bishop of Chichester would not do so. The attitude of the Earl and Sockett was then to get through the required time at university as quickly as possible, and the faculty of Oxford was willing to cooperate.

Exeter College has no record of Sockett's stay there beyond the fact that he matriculated on 24th July 1806, attained his BA in 1811, and his MA in 1814. His matriculation was merely a formal affair; his knowledge of Latin and Greek facilitated his entry to Exeter College where the syllabus would consist almost wholly of classical studies with perhaps some mathematics. He needed to be in residence for the required number of terms, and these were short. For his first term he went up to Exeter on 14th October 1806 was back in Petworth by 11th November; he did not return for a second term until 16th February 1807.

Beyond his description of his visit to matriculate we have no knowledge of Sockett's own experience of the university during his stay from 1807 to 1810. Gibbon wrote scathingly of his experience of Oxford in his *Memoirs*, and Sockett may have been influenced by him one way or another. He was in a strong position, having a notable sponsor in the Earl of Egremont and having the promise of Petworth Rectory; many graduates had to wait around for a considerable time before they were given a benefice and needed to cultivate the owners of advowsons, be they in the hands of a college or a private individual. As a gentleman commoner, Sockett led a relatively privileged life and, as he had Charles, a servant, and occasionally George with him, it is likely he lived in rooms in the city rather than in the college itself.

As well as his studies Sockett seems to have still been acting as personal assistant to the Earl. In 1809 he was, for instance, sorting out confusion over early yeomanry accounts.[142] In 1808 Egremont acquired the living of Tadcaster on the Egremont Yorkshire estates; he gave the living to Sockett, presumably as an income of his own. Henry had by this time gone into the Guards, and Frances had married Sir Charles Merrik Burrell, MP for Shoreham, in 1808. The servant who accompanied Sockett and Charles to Oxford may have been William Pipson, listed in the Petworth House wages book as servant to Sockett in the summer of 1806.

Hayley still took a great interest in Sockett. He wrote to the Earl in July 1808 telling of his extreme pleasure at 'his great Goodness to my Friend Sockett, and I am much inclined your Lordship will have the satisfaction of seeing Him one of our churchmen distinguished by a well cultivated mind and a <u>very grateful heart</u>'.[143]

George Wyndham had recently returned from service in the army in the West Indies. He was for a short time midshipman on the *Amelia* but switched to the army when, aged sixteen, he was equipped at great expense with all the necessary accoutrements for his entry into the 5th Dragoon Guards as a cornet.* At the beginning of December 1803, a large chest containing his bedding and luggage was sent by wagon down from the Old King's Head in London to the port of Deal en route to George on board *HMS Monarch* at anchor in the Downs in the Straits of Dover, and he sailed out of Sockett's care.†

The comment 'if he lives' was no studied pious interjection but a very real possibility for the death rate among the troops was high. Sockett was later to be very anxious for his own son, George, an ensign in the 36th Regiment, who nearly died of fever in Barbados in 1829. George, Henry and Charles Wyndham all went into the army as junior officers when they were barely sixteen; an advanced age compared to their cousin, George, who enlisted in the navy when he was thirteen. Certainly Great Britain was at war, but there was no conscription. The Earl had to buy his sons' commissions but: 'The young men of fashion and birth are bit with a military mania; they all aim at attaining a martial air, and a reputation for strictness in their Militia discipline'. Halevy quotes from Lady Holland's journal of 1793[144] and comments:

> the English officer was essentially an aristocrat, for whom camp life was but the continuation of the life on his country estate, to which he had been accustomed from infancy ... When a young man scarcely sixteen years old bought an ensign's commission and joined a regiment, he found a non-commissioned officer, without prospect of promotion to a higher rank, ready to advise him and to cover his inexperience. And in this old sergeant who inspired or interpreted his orders, the young officer would recognize the old servant who in days gone by on the family estate taught him to ride or to shoot.[145]

Sockett, the tutor of the past, continued to play much of this role for George in later years; advising him and interpreting his orders.

---

* Cornet: an officer in the cavalry who carried the colours, i.e. the flag.

† The bills for his clothing, breeches, hats, swords, saddle, and military trunk, etc., came to about £140. WSRO, PHA 12012, and PHA 8025.

Ever Your Affectionate Father: A Wife out of Westminster, 1810

Woe be to him who buys a horse in Smithfield,
or takes a servant from St Paul's
or a wife out of Westminster

It seems unlikely that the Socketts bought a horse when they lived at Smithfield, or took a servant from St Paul's, but Tom certainly took a wife out of Westminster; 'a woman for whose memory I entertain the greatest affection'.[146]

On Friday, 27th July 1810, the Reverend Thomas Sockett, clerk, of the parish of St George's Hanover Square, bachelor, married, by banns, Sarah Gray, in her parish of St Margaret's, Westminster. They were the second of two couples married that day at St Margaret's, a prestigious church hard by Westminster Abbey and the House of Commons, of which it was the official church. The witnesses to Tom and Sarah's marriage, on a wet day with squally winds, were George, William and Harriet Nicol.[147] Thomas had come a long way geographically and socially from Smithfield. His wife, the daughter of Sarah and Andrew Gray, was born in Craven Street, Westminster, on 21st December 1784, and baptised, in February 1785, at St Martin-in-the-Fields, Trafalgar Square.[148] Two years later the family moved a short distance east into Robert Street, part of the Adelphi complex, where her father was an agent for the Ayr Bank. He died in January 1788, and in 1790 Sarah's mother married Alexander Hislop.[149] In addition to an older sister, Jane, and younger brothers, Henry and Andrew,* Sarah then had half-sisters, Elizabeth, born in 1791; Margaret, born in 1792; and a half-brother, John, born in 1793.

In his will Andrew made provision for his wife and for Andrew Douglass his 'reputed natural son'. He then bequeathed Sarah and any other of her siblings, living or in the womb, a share of his estate. His daughters were to have their inheritance when they were twenty-one or when they married, whichever was the sooner.[150] Sarah was entitled to her share at the beginning of 1805, but this may not have been a great sum for the Ayr Bank suffered several acute vicissitudes in its history, and the Adam Brothers' Adelphi project was never financially successful. After his wife and Andrew Douglass had had their share, there may have

---

* Andrew was born in March 1778, after his father died.

Gray / Hislop / Brydone Family Tree

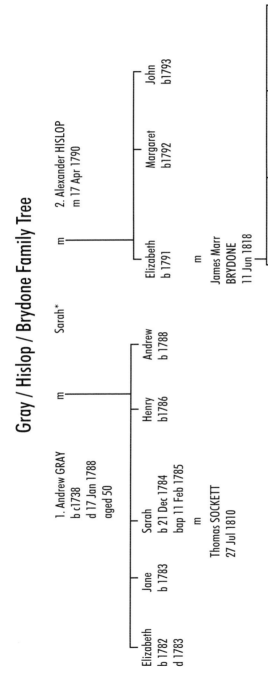

1. Andrew GRAY
b c1738
d 17 Jan 1788
aged 50

m Sarah*

Elizabeth
b 1782
d 1783

Jane
b 1783

Sarah
b 21 Dec 1784
bap 11 Feb 1785
m
Thomas SOCKETT
27 Jul 1810

Henry
b1786

Andrew
b 1788

2. Alexander HISLOP
m 17 Apr 1790

m

Elizabeth
b 1791
m
James Marr
BRYDONE
11 Jun 1818

Margaret
b1792

John
b1793

Henrietta
Jane

Walter
Marr

Elizabeth
Caroline

Henry
Gray

* Andrew GRAY married Sarah GREEN (according to family history but no record found)

* Andrew GRAY (widower) married Sarah WHITE 16 July 1778, St Clement Danes, London

been little to be divided among the other children. Nevertheless, when Sarah's brother, Henry, died in 1810, he left £2,600 invested in annuities, £2,300 of which were left for his half-sisters Elizabeth and Margaret Hislop. Sarah, newly married to Thomas Sockett, inherited a one-third share of the income from a leasehold tenement at the Adelphi.[151] Sarah may or may not have brought a fortune to the marriage, but she brought a desirable social background and some tangible goods including a collection of printed books.[152]

One of their marriage witnesses, George Nicol, was an executor of Sarah's father's will and thereby her guardian. When William Nicol paid his visit to Tom at Petworth House in 1806, he had been a partner for five years in the book-trade with his father, George, in fashionable Pall Mall. George had the reputation of being a kind, good-tempered man and his second wife, Mary, had a countenance which 'beamed with benevolence'.[153] Perhaps they warmed to William's friend. By the time of Tom's marriage, William was married to Harriet. How did Tom come to be friends with William? If Tom had not worked for George Nicol in 1793–1794 perhaps the boys met at school, or perhaps George Nicol had been a friend or acquaintance of Thomas Sockett, Tom's father. They were both booksellers, although it seems unlikely that the poverty-stricken bookseller in Cloth Fair should be well acquainted with George Nicol 'bookseller to the King'.[154] As George was Sarah's guardian, Tom probably met her through the Nicols.

George Nicol, as well as selling books, worked as a printer and publisher with William Bulmer at his press in nearby Russell Court, Cleveland Row.[155] Bulmer had come to London from Newcastle. His notable achievements in London included the setting up of the Shakespeare Press, to produce a fine edition of Shakespeare — in which George, and later William Nicol, was to be involved. The birth of the Shakespeare Press in 1786 was described by Alderman Boydell as taking place around the dinner table at his house in Hampstead; Hayley, Romney and George Nicol were there. Boydell offered him a half share of the letterpress which he accepted[156] and enlisted the support of King George III for the project.

Sarah moved in this coterie of printers, publishers, and bibliophiles. Another strand in this network of friends and relations was that of the Hislop family. In 1818 Sarah's half-sister, Elizabeth Hislop, married James Marr Brydone.* Brydone became a friend and colleague of Tom Sockett, who cared about his half-sister-in-law Eliza, her husband, and their children. The Hislop family, in turn, had links

---

* On 11th June 1818 at Marylebone Parish Church.

with the family of Mungo Park, the African explorer, whose mother, Elspeth, was a Hislop.* [157] In 1799 Bulmer printed and published Park's account of his first journeys to find the source of the Niger.[158] Mr and Mrs Hislop and the Earl of Egremont were among the subscribers to the book which ran through three editions in its first year. When he died in 1830, Bulmer was a rich man living in leafy Clapham. One executor of his will was John Walter Esq., of *The Times*, who kept Sockett company on his visit to Oxford in 1806.[159]

Tom now had a wife and very soon children to care for, and Dunster was not yet dead. Tom did perhaps remember his father's strictures on poor curates for he now needed work and was to be glad to get it from the Earl of Egremont. The Earl had a considerable number of ecclesiastical livings in his hand and was keen to acquire more, for they brought territorial, economic and political power — and foxes.

In May 1811, at the time Sarah and Tom's first son, George, was born in London, Tom was offered the living of North Scarle in Lincolnshire and the curacy of Northchapel in Sussex, both very different parishes in kind and troublesome in their own way. The Reverend Thomas Sockett went up to North Scarle, when George was three days old, to be inducted into the living at the Earl's expense. It was a small village in the flat fen lands ten miles southwest of Lincoln. John Wesley, a Lincolnshire man himself, on a preaching tour in August 1758 said of it:

> I rode to North Scarle, the last village in Lincolnshire, 10 miles short of Newark. Here a great multitude assembled from various parts, most of them wholly unacquainted with the ways of God; indeed to such a degree, that though I spoke as plain as I could on the first principles of religion, yet it seemed very many understood me no more than if I was talking Greek.[160]

The Methodists did concentrated work in North Scarle, for by the time Sockett became rector they had a strong presence in the parish with a chapel and Sabbath school attended by many of the local children, who were taught reading and writing as well as scripture. This rise in the strength and purpose of Dissent in one small village is a striking example of the effect that the Nonconformist church was to have on nineteenth-century church and state. With memories of his parents and his own childhood background, Sockett may have had ambivalent feelings about these Nonconformist rivals. In 1846, writing to the

---

* Elspeth was a sister of Alexander Hislop, Sarah's step-father.

28. North Scarle in 2002.

Bishop of Lincoln, Dr J. Kaye, he was to describe North Scarle as 'a very perplexing village'.[161] It consisted of over two thousand acres of land, largely small copyholds held by a number of families. The census for 1851 listed sixty-one farmers, fifty-six agricultural labourers, and very few servants, a very different social mix to that of West Sussex.[162] The Earl of Egremont acquired the advowson for the sum of £2,000 as an exchange between himself and the Reverend Thomas Raddish, the vicar of Kirdford, for Northstoke, in Sussex.

Sockett had no intention of starting married life in Lincolnshire in 1811. Indeed there was nowhere in the village suitable for him to live. Writing of the rectory in 1829, he said: 'the house is a mere cottage, fit only for the abode of the lowest class of farmer … and could not be turned into a habitation fit for a clergyman without considerable expense'.[163] Sockett sought an income not expense and it was an advantage, in law, to declare the rectory uninhabitable as an acceptable reason for his non-residence. Agreement over his tithes and glebe was not settled for another year for the parishioners of North Scarle laid claim to fifteen of the thirty-two acres of glebe, the legalities of which gave Tyler, the Earl's lawyer and steward, considerable trouble and induced the Earl to declare he did not want to inherit a lawsuit with the advowson. He threatened to withdraw from the deal, or to charge Raddish £200 as recompense for loss of the glebe. The contract was finally agreed without any penalty payments at the end of 1812. Raddish was invited to Petworth for the final settlement at the beginning of January 1813.[164]

Directly the Earl owned the living, he proposed to exchange it for Lancing, and in 1814 for Bignor, neither of which took place, for Sockett was rector of North Scarle until his death forty years later. He paid a few sporadic visits to the village and donated £5 towards the establishment of a Church of England day school and Sunday school, and appointed at least eleven curates over the next forty-eight years.

The situation was reversed at Northchapel, a small village to the north of Petworth, where Sockett was curate himself from the summer of 1811. The Reverend Dr Colin Milne, the rector of Northchapel from 1770, had lived in Deptford for the past forty years, and admitted that he had seldom visited Northchapel in that time, being of 'narrow fortune' and 'loaded with a family of thirteen children'.[165] As rector he was responsible for repairs to the chancel of the church, which he could seemingly ill afford. By 1811 he was also increasingly infirm and confined

29. Northchapel church and rectory, from a late-eighteenth century drawing by Grimm.

to his room, not able to get to the Earl's London house in Grosvenor Place to see Tyler on business, let alone to Northchapel, where he had appointed a series of curates, the last being P. B. Beath, described by Tyler as a 'coarse and low-minded man'.[166]

The Earl of Egremont inherited the living of Northchapel from the Duke of Somerset. St John the Baptist, Northchapel, had been a chapel of ease to Petworth until it became a parish in its own right as St Michael and All Angels in 1717. *The Gentleman's Magazine* said of it in 1833:

> This church was of very small dimensions, and of the coarsest style of architecture ... It consisted of a single aile and chancel, with a small wooden bell turret; it was 60 feet long and 20 wide and the side walls about 8 feet high. The roof was of Horsham stone, a very heavy material, formerly much used for covering Churches in the Weald of Sussex. The whole building was entirely free from any pretension to ornament, except a Decorated window in the chancel (which is still preserved); from which it would appear that the Church had been erected probably about the middle of the fourteenth century.[167]

By 1808, after a salutary visit by the archdeacon, the church and the parsonage were being radically overhauled at the Earl's expense, and indeed they stood in need of attention. For the next few years he paid bills for carpenters, bricklayers and masons, who repaired the parsonage barn and the churchyard wall, repaved the church, mended the weathercock, re-thatched the barn and stable and repaired the 'greap vine'. The parsonage itself had its tile roof mended, the chimney replastered and the drains cleared. In addition, some joists and the floor in the dining-room and parlour were mended; the lumber room's rotten rafters were replaced; and the wood and fowl house had its tiling mended and the north end wall repaired.[168] One can feel sorry for the poorly paid Reverend Mr Beath, earning £30 a year, enduring all this activity around him, but nevertheless he and Milne were increasingly at daggers drawn, largely over money, and by December 1810 Milne was eager to get rid of Beath, and he was eager to go; he was to leave on Lady Day, 25th March 1811. Milne was anxious about a replacement and at first suggested the Reverend Mr Douglas of Chiddingfold, just over the county boundary in Surrey, but was happy to accept as an alternative Mr Sockett, who was 'patronised by the Earl of Egremont' and recommended by Tyler. Sockett was to get £50 a year. Beath, however, was not gone by Lady Day, for in April 1811 he wrote to Milne threatening legal action if he did not settle a payment for salary that was due to him.[169] Milne was horrified at the prospect of a writ being issued against him; how could he endure

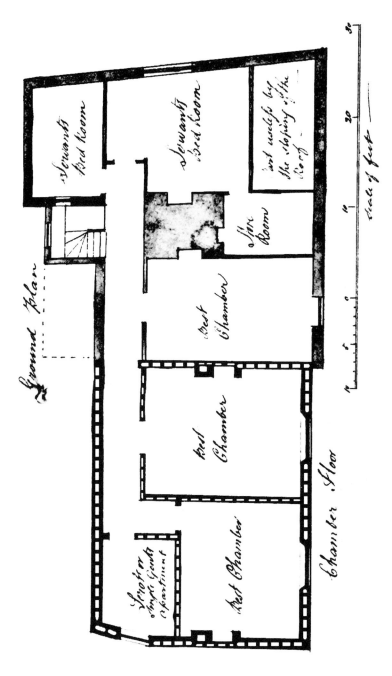

Ground Plan

Servants Bed Room

Servants Bed Room

not useful by the sloping of the Roof

Best Chamber

Lan Room

Best Chamber

Best Chamber

Another single gents Apartment

Chamber Floor

Scale of feet

30. Plan of Northchapel Rectory in 1825, showing the alterations.
The broken wall lines on the left half of the plan indicate the rooms in the west wing that were rebuilt.

The chamber floor (first floor), which comprised two servants' bedrooms and a store room, two 'best chambers' and a 'servants or single gents apartment'.

The ground floor, which comprised (from left to right) water closet, wine cellar, beer cellar, entrance hall, white wine cellar, dairy, pantry, courtyard, coal shed; dining room, drawing room, library, kitchen (with two store rooms, wash house (with boiler), privy and servants' privy.

Church

Coal Shed

Court Yard

Well

Wash house

Privy

Serv[ts] Privy

Dairy

Pantry

Kitchen

Store Room

Store room

White Wine Cellar

Entrance Hall

Library

Larder

Beer Cellar

Wine Cellar

Water Closet

Passage

Drawing Room

Dining Room

Ground Plan

the shame in Deptford? Tyler seems to have acted as arbitrator and the matter was eventually settled.*

Tom finally brought Sarah with their small baby, George, and her books to Northchapel in the summer of 1811. It must have been a considerable change, if not a shock, to come from Westminster to Northchapel, a relatively isolated village in the Weald of Sussex, and from a London town house to a country parsonage. In spite of the repairs, the parsonage was obviously still in a dilapidated state for it was to be declared ruinous by 1825,[170] when extensive work was planned at a cost of over £800, including the demolition and rebuilding of the west wing; the replacement of the damp earth floors with wooden floorboards; and the refurbishment of the kitchens, wash-house, and privies.

It is to be hoped Sarah liked country living for when George was three months old she was pregnant again. Her first daughter, Frances, was born in April 1812, followed by Caroline in November 1813. Doubtless Sarah had help in the house although how much and of what quality is not recorded, but in May 1812 the Socketts did take in a little parish girl, ten-year-old Hannah Mills, for a year — 'the parish to clothe her'.[171] Tom and Sarah were not in any hurry to have their children publicly baptised. Tom doubtless baptised them privately soon after they were born, for George was not baptised by his father in Northchapel church until 4th July 1813, when he was two years old, and Frances and Caroline were baptised together in January 1814 by the Reverend H. R. Stanhope, a prestigious cleric.†

Perhaps George was named after that 'noble youth', George Wyndham, or after King George as many English boys were, or after George Nicol. William Nicol and Harriet came from London to visit Northchapel in September 1812, perhaps to see the new baby, Frances. Whilst they were there, on 20th September, Sockett baptised their daughter, Eleanor, now nearly three years old. Her baptismal entry says she had been born on 3rd November 1809 at the Nicols' house at 2 Stafford Place, Pimlico.[172] Sockett officiated at his first marriage in Northchapel in September 1811. He got on well with his absent rector — probably Milne was greatly relieved to be rid of Beath. The writer in *The Gentleman's Magazine* in 1833 spoke of the inhabitants of Northchapel

---

* Beath became perpetual curate at Capel, near Dorking, Surrey. WSRO, RPHA 850.

† Henry Richard Fitzroy Stanhope, the fourth son of the Earl of Harrington, was educated at Trinity Hall, Cambridge, where he was awarded an honorary degree in 1811. In 1810 he was appointed vicar of Wressell, in Yorkshire, a living in the hands of the Earl of Egremont, who also appointed him to Gatton Rectory in the same county in 1814. In 1819 he became dean and rector of St Burian in Cornwall, a living he held until his death in 1864. He married the Earl's niece, Caroline, daughter of Charles Wyndham.

as 'an industrious peaceful race', with a 'respectable demeanour': 'along the cool sequester'd vale of life; they keep the noiseless tenour of their way'.[173]

This may have been so in 1833, but it was not so in 1811; Sockett's three years at Northchapel were made noisy and turbulent by an ongoing row that harassed Milne, exasperated the Bishop of Chichester, gave Tyler much work, and upset the churchwardens and the parish. The small church had accommodation for fewer than half of its 634 parishioners and, in the past, box-pews had been crammed into the chancel to provide seating for several yeoman farmers. These pews came right up to the communion table at each side of the chancel, thereby severely restricting access to the communion rail. As the Bishop testily pointed out, the only person with the right to a seat in the chancel was the rector and the clerk, anyone else seated there did so by the rector's express permission and goodwill. He proposed cutting the length of the box-pews to give access to the rail on each side of the communion table, restricting the pews' width to give more space in the chancel, and splitting each of two large box-pews, thus providing pews for four claimant families.

There were constant disagreements over these split pews; the chief complainant was George Baker, of Stilland farm, who felt he had been done out of his personal pew in the chancel. He would not share with anyone and would not take a mere seat in the body of the church. The Bakers had been yeoman farmers of note in the parish for generations and, as one churchwarden said testily, Baker wanted 'all or nothing'.[174] The family had a reputation for being difficult. In the 1790s they had already corresponded at length with Milne and the Bishop about the then curate's failure to take two services on a Sunday — services essential in 'this immoral age' — and there was a lengthy and bitter feud over a curtain erected by one of the pew-holders and hacked down by Baker with his knife.[175]

Milne, increasingly old and ill, was reluctant to upset old parishioners and friends; the Bishop of Chichester issued ultimatums that were never implemented; and the churchwardens seemed impotent to come to any satisfactory solution. They wrote to the Bishop, saying that perhaps he would care to come and point out an exact spot that would satisfy Baker, adding tartly that such trouble and criticism as they were enduring would deter people from taking on the work of churchwarden in future. Sockett, as the mere curate, was not called upon to play any official part in this ongoing trouble, but doubtless, being actually there in person, he encountered a good deal of face-to-face argument and fevered parish politics. At the same time he was officiating at services, superintending the repairs to the church, attending vestry meetings and vaccinating ten of the village children against smallpox.[176] He may have vaccinated George at the same time, if not baby Frances. He was also riding up and down to Petworth and is pictured as present on 24th June 1814 when the victorious heads of state in the late war with France visited the Earl of Egremont. Sockett is, perhaps typically, peeping over the heads of the assembled nobility on the far right corner of the picture.[177]

On 24th November 1814 he baptised his fourth child, Sarah Ellen. This was the last time Sockett officiated at Northchapel, for twelve days later the baby and her mother were dead. Sarah, having had four children in as many years, died of fever, presumably puerperal fever.* Sockett disappears from the Northchapel records from then on. There was indeed woe. Having read in his Journal for 1806 of his sorrow at losing his mother, one can imagine his dire distress at this tragedy.

Sarah and the baby were buried by the Reverend John Costhwaite, the curate of Egdean, near Petworth, and services in Northchapel from then on were taken by various stand-in clergy. The three little children were perhaps taken to London to be cared for by their maternal grandmother and Sarah's half-sister, Elizabeth Hislop.

Sockett officially relinquished the Northchapel curacy in May 1815; Milne wrote to Tyler that Sockett had told him himself in 'so very delicate a manner' which did him 'the greatest honor' and has not failed 'to raise him high in my esteem'. Milne himself was dead by October 1815. He died insolvent, and his wife, Jane, asked Tyler to send thanks to 'Mr Sockett for his kind attentions to me'. It was well known that Milne was in desperate financial straits and Sockett's 'kind attentions' may have included the £60 a year that the ratepayers of Northchapel voted for Milne in February 1813, as an addition to his tithe, to help with the expense of repairs.[178]

---

*An entry in *The Gentleman's Magazine* obituaries for December 1814 recorded: 'Dec 1st – At North-chapel, aged 29, Sarah, the wife of the Rev. Thomas Sockett MA. Her death was occasioned by a fever following the birth of her fourth child. And on Dec 5th Sarah-Ellen, her infant daughter.'

MY LITTLE PARISH OF DUNCTON

In April 1815 Sockett became rector of St Mary's, Duncton, a pretty village containing thirty-five houses in 1811, three miles south of Petworth, under the shadow of the South Downs and the hill that gave Cowper so much anguish on his visit to Eartham. The living of St Mary's was another of the many in the hands of the Earl of Egremont. The previous rector, the Reverend Dr Bryan J'Anson Bromwich, died in April 1815. He had been rector for over forty years, but after 1785 a series of curates began to officiate in the parish. Tyler said of Bromwich, at the time of his death, that he was poor with four or five children, although he must then have been at least in his sixties. When Sockett took over, the tithes of Duncton — about £160 a year — were a considerable advance on the £50 he had had as curate of Northchapel and a useful addition to the tithes of North Scarle.

Sockett officiated at his first baptism on Christmas Day 1815, when he baptised Ruth, the daughter of Alexander Dobison, a paper maker, and his wife, Sarah. (The Earl of Egremont had established paper mills in Duncton and Iping.[179]) Duncton Church was tiny; separated from Petworth in 1692, it then became a parish, with a rector in its own right, forming part of the settlement around Manor Farm. Ten acres of land were set aside as land for a house with outhouses for the habitation of the rector and his successors forever.[180] The tithe map of 1838 shows a small free school next to the church, and a stable for 'Rev T. Sockett' — presumably for his horse — but no mention of the rectory, a large house opposite the church. It does not figure in the tithe commutation map, being not liable for tithe, but Sockett paid £7.8s. land tax from 1816.

The rector of Petworth, Charles Dunster, and his wife, Mary, had been absent from Petworth Rectory for considerable periods. In 1813 he had a licence to be absent. In 1815 he was in some kind of institution: 'Mrs Dunster will not think of getting him out till he be regularly discharged'.[181] They had their own house in Petworth, New Grove, by 1816. In May 1814 the Earl offered Petworth Rectory, purely as a place to live, to John Welchman Wynne, the then curate, who refused it as he was quitting Petworth the next month. Wynne was a living blueprint for Trollope's Mr Quiverful of Puddingdale. Whilst he was curate at Petworth, a petition was issued in his name citing his dire circumstances and debts.[182] In September 1814 the Earl then offered the rectory, which was still standing empty, as a home for the next curate, Joseph Brenton Wanton/Wauton. Wanton had second thoughts about taking it for himself and his considerable family, the problem being payment for the fixtures and fittings that he had wrongly presumed went with the house.

After Dunster died towards the end of April 1816, the Earl seems to have been in a hurry to install Sockett as rector, only two days later. Sockett himself was uneasy about the rush. He had followed the Bishop of Chichester to London at the Earl's wish but seemingly against Tyler's advice:

> Should you have any further conversation with Lord Egremont and should his Lordship come over to your ideas on the subject pray let me have a line in Grosvenor Place. Whether it be the best plan or not I think it right for me to act as Ld E recommends be the consequences what it may; unless he sees the propriety of waiting believe me with many thanks for your kind zeal ...

He wrote again the next day, 23rd April 1816, from London to Tyler:

> The Bishop is at Chichester; and does not return to town till Monday next. I shall return to Petworth <u>tomorrow</u> and if Ld Egremont should <u>still</u> think it expedient that I should get immediate institution will go to Chichester on Thursday — <u>I</u> think your plan the <u>safest</u> but must of course feel myself bound to comply with his Lordship's wishes — If you should have any opportunity, perhaps you will have the goodness to explain to him your view of the subject you are perfectly right in saying that my haste in coming to town was entirely owing to my thinking it was <u>Ld Egremont's</u> own wish which indeed <u>he</u> expressed very strongly, believe me truly yours — [Sockett's emphasis][183]

It does seem undignified haste, with Sockett pursuing the Bishop around the country and talk of immediate action and safe plans. Did the Earl think that, in spite of him owning the living, another candidate was going to appear, or that the Bishop would not approve his choice?

Some explanation of the Earl's and Sockett's actions may be found in a letter Hayley wrote on 2nd December 1807 to his friend Richard Watson, the Bishop of Llandaff, asking if he would consider ordaining Sockett before he obtained a degree, as the Bishop of Chichester would not. Hayley notes that the Bishop of Chichester and the Earl were not on good terms. He is also concerned that should the Earl or Dunster die before Sockett was ordained he might 'lose a very good Living by the unlucky Circumstance of not being prepared with the usual Formality to hold it' and would, as an orphan, 'be left indeed desolate in the World.'[184]

Richard Watson it would seem did not grant Hayley's plea, for Sockett was ordained by the Bishop of Chichester in 1810. The Earl was fortunately still alive in 1816 but did he fear, given the animosity between them, that the Bishop of Chichester would not approve his choice of candidate for the Petworth living?

Certainly the Earl and Sockett were anxious, and Tyler hatched a plan. In the event Sockett seems to have caught up successfully with the Bishop, for two days later he issued a mandate for Sockett to have the 'Rectory of the Parish church of Petworth' on 25th April 1816.[185]

31. St Mary's Church, Duncton, in 1745.

My Tumble Down House: Petworth Rectory, 1816

When Sockett finally came to Petworth Rectory[186] the Church of England and the status of its clergy were about to come under acute attack. Within a decade the Anglican Church was to wrestle with changes that upset the relative calm and the assumptions of Sockett's eighteenth-century inheritance. By the time he died there were significant changes. In Petworth the Dissenters had two chapels: Providence Chapel, built in 1775, and the Congregational Chapel, to be built in 1819; the Methodists were making great incursions into the religious life of North Scarle; and at Duncton the Biddulph family of Burton Park, staunch and influential members of the Roman Catholic Church, were to be catalysts of change. The admittance into Parliament of representatives of these groups of Nonconformists and Roman Catholics by 1830 diminished the authority of the Church of England and initiated a painful period of enquiry into its finances and structure.

There were also painful upheavals within the Anglican Church itself. Sockett undertook his ministry in a spirit of humane but ordered belief; he did not embark on a mission of saving souls from eternal punishment. He admired but did not emulate his father's 'enthusiasm' and was not driven by the anguish of the Oxford Movement that was to grip his compatriot, Henry Manning, at nearby Graffham. As long as Egremont was alive, the structure of the old rural hierarchy of order and responsibility held good, although it was increasingly to be challenged by other factors that Sockett was to recognise in his own parish — namely, the growth in population and the changes in the labour market. Sockett himself might be held to a degree responsible for the growth of population by his sponsorship of smallpox vaccination, and if Sarah had lived they two were well on the way to turning Sockett into Mr Quiverful.

It could be argued that Sockett himself was part of the change. He was an educated member of the upwardly mobile middle class with his roots in trade, and he represented in many ways the skills and energy that challenged the hegemony of the landed autocracy. He was London born and bred until he was ten, and brought a business and town background with him to the countryside. Egremont, as his employer and patron, gave him the entrée into the highest echelons of society and power, but with them he was always to a greater or lesser extent an outsider. How he would have fared in the city is open to question. Nevertheless, he kept strong links with London life and thought. Egremont spent a considerable amount of time in his London house and Sockett went with him, as well as visiting the Nicols just over the park in Pall Mall and Stafford Place.

In 1816 it must have seemed to Sockett that a new life was opening before him; the long war with France was finally over and the

Herington Family Tree

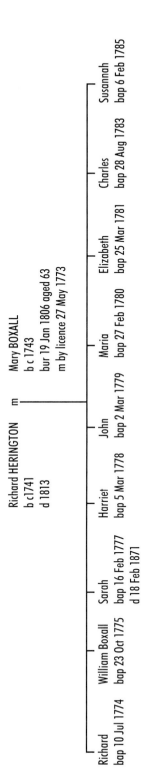

Richard HERINGTON
b c1741
d 1813

m

Mary BOXALL
b c 1743
bur 19 Jan 1806 aged 63
m by licence 27 May 1773

Richard
bap 10 Jul 1774

William Boxall
bap 23 Oct 1775

Sarah
bap 16 Feb 1777
d 18 Feb 1871
m
Thomas SOCKETT
m 1816

Harriet
bap 5 Mar 1778

John
bap 2 Mar 1779

Maria
bap 27 Feb 1780

Elizabeth
bap 25 Mar 1781

Charles
bap 28 Aug 1783

Susannah
bap 6 Feb 1785

triumphant powers were busy trying to put Europe back together, largely on the old pre-war model. He married his second wife, Sarah Herington, from neighbouring Kirdford, on 21st March at Petworth, and on 25th April Sockett became rector of Petworth. He was thirty-eight and was now rector of North Scarle, Duncton and Petworth, three livings that he kept for the rest of his life. Sarah was the eldest daughter of Richard Herington and his wife, Mary Boxall, both of whom had lived in Kirdford for many years as substantial tenant farmers of the Earl of Egremont.[187] Sarah, baptised in February 1777, was some months older than Sockett. She had five brothers and four sisters. Harriet, a year younger than Sarah, was witness at her marriage to Tom and she lived with them much of the time, possibly playing the classic role of the spinster helping to look after her sister's children. She is listed in the census return for the rectory in 1841 and 1851.

At his death in 1813, Sarah's father's household goods and chattels were sold and the proceeds shared among his children. Sarah and her siblings seem to have inherited something less than £200 each, for they each had around £100 plus in the Petworth Savings Bank from 1818 onwards. Sockett was responsible for setting up this bank, one of the contemporary vaunted 'self-help' institutions, and the Heringtons figure large among the entries in its early days.[188] Sockett seemingly did not marry Sarah for her money. Why did he choose her above her four sisters? It was perhaps, to a greater or lesser extent, a matter of expediency. Sarah had presumably shown skill at running a household and managing servants. She had experience of coping with children, being the eldest daughter with younger brothers and sisters, but at thirty-eight would presumably be spared the burden of producing countless children herself at yearly intervals and repeating the bitter tragedy of 1814. She should also have skills at coping with the usual tasks of the farmer's wife or daughter, managing the poultry yard and supervising the dairy.

How did Sockett meet her? Had he and the first Sarah known her in their Northchapel days? Had they met on the local social network and, if so, how much had Sockett been involved in this since his wife's death scarcely more than a year before? Did the second Sarah live up to Sockett's expectations? Was she kind to her stepchildren? Was she liked in the parish? We do not know for there are few references to her in all of Sockett's correspondence after 1816. Letters to and from friends sometimes refer to his daughters but scarcely ever to his wife. She was mentioned rather dismissively, for example, on one occasion when Sockett, writing to Mrs Hawkins of Bignor Park in 1836, says that Henry and he have been struck with influenza and 'Mrs Sockett is also very poorly whether from the same disorder seems hardly ascertained — thus we are a set of poor creatures'. In 1838 he and Sarah had a holiday in the

Wyndhams' Brighton residence, and it is a matter of note that 'Mrs S who before she came had been confined to her room walked out <u>twice</u> down to the sea this day'.[189] It is Caroline, Sockett's youngest daughter, 'my dear active careful Caroline, who is a great comfort'.[190] If Sarah was, or became, a poor creature, she did produce Henry, Sockett's younger son, who was to follow in his father's footsteps and was very dear to him. She did subscribe regularly to the Petworth Girls' School until the 1830s,[191] and she lived to be ninety-four. She did not go to her husband's funeral and is not mentioned in his will.*

Financially, Sockett was now comfortably off with the tithes of three livings at his command. In Petworth he also had 149 acres of glebe spreading to the east and north from the back of the house. In 1819 his yearly income from Petworth was reckoned to be £1,044.14s.3d., including £688.5s.8d. from tithes, and £362.3s.9d. profit from the glebe.[192] Of this, £140 a year came from the fourteen-year lease of the parsonage farm to William Elliot, senior and junior, who were also to supply Sockett with five wagon-loads of wheat straw each year, three as a gift and two at one guinea per load.[193] Several of the glebe meadows Sockett leased as small lots, and presumably the remainder of the yearly income came from the part of the glebe he farmed for himself. This included meadow and arable land, a hop garden, two ponds and a small lake. By 1838 he also owned a small cottage and a cherry orchard, adjacent to the glebe, in his own right.

In addition, he had tithes of £387 net from Duncton[194] and, by 1840, £252 from North Scarle plus the income from thirty-two acres of glebe which he leased to a North Scarle farmer. In accepted contemporary fashion, he also supplemented his income by taking pupils, certainly at least one: his godson, Frederick Henry Arnold. As rector he would have the fees for officiating at births, deaths and marriages and would also make a little money by proving wills — the usual fee was five shillings.[195] His income would thus have been in the region of £1,700, putting him in the top bracket of livings in the diocese of Chichester.

His expenses, apart from his household expenses, included payment for two curates, one at Petworth and another at North Scarle. In 1835 he was paying £159 a year for his two curates; the average income for a curate in Lincolnshire in 1835 was £77.[196] Presumably the curate at Petworth, given a larger parish, would get the larger part. In 1816 they were probably getting less than in 1835. Sockett had received £50 a year at Northchapel. He did not have a curate at Duncton, where he took the

---

* There are two recently discovered letters written by Sarah in 1864 to Helen Wyndham, the daughter of George and Mary Wyndham; thanking her for a visit; urging her to read her New Testament; and referring to a performance of Dr Arnold's oratorio, 'Ahab'. WSRO, PHA 13903.

services himself except for a few occasions when nearby clergy officiated on an ad hoc basis for a fee, until his son Henry took over as curate in 1842. There would also be many parish charities to subscribe to for coal, clothes, and incidental appeals, such as 'buying a mangle for Catherine Yeoman'.[197]

He also needed to employ men to farm his own acreage. In the 1830s he had three. He did not pay land tax on the Petworth living, as this was redeemed in 1800 in exchange for tithes due on part of Petworth Park, but did pay £7.8s. a year for the rectory at Duncton (and he presumably paid land tax for North Scarle). The land tax remained constant, but Sockett was liable for poor rates and these would be an increasing burden. Arthur Young, in his correspondence with the Earl in 1800, had spoken of his anxiety about the alarming state of the poor, as a result of enclosures, the war, and the acutely rising price of grain: 'there must either be some great change in their support or poor rates will swallow up the whole landed in course'. He went on to hope that the Earl of Egremont would think of some plan to 'assist the poor in their misery'.[198] The conception and implementation of a viable plan was to occupy the Earl and Sockett for the next thirty years.

For Sockett, the future looked secure and comfortable, with a new wife to care for the household in a large and socially desirable rectory —unlike that of North Scarle this *was* fit for a gentleman to live in. The living of Petworth, previously a gift of Eton College, had from 1693 been in the hands of the Dukes of Somerset and their successors to the Petworth estate. The rectory had been rebuilt between 1623 and 1641, and the Earl had spent almost £600 in repairs between 1783 and 1785.[199] When Sockett took over, he immediately spent £1,200 of his own money, presumably on more necessary repairs and alterations. Unfortunately, in 1819 some of this seeming security and comfort was physically and financially to fall apart, for the rectory proved not fit to live in. On 23rd February, after stormy wet weather followed by snow, the middle part of the rectory roof, the middle walls, and the whole of the interior — twenty-six feet in length and forty-five feet in breadth — over the hall, the bedrooms over the hall, and the dining room collapsed to the floor.

There were now five small children in the Sockett nursery, including Tom and the second Sarah's two little children, Charlotte aged two and Henry, a baby in arms, but no one was reported as injured or killed. The family may have been living elsewhere in Petworth or Duncton until Wanton left in 1819, when initial repairs were begun at Petworth Rectory, and it was perhaps these incomplete repairs plus the bad weather that brought the roof down.

The rectory was Sockett's freehold responsibility and he faced the bill for the repairs. An estimate by Thomas Chrippes, the local surveyor, came to £1,720.11s.10d., including £128 worth of timber to be used from the glebe. One saving grace in this disaster was the mortgage facility offered by Queen Anne's Bounty, a fund set up to encourage the rebuilding and repairs of rectories and thereby to encourage the residence of the clergy. In 1811 £50,000 was specifically set aside for this purpose and from then on the provision of mortgages, as one branch of the Bounty Board's work, was extensively developed; Sockett was one of its early clients. He negotiated a mortgage, through the auspices of the Bishop of Chichester, with the Bounty Board for twenty-five years at five per cent on the security of his tithes and the glebe rent; his income from these was reckoned at £1,044.14s.3d.; £688.5s.8d. from tithes; £271.3s.9d. rent of the glebe; plus another £91 from the glebe; minus £5.15s.2d. for procurations, tenths, synodals.* His annual repayments would come to about £109 a year. If he was non-resident his interest rate would have been ten per cent.[200]

He said in 1819 he was so poor: 'I cannot afford a cruet stand'.† An amount of £109 a year for the mortgage does not seem a fearful amount out of his total income, but this debt seemed to be a large contribution to the 'weight of corroding care' he says in April 1838 he had carried for nearly twenty years.[201] From then on he certainly pleads poverty on frequent occasions. It would seem that any money Sarah, his first wife, brought to the marriage died with her or was tied up for her children, unless it was part of the £1,000 Sockett had already spent on the rectory. Another chronic financial care was that, if he died, his wife and children would have no income and no home. In his Journal he said did not expect to make old bones, and his income was the only source of substantial money, for he had no family nor family wealth behind him as many Anglican clergy did. Making provision for his family was one constant preoccupation. 'I could not, with a wife and family and a life-income only involve myself in law suits' was to be his tart answer to Mr Wakely, a member of a Select Committee, in 1844.[202] Caroline, his younger daughter, never married, and the eldest, Frances, did not marry until she was thirty-eight. Both the girls were therefore dependent on their father for much of their lives and his sons, Henry and especially George, as adults were a constant expense. Even if he did live to a good age, any of his family who outlived him would inevitably lose their home, as the rectory, on which he had spent so much money, would pass to his successor.

* Money set aside for the entertainment of ecclesiastical dignitaries, such as the bishop or archdeacon.

† Sockett would seem to be remembering Horace: 'He lives well on a little whose family salt-cellar shines amidst a modest table'. Odes Bk II: 16. WSRO, PHA 10547, Sockett to Tyler.

Nevertheless, poor Sockett's loss is our gain. To procure his mortgage, Sockett had to submit a detailed plan of the ground floor, any other floors of the parsonage, and a plan of the elevation of the house. There also had to be written specifications for the repair of the rectory with a description of the old condition of the house.[203] These plans and the specifications give an immediate picture of the lifestyle of Petworth Rectory in late Georgian England.

In common with many mortgage negotiators Sockett reasoned that whilst he was about it he might as well do the job properly. Dalloway wrote that Sockett 'has made great improvements both in the house and spacious gardens. From the terrace 130 yards in length, there is a beautiful home view with the Surrey hills in the northern distance'.[204]

The repairs to the house were finished in 1820, and it was now set in spacious gardens with an impressive drive sweeping in a circle from its tree-lined entrance on North Street. The old stable-yard was now a kitchen garden and there was a laundry at a suitable distance from the house. All a far cry from the bookshop in Cloth Fair and the cottage at Weston Underwood. This was a gentleman's house and over his lifetime Thomas and Sarah filled it with suitable furniture and fittings — including presumably some cruet stands — as the sale of effects at Thomas Sockett's death was to show.

Messrs. DEATH & SON.

By order of the executors of the late Rev. Thos. Sockett, ALL THE HOUSEHOLD FURNITURE, consisting of prime goose feather beds, mattresses, four-post, tent, French, and Arabian bedsteads, bedding, mahogany and japanned chests of drawers, washstands, toilet tables, commodes, wardrobes, toilet glasses, hall, dining, library, and other tables and chairs, sideboards, Indian cabinets, Brussels, Kidderminster, and other carpets, pianoforte, table and other lamps, easy chairs, sofas, chimney glasses, silver plate, plated goods, glass, china, linen, 1,000 volumes of books, pair of globes, busts, paintings, the usual culinary utensils, a patent mangle in good condition, electrifying and galvanic machines, air pump, electro-magnetic rotatory machine, insulating stool, electronometer, a lapidary's lathe, garden lights and frames, tools, ladders, roller, plants, a very fast saddle mare, 8 years old, about 15¼ hands, warranted perfectly free from vice, a six-years' old bay horse, 15½ hands high, warranted perfectly quiet in saddle or harness, a capital pony, very quiet, pony chaise, harness, light spring cart, gig, water tubs on wheels, &c., &c., &c.

32. Auction of Sockett's household goods, from 12th May 1859.

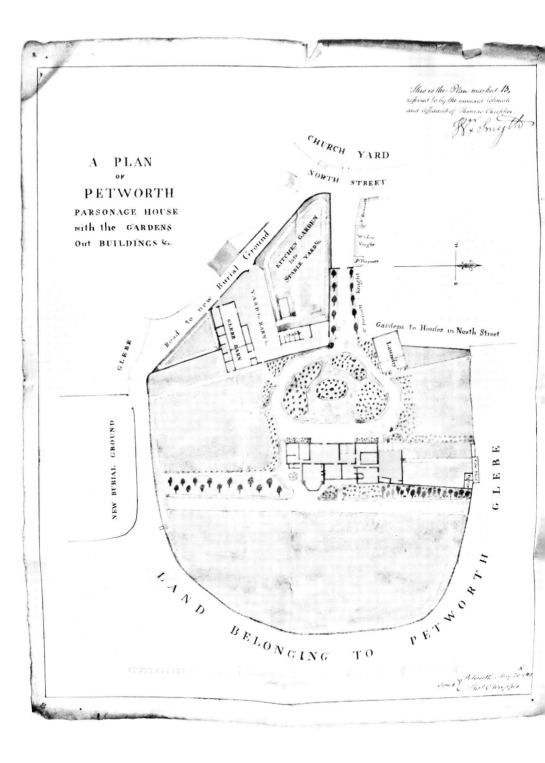

33. Plan by builder Thomas Chrippes of the parsonage house, gardens and outbuildings.

An Estimate for rebuilding part of the Parsonage House of the Rectory of Petworth and for the Outbuildings on the Glebe thereof –

All the Walls to be of Stone with Brick Angles and rough cast on the outside. The Lintels bond Timbers and Joists to dining Room and the Chamber (over Washhouse) Floors and Washhouse and dairy Door cases to be of Oak. The Roofs the naked Flooring over Hall, dining Room and Kitchen and the quarter Partitions to be of memel crown Timber. The West Roof to be covered with Slate the east Roof with Tiles and with a lead Gutter between the two Roofs. a plain Verander to West Front painted Green. a purbeck Stone Pavement to East Front between the wings five feet wide. Two Cellars under dining Room to be Arched with Stone and paved with Brick. The Hall to be restored of the same dimensions as before. All the bed Rooms, the dining Room and the Study to be floored with Deal. The Walls to be plaistered and papered, the wood work both out and inside to be painted. The windows to be sashed and glazed with best Crown Glass. A new folding Gate to the Stable yard. the Stable to be repaired and separated from Coachhouse by a quarter Partition lined with Deal. The Barn to be repaired with one new Pair of Doors and a shilling in the Barn enclosed for a Stable. The Stone Wall at the side of the Road to new burial Ground to be compleated and a piece of low walling to be added on the south side of Road to preserve the line.

The whole to be done in a good and workmanlike manner and according to the Plans prepared and signed by me and will after applying the Value of the Timber and other Materials thereupon fit to be sold or employed about such Buildings amount to the Sum of One Thousand seven hundred and twenty Pounds eleven Shillings and ten Pence –

Thos Chrippes

34. Part of Thomas Chrippes's estimate for rebuilding part of the parsonage house at Petworth Rectory.

Plan of Chamber Floor.

35. Plan of Petworth Rectory 1819. The broken lines indicate the location of the repairs.

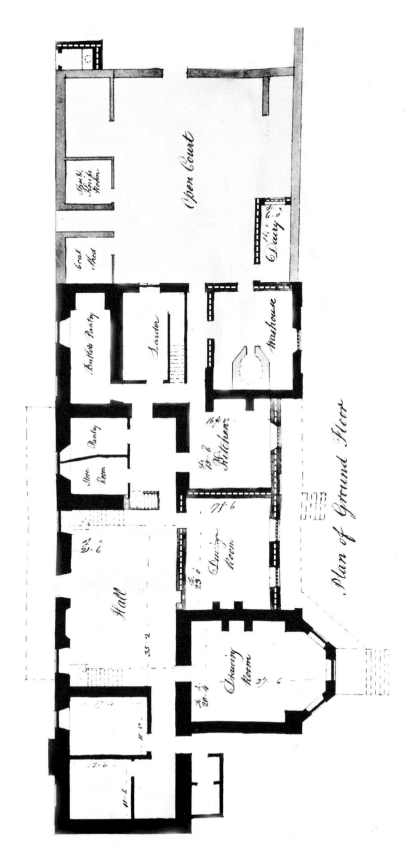

Plan of Petworth Rectory 1819. The broken lines indicate the location of the repairs.

MY TUMBLE DOWN HOUSE: THE DRAWING-ROOM

From the windows of his study Sockett could see who was coming down the drive from the town. 'My house is invaded from morning to night, and it cannot be helped — it is part of my duty',[205] Sockett wrote in despair to Mrs Wyndham at the time of the Earl of Egremont's funeral. Nevertheless his words held true for many days at the rectory. Many of these 'invaders' were visitors to the back door seeking help in spoken or written word, or tangible kind; but a select number would be admitted at the front door and cross the high hall to the large and imposing drawing-room. The Earl and his children presumably came over from the big house; perhaps Sockett or Brightman cousins visited; and Tom and Sarah entertained the nearby Heringtons. Sockett was well liked with a large circle of friends, over whom he took time and trouble: 'It is a sweetener of the bitters of this life, when one has a chance of doing anything for a friend.' [206]

Some were longstanding friends from the days of his Journal, including the Nicols in London, the Guys in Chichester and the Mitfords at Pitshill. Others were encountered and cultivated in his role as rector of Petworth and Duncton, including the Hawkins family, who had lived at Bignor Park since 1806. John and Mary Hawkins had children much the same age as Sockett's own and consulted him over the education of their son, as well as over the board wages that Lord Egremont paid his servants. They asked him to dine (Mrs Sockett is not mentioned): 'my cold is certainly somewhat better & I shall have much pleasure in dining with you on Thursday'; they hope he will come and meet their visitors from Lincolnshire; and in February 1826, on an apparently cold or wet day, they earned 'my best thanks to Mrs H for the loan of her cloak which did me noble service'.

Hawkins was a fellow of the Royal Society and the Geographical Society, and he and Sockett evidently got on well together and shared an interest in the academic and scientific discourses of the day. Hawkins took a personal interest in the discovery of the Roman villa at Bignor and the hypocaust at Duncton in 1811. He and Sockett were both farmers with an interest in crops and the weather;[207] Sockett kept a meteorological journal.[208] Francis Steer said of Hawkins that he had a not unpleasing sense of humour and this may well have chimed in with Sockett's own, which surfaces occasionally in his formal correspondence; correcting Hawley, the Poor Law Commissioner, in 1837 over the cost of individual emigrants, he writes: 'These cheep ones went from Swanington — possibly they swam over'.[209]

Another good and longstanding friend was Adelaide O'Keeffe. She and her father, John O'Keeffe, the renowned dramatist and actor, came to England from Dublin in 1780 to live in Chichester and then, by 1830, in Southampton. Adelaide's brother, John, had been at Exeter College six years before Sockett, and died three weeks after going to Jamaica in 1803. Adelaide and Sockett corresponded with some intimacy, concern and — on Adelaide's part — dry humour, over the years. Staying at Kew in 1840, she was expecting a visit from George Wyndham and his daughter, which would give the owners of the '200 eyes' peering from the windows of Kew Green something to gossip about. Adelaide took a great interest in Wyndham's horses currently racing at Epsom and Ascot but claimed not to share Sockett's interest in old manuscripts and the library at Petworth, and recollected how in the past she had evaded him whilst he hunted for her all over Petworth House: 'I preferred two miles walk in the Park & thro the Gardens for I am an ignoramus as to Books and Mss'.[210] This claim was not strictly true as she had a number of poems for children published in 1808.

Other visitors to the drawing room came from nearer home. Sockett had been friends with the Arnold family since his time as tutor. Benjamin Arnold was music master at Petworth House and organist at St Mary's, where a new organ had been installed in 1812. His funeral in 1816 was one of the few at which Sockett officiated at Petworth. George Frederick Handel Arnold, son of Benjamin and Harriet, was baptised on 5th June 1795. He became organist in his father's stead, assistant master at Petworth National School and vestry clerk. Sockett stood as godfather to Frederick Henry, George and Mary's son, baptised at Petworth on 23rd March 1831.

One family visitor was Elizabeth Brydone, Sockett's sister-in-law. Sockett maintained great affection and concern for Eliza. Possibly she had helped to care for her two little nieces and nephew after their mother died, and she was a link for Sockett with the past. In June 1818, when she was twenty-six, Elizabeth married James Marr Brydone at St Marylebone Church in London. Brydone was a surgeon and a male midwife and, after their marriage, set up in practice at 37 High Street, Marylebone. The practice was evidently not very lucrative for in 1819, shortly after his daughter Henrietta was born, Brydone was appointed surgeon superintendent on the *Eliza* taking 150 convicts to Australia.

He was already a well-travelled Royal Navy surgeon, having been to India and the West Indies, and present at the Battle of Trafalgar. On this visit to Australia in 1820, he took the opportunity to go kangaroo hunting over the Blue Mountains. On his return he was appointed surgeon to Portsmouth dockyard, where his first son was born; in 1823 he went to the Victualling Yard, Deptford, where a second daughter was born in 1825. By 1834 there were four children, half-cousins of Sockett's eldest three children.

Brydone had been anxious about his prospects and future employment in 1827 when Sockett took up his cause in high places.[211] His contact was Colonel George Fitzclarence, one of the sons of the Duke of Clarence — soon to become William IV — and the famed actress Mrs Jordan. Colonel Fitzclarence in 1819 had married Mary Fox, one of the Earl of Egremont's daughters — one of the three little girls who had gone on the trip to Portsmouth in 1805. Sockett was on good terms with Fitzclarence — said to have been 'a most amiable man in private life' — who promised to take up Brydone's case with his father: 'but I understand the Duke says, he has so many applications for all sorts of things that he knows not which way to turn'. Sockett urged Brydone to keep an eye open for future possibilities and 'perhaps Eliza's ingenuity may suggest some more efficient mode of application that may back up mine'.* Sockett promised to keep Brydone's name before Fitzclarence and to introduce Brydone to him in London. Fitzclarence, Sockett noted, was often to be found at the Admiralty, which might well be, given that his father, the Duke, had served in the Royal Navy since a boy, and had in April been appointed Lord High Admiral, a title resurrected for the Duke's pleasure by the new Prime Minister, George Canning. When the Duke became King in 1830, he made George Fitzclarence Lord Munster. After a brilliant if controversial career, Munster shot himself in 1842, and Mary died a few months later leaving three sons and three daughters.[212] Henry Wyndham became guardian to the children. Lord Melbourne did not consider Munster a 'most amiable man' and on hearing the news wrote to Queen Victoria:

> Charles Fox attributes it entirely to the vexatious and uneasy life which he led with Lady Munster, but he was always, as your Majesty knows, an unhappy and discontented man, and there is something in that unfortunate condition of illegitimacy which seems to distort the mind and feeling and render them incapable of justice or contentment ... application may be made to your Majesty for the continuance of the pension upon the Privy Purse to his son. As Lord Melbourne advised your Majesty to continue these pensions upon the late King's death, perhaps it may not be improper that he should now say that it is his strong opinion

---

* Eliza may have had some family connection with Sir Thomas Hislop to whom George Fitzclarence was appointed aide-de-camp in India in 1814.

that they should not be continued further. There is no reason for it. They are not very rich but neither are they poor, and they have very opulent connections and relations.[213]

Melbourne might well speak of the 'opulent connections and relations', for it was widely believed that he himself was a son of the Earl of Egremont: 'resembling in character and manner, as he did remarkably in feature, his father, the late Lord Egremont', wrote Charles Greville.[214]

In 1834, with the reduction of naval personnel, Brydone was finally made redundant. Sockett again took up his and Elizabeth's cause but now with the Duke of Richmond, his neighbour:

> I have just received a letter from my sister in law, written under the most anxious feelings, as an order had just come down, the effect of which will be to remove her husband from his present post, and not conveying any intimation as to his future destiny. I cannot help forming a hope that this may be only a preparatory step towards placing Mr Brydone in a situation better suited to his talents and his services, but in the mean while his wife, a very delicate woman with four children under 13 is sadly agitated & I dread the effect upon her health.[215]

Sockett was rather vague as to the children's ages for Henrietta would be fourteen coming fifteen. In another letter in March of the same year he seems unsure whether Brydone and Eliza have five children or four,[216] but his concern was genuine and practical. It became increasingly obvious that Brydone was not going to get another naval appointment, and Sockett turned his attention to persuading him to take charge of the ship being sent by the Petworth Emigration Committee to Canada, leaving very shortly at the end of April. The 1834 PEC ship, the *British Tar,* was in need of a good, experienced surgeon–superintendent and Brydone could well be the right person. In his relationship with Brydone and in their correspondence, Sockett was at his most forthright and forthcoming on an equal man-to-man basis: 'I have no doubt that you have been darkly dealt with; but the difficulty would be in bringing the matter to <u>light</u>: and if you did — now for another old saw — one such victory might be worse than a defeat — <u>All big wigs hang together</u>'.[217] An observation gathered, one suspects, over years of being the man on the fringe of affairs, and the lowly observer at the tables of influential administrators of local, and lofty, policies and decisions.

Brydone took the post on the *British Tar* and from then on, with Sockett's encouragement and his influence with Egremont and George Wyndham, he was to work for the owners of Petworth House, and settle in the town, and his children after him. At some time between 1834 and 1841, Elizabeth Brydone and the children moved into part of Petworth Rectory; Elizabeth and James Brydone appear in the 1841 census at the Rectory. Elizabeth was probably glad to be well settled whilst Brydone was away in Canada and later in Ireland, and the nurseries were presumably reopened at the top of the house. It is to be hoped that Elizabeth and Sarah, Sockett's present wife, got on together. The Brydones would surely have paid some rent which might have eased Sockett's 'corroding care'. There were plans to build an extra wing on to the south side of the rectory and to divide the large hall, presumably to give the Brydones a dining-room, kitchen and pantries of their own,[218] but there is no evidence that this was implemented; perhaps Sockett did not relish the expense.

MY TUMBLE DOWN HOUSE: THE STUDY

Sockett's especial kingdom was his study and library. Here he wrote the voluminous correspondence he maintained on behalf of himself, his parishes and the Earl of Egremont. Brydone spoke with appreciation of the hours he spent in Sockett's 'snuggery'.[219] Of his sermons we know very little; if he followed common practice, he used the volumes of published sermons widely available to the clergy at the end of the eighteenth century. The famous painter Joseph Turner, friend of the Earl and a frequent visitor, painted a picture of a preacher in the pulpit of the chapel in Petworth House, and this may be Sockett in his role of chaplain to the Earl.

He may seldom have written his own sermons, but he spent hours every day writing letters. Letters were taken by hand by a boy around the town; others went with Sockett's 'man' on horseback to the great and not so great in the wider neighbourhood; others were loaded on to the daily mail-coach for delivery to London and the country at large. Early in his career Sockett created a very distinctive signature for himself which he used throughout his life, and his writing is bold and clear; a factor that recommended him to Hayley, Lord Sheffield and the Earl of Egremont. Sockett's business letters are clear and concise in content and, although he uses due deference in his correspondence with the Duke of Richmond, for example, his style is not sycophantic for its time but straightforward in its requests and information. One has the feeling that Sockett enjoyed much of the mechanics of the administration, which he admitted he 'cheerfully undertook' on behalf of the Earl.[220]

All of Sockett's business correspondence was copied as a record. He may have done some of this copying himself, but sometimes Caroline and Frances were seconded to help and perhaps earned a little money: 'if my daughters were here they would speak most feelingly upon the subject, because the poor girls have had many things to copy which otherwise I should have slipped in'.[221] Giving evidence to the Select Committee on Postage in 1838, Sockett argued for letters to be charged by weight rather than by the number of sheets, each piece of which was then charged as a separate letter. As well as being a useful private code, his use of shorthand was a practical means of taking down letters for later transcription and providing copies of written correspondence. In later years he used the newly developed copying system whereby damp tissue paper was pressed on to a mirror image of the original document impressed on a stiff jelly in a tray. This was a great time saver and released Caroline and Frances from much labour, but from the later reader's point of view these tissue copies are difficult to decipher and handle for they are faint and fragile and stick together.

Many letters were carefully kept by their recipients. Squire and Mrs Hawkins kept at least some of theirs, as did James and Elizabeth Brydone. Letters to the Duke of Richmond were filed in the Goodwood Archives, and hundreds of others are stored in the Petworth House Archives. Tyler, Egremont's steward, must have been responsible for many retained and stored with a lawyer's prudence and efficiency. Nevertheless, there must have been many letters to and from the rectory now lost, some of them of a personal and informal nature.

Whilst the Earl was alive, Sockett could get franks to cover the postage of his letters, a facility he used extensively, but 'even that facility I did not use to the utmost of his lordship's kindness I often hesitated to ask him for franks'.[222] When he was organising the emigration scheme after 1832, he received countless letters and used some initiative in dealing with them:

> When I first began this system of emigration, I had letters from various gentlemen, making inquiries on the subject. I found that it was absolutely impossible to answer all those letters. I therefore sat down once for all, and wrote a little pamphlet, which I entitled 'A Letter to a member of Parliament' ... At that time I took care to have it under an ounce in weight. I sent a copy to nearly every Member of both Houses of the Legislature, because I could send them for free.[223]

One can envisage Sockett in his study working on this letter, outlining the desirability of sponsoring parish emigration and the method that the Petworth Committee took in implementing it, and the anxiety and authority with which he sent it out into the world. The same concentration and effort must have gone into the compilation of the chart of emigrants, by parish, number and date, which he put together in 1836. Caroline and Frances must have helped him with this.[224] It is small wonder, that with all this correspondence coming and going from the rectory, Sockett claimed to be well acquainted with the postmaster of Petworth and much in the habit of passing by the Post Office.

Sockett's signature.

My Tumble Down House: The Nursery

Apart from the corroding care of his mortgage, Sockett had worry and expense with his children, the lot of the anxious parent throughout the ages. Charlotte Agnes was born nine months after Sockett and Sarah Herington married, and Henry eighteen months later; it may be these successive births that accounted for Sarah's ill health. However, there were to be no more children, and Sarah, who was thirty-nine when Henry arrived, was spared the constant pregnancies and premature death of the first Sarah. She did, however, have the sorrow of losing her first-born when Charlotte died in 1824 aged seven. We can imagine the sorrow that her mother and father underwent from the anguish her father described later when Henry nearly died of influenza in 1836:

> the preservation of his life to us, and restoration of his health is felt by me, I think, hope and believe, with deeper sentiments of gratitude to a merciful God, than I ever before experienced on any occasion — it is agony to think how ill I was prepared to say from the heart 'thy will be done' had that been different.[225]

The rebuilt nurseries were under the roof over the high hall, a storey above the study and library. With five young children to care for, Sarah would expect to employ at least a nurse and a nursemaid, one of whom would sleep in the night nursery with the children. How did the three eldest children get on with their stepmother? George went away when he was seventeen, but Caroline and Frances lived at home for many years. There is never any hint in Sockett's correspondence that he feels them to be an untoward expense, and they certainly helped their father in his study and the parish, and doubtless their stepmother in the running of the house.

How were George and his sisters educated? With his experience, Sockett probably taught them himself along with one or two paying pupils. The girls may have had a governess, at least for short periods, and Frances went to school in London, probably to a young ladies' academy, for a year or two, when she was fifteen or sixteen.[226] George may have gone to school or had lessons from another tutor in the town. It is unlikely that Sockett sent him away to school after George Wyndham's experiences. The children had plenty of space to run around in Petworth itself and on their father's glebe lands, and went to the seaside at Littlehampton where Sockett rented a house, No. 15 Beach house, in the 1820s and 1830s.[227] Mrs Sockett was there in November 1827: 'not very well I am sorry to say'.[228] On one occasion, perhaps as an eleventh birthday treat,

George accompanied his father to the Egremont's Brighton house.[229]

On 21st November 1828, at the age of seventeen, George went into the army. There is no evidence that he thought of going to Oxford, as Henry was later to do. Perhaps he had no inclination, or perhaps there was no money with four other children at home, but Sockett did spend about £500 buying George a commission as ensign with the 36th Regiment of Foot, and then in 1832 as a lieutenant in the 36th Herefordshire Regiment of Foot.[230] Perhaps George chose to go into the army in emulation of the army careers of the young men of Petworth House. He served in Ireland and in the West Indies at the time of the great hurricane of August 1831, from whence he was sent home in 1832 suffering from fever. His father wrote to the Duke of Richmond asking that George should not go back to the West Indies:

Petworth Sept 13th 1832

My Lord Duke,

I have this moment (10pm) received your Grace's very kind note with the enclosure from Sir J MacDonald the contents of which afford us the greatest comfort & I lose not an instant in begging your Grace to accept my warmest acknowledgements & those of my son for the great kindness you have shown towards us in the whole business — This reprieve from the W Indies will afford us time for consideration ...[231]

A later letter thanked the Duke for expediting George's transfer to the 15th Horseguards, now stationed at Newcastle but due to go to Canada.[232] Meanwhile, whilst he was home, the unfortunate George broke his leg, which delayed his return to his regiment until March 1833. He was disappointed at not getting a posting straightaway to Canada. In April 1833 he wrote from Newcastle that he had offered to take another officer's place without success: 'I am quite sure of going in the next draft but I fear that will not leave the country till next year about this time'.[233]

As a result, in August 1833, George precipitously sold out his commission and came home still set on Canada. However, unless he went almost immediately, he could not sail until the following spring after the St Lawrence River had unfrozen. Therefore, after much 'hurry and turmoil', he sailed at 9:00 a.m., on 29th August 1833, on the *Ottawa* from Gravesend. The previous day his father accompanied him to London, where they stayed overnight with the Nicols in Pall Mall. It was a rough, stormy day:

you will rejoice with me in the escape of my dear boy thro' the favor of a kind providence from the dangers of such a gale as the ship was exposed to in the Downs — several broke away from their anchors, and more than one was lost, but she rode it out gallantly and went away cheerily with the first fair wind and is I trust eer this half across the Atlantic.[234]

Sockett's experience was shared by many families saying goodbye to their kith and kin sailing away on emigration ships, including the Nicols' son, William Bulmer, in 1835.

A considerable amount of money was to go out to Canada from Petworth Rectory over the ensuing years to buy land and maintain George on a farm at Eramosa, near Guelph. There was also a steady flow of letters. Frances and Caroline were obviously fond of their brother and wrote often. Sockett, the two girls, and Henry — Sarah Sockett is not included — wrote a joint letter, each having part of one large sheet of paper which folded up could then go for the cost of a single letter: if the postage was not so expensive, 'My daughters would be frequently writing; they would write to their brother whenever any little thing occurred'.[235]

My Tumble Down House: The Piggery

Across the yard from the kitchens and outhouses was the piggery. Pork, bacon, ham and sausages played an important part in the domestic economy of the rectory dining-room, and the lesser cuts, offal and trotters, would be eaten in the kitchen or given to the poorer inhabitants of Petworth. The Sussex pig was bred from the large Berkshire spotted pig or a cross between this and a smaller breed. Cobbett reported that the pigs around Petworth were all black and thin-haired and 'precisely the same sort ... with which I pretty well stocked the American states'.[236] Sockett did his bit toward stocking Canada, with the hogs that Edward Longley took over on his behalf to George Sockett in 1835.[237]

Sockett's pigs in 1819 were doubtless taken from the Earl of Egremont's stock, although their sty would have been a smaller, simpler version of the impressive piggery erected by the Earl at the turn of the nineteenth century.[238] Arthur Young tells of the interest of the people of Petworth in the fattening of the pig. He describes the weighing of a very large Berkshire stag hog in Petworth market-place and discusses the fattening of hogs in detail. The Earl experimented with the two extremes of either letting them run free in the park or fattening them up in a battery system. Pigs were commercially fed on barley, pease, oats, or potatoes; Sockett's pigs doubtless had some of their food from kitchen waste.

Sockett, we trust, had never been acutely hungry, although, as a lad, food was probably austere for economic reasons when his father was bankrupt and the bailiffs called, and during the austere lifestyle practised at Eartham. It was perhaps difficult to have more than enough if one was perpetually a dependant at other men's tables. Sockett took a direct and concerned interest in the provision of food in his work as rector of a parish, as a visitor at Sutton Union, and in the rations for emigrants on the Petworth Emigration ships. 'I think they ought to have, to use a coarse phrase, a belly-full' was his tart rejoinder to Sir James Graham in 1837 when they crossed swords (or perhaps knives) over the provision of meat puddings to paupers.[239]

The meat that the ordinary working man or woman ate was bacon. 'We *must* and *will* have *that*', said the young turnip hoer, eating his breakfast under a hedge near Upwaltham, to Cobbett, who in 1823 'saw with great delight, a pig at almost every labourer's house'.[240] Ten years later, in the early 1830s, the *must* and *will* were being spoken with increasing desperation. In the face of increasing unemployment, the high price of grain, rising poor rates, and the rigours of the new poor law, the labouring man and woman in Sussex were having to live on less and less. Indeed, as many commentators, including Sockett, were to point out, a man with a family could scarcely earn enough to eat at all:

A labouring man at the present wages, the out-door relief being taken off, cannot keep his family in anything beyond bread; in many instances he has been obliged to cease to keep his pig; which is a great comfort to a labourer.[241]

Another Sussex man remembered:

When it was possible for father to do so, he bought two pigs every spring — paying seven shillings or a little more for each. We fetched in ferns and leaves off the rough to make their beds, and fed warm vegetables to them which I used to boil and stir up with a little meal. We could not pay a big score to the miller so father hired a quarter of an acre of land and sowed it with oats in order to get grain to ripen the pigs. The second pig we always sold, so the money over, after we had paid the miller, went to buy material for clothing for us all. Then the manure made the garden stuff grow. [242]

Mr Butt, a local farmer of forty years standing, and a guardian of the poor, spoke vividly of the hunger in the 1830s: 'I have seen the difference even in the faces of the people'. There was now no money to spare to buy barley for the pig. Under pre-1834 regulations Butt had given sacks of barley as 'out-relief' to labourers fallen on hard times; under the new poor law commissioners' regime he was forbidden to do so.[243]

Sockett lent money to his parishioners — farm labourer William Dearling was one — to buy a pig. Sockett was exasperated by the policy of the Sussex Agricultural Society — offering prizes for married labourers who had voluntarily supported their aged parents or made provision for their own old age.[244] In his judgement, it was impossible for a family such as the Dearlings to do so; they had five children under the age of thirteen and could scarcely live, even when their income was supplemented by the meagre amount the industrious Dinah Dearling could earn by taking in washing.[245] Bacon appeared less and less on the family menu, giving way to bread and a little cheese. In 1833, when Sockett headed the local vestry administering Petworth Poor House, bacon or pork appeared on the dinner menu three times a week alternating with cheese and soup. From 1834, after the implementation of the new Poor Law Act, Petworth became part of the Petworth Union in which Sockett refused to act as guardian. The diet was now governed by the stringencies of the Poor

Law Commission. Sockett compared this unfavourably with the food provided by Sutton Union in which he was still a visitor:

> In the Sutton workhouse the people have, four days, plenty of meat and it is not weighed out to them by ounces and half ounces; they have a reasonable supply, and they have what is a very great comfort and luxury to a poor man, they have what is called a meat pudding.[246]

The rations provided for the emigrants sent out between 1832 and 1837 by the PEC were much the same. They had meat four times a week, beef on two days and pork or bacon on another two. Beef was considered superior to bacon and seldom appeared on the tables of the poor in the 1830s. The first PEC ships carried highly salted Irish beef, which the emigrants universally rejected: 'they could with great difficulty eat it, and would have preferred living entirely on dry bread or biscuit'. Consequently, from 1833 on, the ships were supplied with local salt beef, bacon and pork, 'that had been cured for the express purpose at Petworth' — a slice of home.[247]

St Mary the Virgin: Petworth

A church in Petworth is noted in the Domesday Book. Peter Jerrome in his two volumes of the history of Petworth, charts the history of the church and its clergy through the ups and downs of English history and religious practice.[248] When Sockett arrived in 1816, the Anglican Church had been experiencing a relative calm, although change and decay were now attacking its foundations. St Mary's was to suffer material decay and change in the understanding of its role and supremacy. Nevertheless, change was not all bad. Music at St Mary's may well have come from a group of instrumental players before the advent of the organ; Northchapel had a band with a flute, clarionet, bass viol, and drum.[249] Benjamin Arnold, the organist of the new organ in 1812, was a keen musician, and singing by the whole congregation was part of the service at St Mary's. For the service of consecration of the organ, Arnold suggested the 'Old Hundredth — All People that on Earth do Dwell' and, from *Olney Hymns*, a hymn for spring especially favoured by the Reverend Mr Dunster:[250]

> Now the smiling spring appears,
> See each grove new beauty wears
> Hark the birds with cheerful lays
> Warble their creator's praise!
> See where lately all was snow,
> Flowers in loveliest clusters grow;
> And the fields in green array,
> Speak the future harvest day.

An appropriate hymn for a country parish, it had little didactic content apart from the birds' praise, and the perhaps implied deeper connotation of the 'future harvest day'. Dunster put together a collection of psalms and hymns for the use of country churches with instructions how they should be sung:

> To my Parishioners this collection of Psalms and Hymns, compiled for their use is affectionately offered and it is recommended to all, who are able, to join in singing them To the Praise and Glory of God, Thereby rendering our Psalmody, what it certainly ought to be, the Devotional Act of The Whole Congregation.[251]

Sockett, as a child, would have sung in the Nonconformist chapel as part of the service, and he followed in Dunster's footsteps at

St Mary's. In 1820 James Goldring reprinted a small volume of fifty-two pages of metrical psalms and forty pages of hymns 'principally selected and adapted by the late Rev. C. Dunster, M.A.', for the use of Petworth Church. There were hymns and psalms designated for the religious and pastoral year, and others chastening or comforting for human weakness and sorrows. Dunster's taste had been eclectic including hymns from Tate and Brady's collection of 1696, *Olney Hymns* of 1799, and the Magdalen collection. Hymn writers included Sockett's old neighbour and friend William Cowper, Thomas Kenn, the Bishop of Bath and Wells, Charles Wesley, Martin Luther, Walter Scott and Mrs Barbauld. Dunster's collection was one of several produced in Sussex at the same period. One was composed, selected, and adapted by T. Bennett, the organist at Chichester Cathedral, and another by Nathaniel Cooke of the parish church, Brighthelmstone (Brighton).[252] At the end of the nineteenth century Henry, Sockett's son, was to publish a collection of sixty hymn tunes he had himself composed, 'during the Sixty Years of Her Majesty's Reign'.*

The congregation at St Mary's, in the early-nineteenth century, sang hymns that were part of many peoples' cultural and religious experience for generations to come including, in addition to 'All People that on Earth do Dwell', 'Guide us o Thou great Jehovah', 'Awake my Soul and with the Sun', 'Lo He Comes with Clouds descending', and 'Brightest and Best of the Sons of the Morning'. Some hymns would be recognised today in slightly different array, for example, a hymn for Christmas Day:

> On Judah's plains as Shepherds sat,
> Watching their flocks by night,
> The Angel of the Lord appear'd
> Clad in celestial Light.

This carol was altered to today's official version in *Hymns Ancient and Modern*, published in 1861. Metrical psalms were verse paraphrases intended for congregational singing as with Psalm 23:

> The Lord my pasture shall prepare:
> And feed me with a shepherd's care...

---

* An advertisement in *The Times*, 30th October 1897, 2, announced the collection, published by Messrs Weekes and Co, Musical Publishers.

As well as encouraging singing in church, Sockett often led the singing at tithe dinners and other parish occasions; perhaps he also played on his flute.

'The Spire looks admirably now all the scaffolding is removed from it', Sockett was pleased to say in November 1827.[253] St Mary's had been given a new spire, paid for by the Earl. Unfortunately, Sockett's pleasure was short-lived, for two months later the tower showed signs of cracking under the strain and the church was closed. Services were held in the town hall for the next two years, whilst extensive rebuilding and renovations, designed by Charles Barry and costing more than £1,600, were carried out. By October 1829 services were being held once more in the church, but the pews in the nave, the reading desk and the pulpit still had to be erected.

A circular stained-glass window was added in the east end of the chancel, replacing the old, wooden-framed one, and three smaller windows were installed to the south side, also glazed with stained glass. Under the east window was a stone tablet inscribed with the Ten Commandments, the Lord's Prayer, and the Belief, and under this a stone table enclosed by a new gothic railing for the administration of the Holy Communion. The foundations of the tower were strengthened and the six old bells augmented to a ring of eight bells; bells sound large in all the festive days in Petworth, and more solemnly at funerals. Hot water heating apparatus was also installed which doubtless added greatly to the comfort of the clergy and congregation. There were 274 sittings in the new pews, 268 of which were free.[254] These pews were in addition to the old for in 1851 St Mary's was said to have 1,366 sittings in all, 572 free and 794 other.[255] In 1846 Sockett had a window in the chancel, reputed to have been closed for 150 years, reopened.[256]

In common with the practice in many eighteenth- and early-nineteenth century Anglican parishes, confirmation services in Petworth Church had been neglected, but in August 1841 there was mass confirmation in St Mary's of hundreds of candidates from Petworth and surrounding parishes. Two hundred and seventy-eight candidates came from Petworth alone, 107 males and 171 females; the clergy seem to have cast their net wide on that occasion to gather up long lost souls. There was a grand organ voluntary by Arnold, prayers by the curate Klanert, and a sermon from the Bishop. The hymn was one of Cowper's, 'Bestow, dear Lord, upon our youth, the gift of saving grace', and a setting of Psalm 26, 'I will wash my hands in innocence'.[257] In 1844, 300 more young people were confirmed at Petworth, but this was as nothing to the 700 confirmed at one service in Brighton.[258]

The Parish: A Nice Market Town

'Petworth is a nice market town, but solid and clean', wrote William Cobbett approvingly in 1822; another visitor, from Cobbett's hated great wen of London, in 1824 scathingly spoke of the 'boors and clowns' of this 'barbarous and outlandish spot'.[259] Cobbett approved of Egremont and Richmond as landowners with traditional values, and he did not encounter Sockett, or at least he does not appear in one of Cobbett's forceful attacks on the frailties of the parson. In 1821 Petworth had a population of 2,781: 1,361 males and 1,420 females; 543 families were living in 457 houses; 158 families were said to be engaged in agriculture, 213 in trade and manufactures, and 172 'other'. Duncton had a population of 246: 128 males and 118 females, living as 45 families in 37 houses; 36 families were engaged in agriculture, and 9 in trade.[260]

As rector of St Mary's, Sockett officiated at few of the baptisms, marriages, and burials in his parish church, almost none of the baptisms and only about six per cent of burials and seven per cent of marriages between 1816 and 1859. In 1816 he inherited J. B. Wanton as his curate, followed in 1819 by W. R. Wake and in 1820 by James Knight Greetham, who stayed for eleven years until he had the gift from Egremont of the living of Northchapel. The services that Sockett did take, as might be expected, were those of the Wyndham family, the Herington family, and his friends, but there were occasionally others of less note, for example, the baptism of a child of a vagrant mat maker in 1821, and the hasty marriage of a farm labourer, Charles Moore, a minor, and Rhoda Willett just before they emigrated to Canada in 1832.

In Duncton he took, with few exceptions, all the baptisms, marriages, and funerals up until 1842 when his son Henry became curate. Duncton was a very small parish and the actual number of these services was tiny compared to those in Petworth, but they were at a distance from Petworth and therefore more trouble. Sockett would need to ride over, rather than walking for a few minutes up the road. Having no curate at Duncton, he probably was constrained financially to act himself rather than paying ad hoc clergy.

It was certainly the curate's function to officiate at Petworth. As the Reverend Sydney Smith wrote, slightly tongue in cheek but with a large degree of truth, in 1805: 'as there must be hewers of wood and drawers of water in every community, so also in the Church there must be makers of Sermons and baptisers and burriers [sic] of the dead. The sweet privilege of doing nothing cannot be enjoyed by all — The Will of God be done'.[261] Sockett, nevertheless, did not have 'the sweet privilege of doing nothing'. As Sydney Smith said of himself, 'I have also played my part in the usual manner, as doctor, justice, road maker, pacifier, preacher, farmer, neighbour and diner-out'.[262] Sockett was not called upon to play his part as a justice of the peace, as this was forbidden in Sussex, but all the other roles were his and that of neighbour and diner-out were perhaps more demanding than normal in that the neighbour was the Earl of Egremont, who made considerable demands on Sockett's time and energy, and the dining out at Petworth House was often with influential local and national personages.

He seems to have been well liked among the farmers and tradesmen. His tithe dinners were convivial affairs, and the townspeople gave him enthusiastic dinners to commemorate the anniversaries of his induction to Petworth:

> the twentieth anniversary of the Rev. Mr Sockett's induction in this parish was celebrated on Tuesday 26th April last, by a dinner at the Half Moon Inn. The morning was ushered in by our well-known ringers giving a merry peal, which indicated to the inhabitants that something was on the tapis, and it was soon ascertained that the principal gentlemen of the town & neighbourhood intended to dine at the Half-moon and to invite the reverend gentleman. Upwards of 50 gentlemen sat down to an excellent dinner, provided by the worthy host and hostess, Mr and Mrs Lee. The company separated at a late hour. There were many good speeches, and the chaunters were in good tune.[263]

Sockett had not embarked on his vocation as a wrestling with sin and everlasting damnation but with a mission to improve, not so much the spiritual, as the moral and secular state of his parish. This moral and secular respectability was to be encouraged by approved methods of self-help, although, as with the Dearlings, Sockett had reservations about how much self-help should be expected from people who were scarcely clothed and fed: 'I think it quite a mockery to propose a medical club to a man that has not shoes to his feet'.[264]

One of Sockett's first actions as rector was to form a sub-committee in support of Petworth National School. This school, under the auspices of the National Society for the Education of the Poor in the Principles of the Established Church, had been mooted since 1811 — the same year as the foundation of the society itself.[265] There was interest in the education of the poor in Petworth before this. Elizabeth Ilive paid 6d. a week for thirty weeks in 1800 to William Newman for teaching John Herrington and John Yeoman,[266] perhaps her servants or grooms. Later, in 1813, Benjamin Arnold received £2.15s.10d. for 'evenings schooling to groom apprentices', and the groom lads were being taught to write by George Arnold in 1814.[267]

Dunster acquired a book on *The Education of the Poor*, written in 1809, and, later, Fred Iremonger's *Suggestions to the Promoters of Dr Bell's System*, written in 1813. Egremont bought five copies of 'Lancaster's system of Education' for £5 in 1811.[268] This system, devised by Quaker Joseph Lancaster, and that of Dr Bell, were both based on a plan of monitorial teaching and were rivals, the Lancasterian system being taken up by the British and Foreign Society favoured by Dissenters, and the Bell system adopted by Anglicans. It is unlikely Egremont toyed with the idea of supporting the Lancasterian system; perhaps he was interested to see how their scheme worked before he invested his money otherwise. The idea of education as a desirable personal and social attribute was increasingly in the air, but the question was what kind of education and by whom? Hayley's hymn, written for the children of Petworth School, encapsulates much of contemporary dogma:

> We honour all, who raise our thought,
> Above the Valley's clod,
> All, by whose Bounty we are taught,
> To know and serve our God.[269]

The National Society was formed with the intention of keeping education of the poor in the hands of the Anglican Church, promoting the liturgy and catechism of the Established Church, encouraging attendance at divine service, and insisting that teachers should be members of the Church of England and that the curriculum and control of the school should be subject to the superintendence of the parochial clergyman. Petworth National School was Sockett's responsibility.

Subscriptions for a school had been sought since at least 1813, for a meeting of the sub-committee in 1818 chased Mr Bridger and Mr Newland for their subscriptions, in arrears for five and four years respectively. There were six classes in the National School of 1816. This does not necessarily mean six teachers for the monitorial system organised a labour-saving pyramid system of instruction from one teacher down to monitors, who then taught their rows of children. The sub-committee initiated a system of rewards for hard-working teachers who attended regularly: 4d. a week for teachers, 2d. a week for assistant teachers, and 4d. for the usher.

George Arnold was an assistant master at the school, becoming master at a salary of £30 a year when James Goldring retired in 1818. Goldring, the local stationer and printer, was awarded a payment of £10 a year as a reward 'for the pains he took in the original foundation and subsequent management of the school'. Goldring had been master of Taylor's charity school in Petworth, established in 1753, providing for the education of ten boys and ten girls, and he seems to have had his own boarding-school grafted on to this; another shoot was that of the free National School.[270] This first day-school was for boys, but by 1822 was joined by a school for girls.

As rector, it was one of Sockett's tasks to gather subscriptions for school maintenance from the local gentry, farmers and tradesmen. This was a trying and unrewarding task; not all farmers nor local employers were convinced of the need of education for their labour force, and parents were often 'too careless to keep their children at school even when they may send them free of expense'.* As compulsory education was not to be introduced for another fifty years, employers, parents and children could continue to be careless if they wished, or, in the case of some parents and children, against their wish.

When Sockett sent in the Petworth return to the Select Committee on Education of the Poor in 1818, he cited a day — and Sunday school 'on the national plan, containing about two hundred boys and sixty girls, supported by voluntary contributions'; the town had, in addition, two fee-paying schools, a long-established endowed school for ten boys and ten girls (Taylor's school), and nine dame schools. The Sunday school, a new departure, probably accounted for the sixty girls in Sockett's return.

Sunday schools, teaching scripture, reading, and perhaps writing to children who could not attend a day-school, were well established nationwide especially in manufacturing areas and among Dissenters, as at North Scarle, but there were already several in Sussex.[271] The Sunday school does not appear officially in the Petworth sub-committee minutes until 1824, when the master's salary was raised from £30 to £40 a year with the proviso that the boys' school should be considered as a Sunday as well as a day-school. Sockett meticulously kept and audited the donations and subscriptions to both the boys' and girls' schools from 1822. He himself gave two guineas a year and the Mitfords and Hawkinses gave generously. Subscriptions overall for 1823 came to £47.5s.5d. and expenditures to £44.10s.9d., including salaries. Items appearing regularly under expenses for both schools were brooms, brushes, mops, 'sope', and dust pans; cleanliness was certainly next to godliness.

---

* Select Committee on Education of the Poor etc. (1818), Sussex. Sockett was either dilatory in his returns to the committee or they were mislaid for the information appears in the supplement to this report.

Charlotte Wyndham provided clothing for six school girls in 1823.[272] The wives of the subscribers to the Boys' School largely supported the Girls' School; one would like to think they did so out of regard for the education of their own sex but it was probably with the pragmatic wish of ensuring a steady supply of acceptable servants. Mrs Sockett donated one or two guineas each year until 1831, and Miss Sockett and Miss Wyndham gave contributions from 1827 onward. After 1829 the school was not totally free, for there were added contributions from 'pence' — the pennies that pupils brought for tuition. From the early 1830s onwards Sockett no longer kept nor audited the donations and subscriptions. Listed subscriptions ceased and the schools' income came from Egremont's endowments of £1,333 for each school, invested in three per cent consuls, and, in the case of the Girls' School, some fees of 2d. a week, plus collections in church following sermons in aid of the schools. In 1830 a sermon by the Reverend Mr Ridsdale yielded £15.0s.2d.[273] By 1834 forty girls were being taught reading and needlework and — for the 'competent' — some writing and arithmetic. All the children in the Boys' and Girls' Schools were expected to go to church twice on Sundays and on Christmas Day.

The little National School at Duncton was affiliated to the Chichester Diocesan Society between 1815 and 1816, and Mrs Wyndham and Sockett both contributed towards the education of the children and Mrs Leggatt's salary. The Wyndhams paid for twenty children at 3d. per week and Sockett kept 'six children constantly at this school' and paid £1.1s.0d. a year towards the Sunday teaching.[274] Sockett's children may have gone at some point to the Petworth fee-paying schools; they would certainly not have gone to the National School. Frances and Caroline may have helped to teach in the school, as daughters of the rectory often did in the early days of the village school. One of their roles was frequently to oversee the needlework which, with basic literacy, formed by far the major part of the girls' curriculum. By 1852, as well as plain seams, the girls were expected to gather a cuff, make a buttonhole, and turn a heel.[275] In 1838 Sockett gave credit to the National Schools for the improvement in literacy among his parishioners in the past twenty years:

> There are very few boys now of 12 years old who could not write something in the shape of a letter ... when I first knew Petworth it was hardly the case at all; but even when I first had the living it was not the case to the extent to which it now is.[276]

In 1816, when he first had the living, 55 per cent of the men and women getting married in St Mary's signed their marriage certificate with their name instead of a cross. By 1844, when the National School had been open for thirty years, 74 per cent of people could write their name,[277] although the increase may be partly ascribed to the fact that after thirty years of the local school they would be expected to do so, and did.

The reinforcement of the doctrine and authority of the Anglican Church was the foundation stone of National School education, but its curriculum was of great if subsidiary importance. Basic literacy was a practical and moral means of improving the 'boors and clowns' of Petworth. Sockett did not see his parishioners as such, but education was one means to desirable respectability. It is not surprising that Sockett was enthusiastic about education, for it had fostered his climb up the social ladder and had been his profession. Petworth National School did not teach its pupils Greek nor Latin, and was not envisaged as a means of change in the social hierarchy, but it was a means of promoting virtue instead of vice and of cultivating honest and industrious people. Whether Sockett was totally committed to the social hierarchy as he found it is open to question, but he had lived through the upheavals of the French Revolution and now, aged forty, he did not perhaps espouse change so much as order.

Advocates of education for the poor towards the end of the eighteenth century concentrated largely on the teaching of reading. People had the right to be able to read Holy Scriptures for themselves, thereby to obtain salvation, and learn the way of Christian life and death, although it was distressing that many then went on to read infidel and subversive literature, sensational newspapers, or worthless fiction instead.

By the time Sockett was at Petworth Rectory, the teaching of writing was increasingly accepted, although it was not taught in Petworth Union Workhouse school as late as 1837.[278] Sockett promoted basic literacy as a means of practical morality. A letter was a tie of affection between family members, at a time when the population was increasingly on the move; but could also be a moral tie in that good advice and counsel could pass from parent to child and vice-versa'.[279] Such a two-way flow of affection and counsel was doubtless found in the letters between the Socketts in Petworth and Socketts in Canada, as it was in letters between other emigrants from Sussex and their families. A desire for literacy must have been greatly fostered by a wish to read letters home from kith and kin overseas, and write in return. Illiteracy made one vulnerable. Sockett was aware of people duped by false carriers of news. Hearing of one man who paid for false news of his sons in Canada, Sockett scolded: 'How could you be so silly as to be imposed upon by that fellow?' 'Oh Sir', said the father, 'I was so glad to hear of my poor boys'.[280]

Sockett did not have undisputed sway over the education of the poor of Petworth. In 1820 a new Independent Chapel opened in the town when the Reverend J. Edwards of the West Sussex Sunday School Union preached from Numbers 23: 23, 'What hath God wrought'.[281] As well as a Sunday school, Mrs Nevatt, a blacksmith's wife, mother of four children, and a member of the chapel, had been 'running a day school at Petworth for some time' before 1831. She and her husband applied to be trained at the British and Foreign School Society in the Borough Road, London, and in 1831 they were granted 15s. a week to attend for three months. They left Petworth and went to London, eventually being sent to Lancaster to teach in a new British and Foreign Society school.[282]

36. 'Reading Sentimental Novels'. George Cruikshank.

The Parish: The Not-So-Respectable

The Earl of Egremont was in almost all respects the direct opposite of Thomas Love Peacock's Sir Simon Steeltrap, who by 1831 had

> enclosed commons and woodlands; abolished cottage-gardens; taken the village cricket ground into his own park, out of pure regard to the sanctity of Sunday; shut up footpaths and ale-houses ... put down fairs and fiddlers; committed many poachers; shot a few; convicted one third of the peasantry; suspected the rest; and passed nearly the whole of them through a wholesome course of prison discipline, which has finished their education at the expense of the county.[283]

The Earl had enclosed Duncton Common and did commit some poachers to Horsham Gaol, although he appeared only at the apex of a process, beginning with his gamekeeper, James Dilloway, and his son, and passing upwards through the hands of his steward and lawyer, William Tyler. Sockett's parishioners were not just the socially desirable friends and farmers, respectable tradesmen, and deserving poor. Some hungry labourers did not borrow money from him to buy a pig but sought meat for free in local fowl houses and in his Lordship's park. One might think the Earl could certainly spare some rabbits, he was a generous man, but it may have been that he was very ready to give, but did not favour those who took. Numerous dead rabbits went on the twice-weekly wagons from Petworth to the London house, possibly to appear on the Earl's table but more probably in the servants' hall. Tyler wryly remarked, 'most of the game-keepers regard with an evil eye any persons getting rabbits except themselves'.[284] After the Earl's death, Charles Klanert, the curate, had to appeal to George Wyndham for the gift of a rabbit 'occasionally', a request that was graciously granted with the additional instruction to the gamekeeper that the Socketts should have a brace of pheasants every week.[285]

Four poachers figuring large in Tyler's 1830 letter books were young lads between the ages of eighteen and twenty. It would be pleasing to see them as caring, independent sons seeking to fill their widowed mothers' cooking pots and feed their little brothers and sisters — and to some extent this was so. In this case, however, these four youths were younger members of their families with grown-up siblings, a factor which may have determined the Earl to proceed against them. They were unemployed and the thrill of the chase, defying the forces of law and order, and making some money with sales on the side were significant factors in their compulsion to take nets and traps and invade Petworth Park.

The unemployed single labourers of the parish had a hard time in these times of hunger and distress in that many of the farmers, and the parish vestry, gave work and relief as a priority to married men with families, a policy that was reinforced after 1834 when out-relief in the form of allowances of money or flour for families with three children or more was arbitrarily cut off. The single men were left to get work and wages where they could and were often ground down to 1s. a day or less. Sockett maintained that farmers could get casual labour from single men at any wage they chose to offer:

> I believe now you may have them at almost any thing you choose to give them ... I have heard many instances of single men, twenty years of age working for 1s. a day, and still less ... I do not myself employ the single men, in mercy to the married men.[286]

Petworth vestry, of which Sockett was chairman, gave unemployed single men relief of as little as five shillings a week. Edwin Chadwick, secretary to the Poor Law Commission, kindly presented to the Select Committee of 1837 a plan for a single man to live on six shillings a week consisting of 14lbs. of bread, 28ozs of cheese, 48ozs of bacon, 7 pints of beer, and 9d. for lodging and washing.[287] Asked, rather sharply, why he himself then needed a guinea (21s) a day as living expenses when he was away from Somerset House, he replied, 'I hardly know how to answer that question'.[288]

One constant poacher was George Vinson, who had several grown-up brothers and sisters. His father, William, had died in 1831. George was involved with William Shepherd, a labourer, in a case of trespass in Petworth Park in 1832. If no evidence of poaching was found on the accused in the shape of game itself, or instruments to procure the same, then the legal proceedings were to issue a notice to the people involved that they were not to trespass in future and, if found doing so, an action would be taken against them for damage to the grass, hedges, fences and so on. Egremont took no action against Vinson and Shepherd on this occasion largely because it was hoped they would sail away to Canada on the first PEC ships of 1832.

Shepherd apparently did leave, but he was soon home again for in March 1833 he and Vinson were accused with James Meachen and John Habbin of trespassing in the Home Park, after receiving due notice not to do so. Daniel Steer, who lived at the lodge, saw them go into the park on 13th March. He told them that John Dilloway, the gamekeeper, was nearby; at which they swore, and said they did not care about Dilloway. On 19th March Shepherd was observed apparently setting and checking wires but he escaped over the wall.

On 11th April, Lucy Meachen, Elizabeth Habbin of Damer's Bridge, and Mary Vinson, the mothers of three of the men, and William Shepherd himself received summonses for the men to attend the court at the Half Moon Inn, Petworth on 29th June 1833. There they were issued with a fine of £50 for damages to the park and a bill for costs of £1.18s.6d. As they had no money to consult an attorney nor any money to pay the fine, on 7th August they were taken to Horsham Gaol where they subsisted on the gaol allowance of bread and water, supplemented by a little money their mothers scraped together and sent to the gaol to buy food, along with a small piece of meat and some apples and onions. In November the four prisoners sent a lengthy petition to Tyler describing their dire situation and saying that, unless the court would take into consideration their plight and order them to be discharged they must remain in prison for life, having no means whatever to discharge the amount of the said damages and costs.

By the beginning of December, Habbin and Meachen weakened and wrote an abject letter to John Lucas, of Pound Street, the Petworth constable, asking him to take it to Tyler or His Lordship:

> Sir, I write to you hoping you will be so kind as to take this letter to the Earl of Egremont or to Mr Tyler an humbly of his Lordship to forgives us what we have done as we acknowledge we have done wrong an we will never do any think to annoy Lord Egremont or Mr Tyler Esq if he will forgive us this time an we hope we shall git our liberty sone an come home and give all our friends good advice and Mr Lucas an if we ever do any thing wrong we hope you will do every thing you can to punish us for the time to come as we have bean upwards of 4 months living upon bread and water an lying upon straw an we hope his Lord Ship will forgive us this time an we will never do anythink to anoy Lord Egremont again an never get on his land any more or any one does to do the like again so we remain your obedent servents. wroght by J Habbin, [Signed by] J Habbin, J Meachen.

If John Habbin had been a pupil of Petworth National School, his teachers had done a little toward teaching him to write something 'in the shape of a letter'. A pencilled note on the letter says: 'on shewing Lord Egremont this Letter his Lordship said <u>why don't they write to me?</u>'[289]

145

It would seem that they did so and were duly released but not until February 1834. Vinson and Shepherd, however, stayed in gaol for they 'persisted in saying that when lose [sic] they would continue their poaching — having made nets for that purpose whilst in prison'.[290] It is questionable where they got material with which to make nets; perhaps they wove them out of straw. It was suggested that Lord Egremont would release them when the shooting season was over, and he must have soon done so, for in March 1834 Shepherd appeared again in a writ for damages and costs for trespass, and Vinson appeared again in 1835 for chopping wood from an oak tree in Rushout Wood, presumably for firewood.

Amongst all these activities, in August 1834 Vinson appeared in a case at Lewes Assizes accused with Charles Herrington, Edward Meachen, and David Clousely, otherwise known as David Sharp, on an indictment of 'wicked and malicious libel'; that is, parading with an effigy of two men hanging on a gallows and defamatory placards in Petworth on market day and at Egdean Fair. The larger of the two men on the gallows was obviously intended to represent Mr Tyler. The judge said that, as the figure accurately represented Mr Tyler, it amounted to libel, especially as this took place when most of the respectable farmers who knew him would be in Petworth. If passed unpunished, the judge thought, this kind of activity would destroy the peace of society. Herrington went to Horsham Gaol for twelve months, and the other three men for one month each.

Charles Herrington came from a family of carpenters and was the black sheep of the family. Tyler remarked to the Earl of Egremont: he is 'a poacher and always ill disposed tho' he is the brother of your London carpenter, and the son of as civil and industrious a man as may be'.[291] Tyler was obviously heartily disliked by many.[292] He and Sockett, however, seem to have been on good terms: Sockett was an executor of Tyler's will in 1835. He gained from Tyler's status in that defaulters in the payment of his tithe were liable to get a letter from Tyler demanding payment or threatening distrainment of goods, a power that many other clergy did not so easily possess.

David Clousely (with his family) and George Vinson's younger brother, Wellington, later emigrated to Canada with the Petworth scheme. One important pleasure and sustainer of life in Canada was that there were no game laws: 'we have nobody to run over us here, and to order us out of their fields. We can take our gun, and go a deer hunting, when we likes'.[293]

While David Clousely was in Horsham Gaol, his wife, Clara, applied to Fittleworth parish for poor relief, a procedure with which she and Sockett, from different points of view, were well acquainted. Sockett was involved with two poor law administrations, that of Petworth as chairman of the local vestry, and from 1819 as visitor and auditor of the Gilbert Union of Sutton, of which his parish of Duncton and the Clousely family's parish of Fittleworth were members. Gilbert Unions, set up under an Act of 1782, gave single parishes or incorporations the right to appoint guardians, representing each parish involved, who met monthly with parish officers to collect the poor rate. The union would set up a suitable joint workhouse in the charge of a governor responsible to an appointed visitor. The guardians, as well as being responsible for the workhouse, could also give out-door allowances to able-bodied paupers with low wages and large families.

The Sutton Union was formed in 1791; Fittleworth became a member in 1804, bringing the number of parishes in the union to fifteen. The Sutton Workhouse, when Sockett became visitor, housed largely the elderly and children who were in need of support beyond that available from kith and kin. The Clouselys, when they appeared on the overseer's accounts — as they often did — were awarded out-relief. David, when unemployed, was found work on the roads or there was relief for him, Clara, and children David, Sarah and Edmund in the shape of money, flour or bread. When George, the fourth child, was born in 1835 there was a regular weekly child allowance for him; the rent was paid for their cottage; and, when Clara and a child were ill in 1831, they had medical care.[294]

The same system applied in Petworth, which had its own poor-house with one acre of garden and two acres of meadowland. The house could accommodate sixty-five men, women or children but on average had fifty inmates, usually old people, young children and females confined of 'bastard children'. There were few of the latter, and Petworth was noted for its policy of not legally pursuing the mothers or fathers of illegitimate children. Sockett felt that bastardy was not to be checked by legal enactments; perhaps he felt it was not expedient nor appropriate to say or act on the question in light of the fact that he had lived and worked amongst 'bastards' for much of his life.

In 1833 the care of the workhouse inmates was farmed out to a contractor at 3s.6d. a head. There was a certain amount of sacking and rope making for the older inhabitants. The young children were taught to read and the older children went to the National School.[295] The care of the workhouse was one facet of poor relief, but both Petworth and the Sutton Union valued the authority they had to assess and award out-relief and stressed the importance they laid on the due consideration of the needs and reputation of the applicant. Much of this responsibility, particularly in the case of Petworth, fell on Sockett, a state of affairs he may have appreciated for its power but deprecated for some of its consequences. It may have been difficult for him having grown up amongst the people of the town — 'men whom I have known from their boyhood, who were boys with myself; men whose habits I know, into whose cottages I frequently walk, and at the side of whose fire I often sit'[296] — to now have the power to give or refuse relief. If relief was discretionary then he bore the thanks or dislike for the giving or refusing. If he gave, then the poor rates rose and rose, from £2,270.6s. in 1829 to £3,613.19s. in 1832,[297] a factor which made him unpopular with the ratepayer and caused him personal dismay as one himself. If he refused relief, he would be execrated as mean. Petworth vestry was an open vestry; all the inhabitants liable for poor-rate had the right to attend, and meetings were held monthly after due notice had been given in St Mary's. In common with local government over the ages, not many people chose to attend unless there was a controversial issue at stake. Charles Maclean, reporting on his visit to Petworth vestry in 1833, said that on this occasion there was the clergyman and four ratepayers present.[298] Sutton Union did better in that the guardians from the associating villages were fined for non-attendance. Sockett was fretful about the members of Petworth vestry:

> I could hardly ever get them to come and help me. My general complaint was "Why do you leave it all to me?" and then if there was anything uncomfortable, I had to bear the blame of it, and I often sent round to the parish to beg that they would come to the vestry[299]

The parson of the early 1830s did not need to seek for issues over which he had been made to feel uncomfortable or be blamed. In the southern counties of England, he was one scapegoat in the unrest, violence, and distress of the 1830 Swing Riots.[300] He was blamed by farmers and their labourers. The farmers, under stress, maintained that, if they did not have to pay so much in tithe, they could afford to pay more in wages to their labourers and would employ more men. It may have been an attack on parsons in general, a personal vendetta against him, or mindless vandalism, when, on 27th July 1831, 'about forty young oaks' planted by Sockett on his glebe verging on the New Road were cut down. Three days later a barn, part of a stable, and hayrick at Northlands, in the hands of two of his tenant farmers on a distant part of the glebe, were set on fire. Tyler wrote to the Earl of Egremont at the Grosvenor Place House giving details:

> All the Horses had gone out at one o'clock that morning to fetch corn from Arundel and the Incendiaries must have watched the Carters off the premises and have immediately set Fire to the Straw at the End of the Barn most distant from the Stable, where the Carters were; and who know that the only candle which they had had was extinguished before they left the premises.

Tyler was of the opinion that this was a wilful act to spite James Green, one of the Petworth overseers, and accused Charles Edwards and Edward Lucas, 'both loose and runagate fellows'.[301] One institution often cited as encouraging 'loose and runagate fellows' and fomenting the 1830/31 Swing Riots was the beer shop. Sockett agreed with Maclean, the Assistant Poor Law Commissioner, who in his 1834 report on Sussex said that beer shops were 'prolific in generating and extending every kind of vice and immorality among the lower orders'. Beer shops were facilitated by an Act of 1830 intended to provide good and cheap beer as an alternative to spirits. However, they fell outside the jurisdiction of the local magistrates, did not need licensed premises, and were soon perceived as centres of gambling and 'inflammatory conversation', providing opportunities of 'pursuing seditious publications' when their clients' time might better be spent 'cultivating a garden or in the instruction of his children'.[302]

Maclean said such beer shops were usually situated in remote and unfrequented places, but in Petworth there were at least four recorded in the 1841 census, two in North Street, one in East Street, and another, in a more remote spot, at Low Heath. 'Beer shop boys' were a thorn in Sockett's flesh and a matter of pastoral concern. Writing in January 1834 to the Duke of Richmond, he cites his anxiety: 'Your Grace saw too clearly, at the Sessions, what a state we are in — this Parish has sixteen individuals (all mere boys) beer shop boys in jail at this moment, for various offences'.[303] Four of these boys were, of course, Vinson, Habbin, Meachen and Shepherd. There is no record of what pastoral care Sockett gave them and their mothers.

17 Drummond Hill, near Taymouth, and Paul.

The Parish: Petworth House

In February 1822 the Earl of Egremont gave a grand ball to celebrate fifty years since his accession to the title. One thousand invitations were sent out, and delight and joy prevailed as the guests danced until morning and took supper in the tennis court transformed for the occasion. After they finished, the servants moved in and dined well on what was left.[304] Sockett was personally involved in the celebration arrangements — by this time he had known the Earl for thirty years.

Dominating Petworth parish economically, socially, and geographically was Petworth House and Park. Indeed, for many people Petworth was the House, and it absorbed a great deal of Sockett's time and energy. When the Earl gave Sockett the living, he saw it as a useful way of keeping Sockett at his side, and indeed in his Journal Sockett recorded his first reactions to the offer: 'I think there cannot be a more convincing proof [than] Ld E's wishing to settle me close to his own door'.[305] Whilst the curate officiated at the baptisms, marriages and funerals, Sockett was occupied with business for the Earl, as he had been as tutor and aide, not only at Petworth but at the London and Brighton houses.

Thomas Creevey, in his description of a visit to Petworth, gives a delightful picture of the house on an August day in 1828. Doors and windows were standing wide open to family and visitors, and Lord Egremont was slouching about with his hat on and his hands in his breeches pockets, talking about his vast collection of pictures, arranging visits to the stables for the men and drives in the park for the ladies. Sockett was seemingly present as 'a chaplain', dining with the party on venison, game and turtle. Turtles, imported live from the West Indies, were frequently despatched in a basket from the London docks to Petworth. They were expensive; one destined for the victory celebrations of 1814 weighed 88 lbs at 3s.9d. per lb. It was perhaps a significant mark of Sockett's standing among this sociable group that he did not warrant a name, but it is pleasing to find him enjoying a last glass of wine and water before going home to bed. Creevey said that his bed at Petworth House would have slept six people in a row without the slightest inconvenience to each other.[306]

Creevey was told there were more servants of both sexes in Petworth House than in any house in England, and the Earl was a central figure in the economic structure of Petworth. Charles Maclean reported in 1833 that Lord Egremont had 132 parishioners in constant employment plus forty labourers in the woods from mid-November until mid-March. Women and children were employed at haying, harvesting, potato picking and weeding.[307] Local girls and women, men and boys were also employed in the London or Brighton houses. In 1818 Lord Egremont ordered the apprentice, Bishop, to come to London to occasionally ride out behind him: 'he is to have a groom's waistcoat and breeches, fitting him well and a pair of boots; which can be made in Petworth. He must take care to behave civilly and keep himself clean — and only wear the livery when he goes out with my Lord'.[308] In July 1823 James Randell was sent to London to be trained as a postillion at 7s. a week: 'try what you can make of him'.[309] In 1819 William Moore went to the Egremont house in Brighton to do general work — which included beating the carpets — Mrs Peacock, the housekeeper, was to find him a bed, and he was paid 12s. a week when the family was absent, 5s. a week and board when they were in residence.[310] The Brighton house was important — the Earl often visited half a dozen times a year, for sea air, to visit friends, including the Prince Regent at the Royal Pavilion, and to go to Lewes races. Catherine Peacock had been a maid in the London house in the early years of the century before she had taken over as housekeeper in Brighton in 1814.[311] We do not know how Sockett got on with Mrs Peacock, but there was constant friction between her and Tyler.

As newly appointed rector, Sockett went to Brighton with his servant and Tyler on business in September 1816.* Tyler instructed Mrs Peacock to get 'a little fish', perhaps whitings, 'a good Beef Stake broiled with Oyster Sauce, and some sort of Pie or Pudding at 4 o'clock. We shall bring some vegetables and Fruit'.[312] One package often carried on the Earl's 'caravan' between Brighton and Petworth was fish for the Earl's table. There was correspondence for years over fish, both in Brighton and London; there was not enough, it was too expensive, the Earl grumbled he has too much cod, and so on.[313] The Brighton fish was bought from two fish-women, Martha Humphrey and Sarah Marchant, and Tyler was concerned that they should be paid regularly for they were 'miserably poor'.[314] He was also concerned that Mrs Peacock should air the beds well. All the linen from the Brighton house was taken in the wagon to be laundered at Petworth, and Mrs Peacock was constantly in trouble for missing items of laundry, for her profligate use of coal and for not having the tradesmen's bills ready for Tyler to audit and pay. On one occasion Sockett brought them back with him when he returned home.

---

* Sockett was challenging, in the courts, a composition for tithes due 5th April 1816. WSRO, PHA 10534.

In 1819 Tyler gave Mrs Peacock six months' notice for being drunk and disorderly and 'exposing herself to the contempt and ridicule of her fellow servants'; the six months was a concession to a long-time servant since otherwise it would have been instant dismissal; nevertheless, she did not go. Tyler wrote irritably in December 1821 that she was a foolish woman with no end to her irregularities, but 'as his Lordship knows her infirmities and still keeps her there I cannot help it'.[315] Creevey said of the Earl's servants that they were all bred upon the spot and all related to each other.[316] One does wonder about the relationship between Catharine Peacock and William Carleton, Sockett's friend and tennis opponent. Carleton appears in the wages book as 'Peacock alias Carleton'; perhaps the Earl had good reasons for 'keeping her there'.

As well as organising festivities and food for rich and poor in the house and gardens, Sockett did more serious work on behalf of the Earl, much of it concerned with administering his charities. There were bounties of clothes, shoes, coal and food to be distributed in the town itself and in neighbouring villages, and formal charities with which Petworth was well endowed.[317] The Earl gave gifts of clothes each year through the local clergy. Each parish in the area was allotted a number of suits, consisting of a smock frock, jacket and trousers, to be distributed on the recommendation of the local clergyman or landowner. In 1831 one hundred such suits were given among ten villages around Petworth. James Dearling was one recipient in Petworth.[318]

In 1832 fifty pairs of blankets were bought from Mr Mance at the Bridewell (i.e. prison) for distribution. Such bounties were restricted to the deserving poor, although the local clergyman or landowner presumably put his own definition on 'deserving'. This work could give a pleasing sense of power, of wrong-doing punished or virtue rewarded. Mr Rapley was given clothes in January 1831 for he 'had not been concerned in the mob'.[319]

Mr Rapley may not have been, but other men and women in parishes largely under the eye of Egremont were. As the Swing Riots against threshing machines, unemployment, hunger and misery moved westwards across Sussex, rumour and reality ran riot at home and abroad in the neighbourhood. At the beginning of December 1830, it was rumoured in Petworth that a mob collecting in Kirdford and Wisborough Green intended visiting the town to extort from the magistrates a promise that young single men, employed as parish labourers, be paid the same wages as married men; the mob presumably also had its eye on Sockett as chairman of Petworth vestry.

Egremont requested — or expected — all his tenant farmers to enrol as special constables, and Sockett had permission to put stores of arms in the hospital grounds in readiness. Hasler and King, accompanied by two or three special constables, went to Kirdford where they found about 150 men marching from place to place urging others to join them. They arrested two of the ringleaders and two others, and the rest were said to have immediately dispersed, claiming they had been forced to join the crowd; since then the neighbourhood had been perfectly quiet. The Earl, with his usual hospitality, on Tuesday and Wednesday when the special constables were in attendance, gave the whole of them (in number about 300) a sumptuous dinner, with strong beer.[320]

The Earl provided wine for the sick and, in 1803, sent Ann Meachen to train as a midwife at the Brownlow Street Lying-in Hospital.[321] Another grimmer bounty was the right the Earl had to nominate patients to a hospital or asylum. One of Sockett's functions was to facilitate entrance into the Bethlehem Asylum for Poor Lunatics in London. One patient in November 1823 was a woman from Northstoke 'The woman must be at Bethleham Hospital on Thursday morning next at ten o'clock — there will be four pounds to be paid with her (being a pauper). Mr Sockett will bring on Sunday the printed notice for her admission'.[322]

'Flying to a Distant Country': 1832

> And God blessed Noah and his sons and said to them, 'Be fruitful and multiply and fill the earth, The fear of you and the dread of you shall be upon every beast of the earth and upon every bird of the air, upon every thing that creeps on the ground all the fish of the sea; into your hand they are delivered.' Genesis 9:1

For Sockett, a priest in the Church of England, God's message to Noah after the flood was divine ordinance. Man should be fruitful and multiply, fill the earth, and subdue it. Malthusian harsh doctrines of overpopulation checked by plague and starvation were not God's plan for man. Nevertheless, Sockett admitted that there were at this time acute problems with an ever-increasing population in Sussex, combined with contracting rather than expanding avenues of employment. The result was unemployment and dire poverty, and an increasing strain on traditional avenues of parish relief and charity. The vestry, often grudgingly, did what it could, but local ratepayers, including Sockett himself, deplored the constant rise in the poor rate. In his neighbourhood the Earl of Egremont provided employment, lowered his rents to his tenant farmers and cottagers, and gave food and clothes, not only in Petworth but in the surrounding villages in which he owned land. He and Sockett initiated a scheme whereby the rate of wages was tied to the price of wheat.[323] Sockett proposed this scheme and practised it with his own four labourers, but, since he dismissed one labourer to finance the scheme to the other three, it was something of a mixed blessing. Other landlords were not as philanthropic as the Earl, and lacked his care and concern. The poor and unemployed did what they could — Mrs Dearling took in washing — and some resorted to stealing from local fowl houses, Petworth Park, and local sheep farmers, and at times to noisy or violent protest:

> Ye Gods above send down your love
> with swords as sharp as sickles
> To cut the throats of gentlefolks
> Who rob the poor of victuals.

sang the people in a Lewes public house before two men and a woman were taken into custody in December 1830.[325] One viable answer was social protest and uprising with a call for change in the social, political, and economic structure of society. The Reform Bill of 1832 was one small step in this process, but there were to be several generations more before there were any great changes in the nature of the Sussex countryside, other sources of food, and means of controlling the birth-rate that were inadmissible in 1800 to the Reverend Thomas Malthus. One less disturbing answer was to persuade people to move elsewhere — to other possibilities of land and employment.[325] They might migrate within the United Kingdom to the growing industrial midlands or north; go to work as navvies building the spreading network of railways; or go and be fruitful and subdue lands overseas — preferably those in the British colonies. The newly appointed Poor Law Commissioners of 1834 were eager to persuade people to migrate within the United Kingdom; and indeed people were moving to the factories and mills of the midlands and north; or to service the ever-growing city of London and the seaside towns along the south coast.

On the whole, Sussex people were not keen to move into industry — 'to explore these manufacturing districts is much dreaded by these Sussex babies'[326] — and the agricultural labouring population was not equipped to do so. Factories and mills wanted nimble-fingered, cheap labour from women and children; the Sussex babies might well dread the mill. Farmers, agricultural workers and skilled craftsmen might be more easily tempted to go overseas where there was the prospect of land of their own and profitable calls for their crafts.

The topic of emigration was much in the air by the end of the 1820s: local newspapers printed letters home from erstwhile neighbours overseas, particularly in Canada; there were debates in parliament; and books, articles and pamphlets were being distributed, by one means or another, around the countryside. The *Hampshire Telegraph and Sussex Chronicle* and the *Brighton Guardian* in 1831 and 1832 carried long, encouraging letters from James Knight of Wisborough Green, who had emigrated in 1821. The *Brighton Herald* reported in March 1832 that there was not a single person dependent on parish assistance left in Yapton, West Sussex, all of them having sailed the previous week for America. There were published reports on emigration from His Majesty's Commissioners for Emigration, and shipping agents, such as Carter and Bonus, wrote to parish vestries throughout the south of England with advertisements for ships due to sail from Portsmouth and Bristol. Eleven wagon-loads of emigrants departed from Frome in Somerset via Bristol to Canada in April 1832.

Emigration was one thing that a concerned clergyman might organise without entering into overt controversial political, economic or social debate and action — talk and action that might be considered outside his mandate as a priest, or might grievously upset the local hierarchy, of which, by birth and breeding, he was often a part. He was not called upon to change the system but to relieve it of troublesome facets and relieve some of its victims. There were, of course, questions as to whom one should conscientiously encourage to emigrate. William Cobbett was, as ever, outspoken in his opinion, advocating the emigration of fundholders and government pensioners living more generously than the pauper on taxes, and absentee clergy living on tithes.[327] Some professional people were already taking themselves or sending their children overseas, as Sockett and the Nicols were to do.

Malthus considered that the poor, who could not organise their own emigration because of a lack of resources, should be helped, if not by government then by leaders among the higher classes urged by the spirit of avarice, enterprise, or religious or political discontent. Sockett was urged by Christian teaching, by a degree of avarice, and certainly by enterprise and some political discontent. He said the catalyst for the setting up of the PEC came on Christmas Eve 1831 when he received a statement from a Petworth poor law guardian showing that there were 103 people on parish relief, a figure that was to rise to 114 in January; when the wives and children of claimants were added, the number reached 330. When accounts were added up at Easter 1832, the expense of these labourers and their families was £1,401.6s.3d. With the feelings of a man, or woman, who has received notice of their tax bill, Sockett laid the Christmas Eve figures before the Earl — perhaps with his season's good wishes — saying: 'My Lord, these labourers have eaten me up, and they will very soon eat your lordship up if something is not done to stop it'.[328] This metaphor of being 'eaten up' by the pauper was popular. Arthur Young, in 1800, had warned the Earl of the fear of the poor swallowing up the landed interest. Chadwick, in his report on the work of the commissioners' investigation into the administration and operation of the poor laws in 1833, said that the published 'extracts' were an instant success and created 'a sort of panic among the possessing classes; that rates were eating up property and soon the landlord and farmer would give way to the pauper'.[329] It should, perhaps, be said that it would be a long time before the Earl of Egremont was eaten up; indeed, it was a grim metaphor as in reality the pauper was scarcely eating at all.

Financial gain and expediency, if not quite avarice, were powerful and attractive factors in Sockett's promotion of emigration. He used them to good effect in his propaganda and public relations at local and national levels. By raising money to send paupers and the poor to Canada, the local vestry could save on existing poor relief and on the prospective relief of growing families. Money lent, or given, by local landholders for emigration would be well invested and yield tangible return in lower taxes for himself and for the parish.[330] For the emigrant, there was the prospect of land and work, and for those who stayed at home there was to be, at least in theory, increased wages and work as a result of the decrease in the potential labour force.

One could not cite the Earl as being spurred by avarice. He spent around £5,000 on the Petworth Emigration scheme between 1832 and 1837,[331] giving the whole of the £10 passage money for people who lived in the parishes in which he owned the larger part of the land, and in proportion to his land holdings in other parishes. Nevertheless, this amount of money was not pinching to a man who spent over £3,000 on corn and hay for his horses and livestock in the year 1835–36.[332] And it would be untrue to say that it was merely economics that fuelled Sockett's energy and enterprise. One gets the impression, particularly in its early days, that he enjoyed getting his teeth into the scheme. He was literate and a proven administrator with considerable experience of running affairs in his local vestries and for the Earl. He was used to mingling with the great and good, had a network of useful contacts, and cared about his flock, for he had been poor and had known what it was to be patronised.

The Earl did not need persuading to let Sockett have his head. He was an old man, a generous man, a known philanthropist, and, as his son George Wyndham remarked some years later, he liked to be liked. He was very willing to try out the scheme as the purse and sleeping partner, only stirring into action if he was anxious or displeased. Sockett astutely only had three people on his emigration committee. He knew Thomas Chrippes and William Knight as friends and professional acquaintances. It was convenient to have to communicate with only two other members and get decisions out of them. His experience with Petworth and Sutton vestries was a salutary example of the difficulty of getting decisions from unwieldy, unreliable groups of people. He worked closely with John Phillips, the local stationer and printer. Sockett had a background knowledge of printers and stationers from his father at the shop in Cloth Fair and from the Nicols. Phillips printed up leaflets, posters, and information on emigration opportunities, and the details on the departure of ships.

Sockett, as rector, had a ready-made network of distribution points in his neighbouring clergy friends and acquaintances and the twelve Sussex parishes in which the Earl held the living of the church. The clergyman could be an agent between the big house, the local farmers and vestry, and poor parishioners; a two- or three-way process.

The Earl held the living and therefore the rector in his hand, and could put implicit or explicit pressure on him and the vestry to promote and facilitate emigration from their parish. Where the Earl did not hold sway, word still went around at a high level between the 'big-wigs'; the Earl of Chichester, who sent a considerable party on the 1834 PEC ship, the *British Tar*, was a member of the Sussex aristocratic coterie. He headed both the Lewes and Brighton Emigration Committees. Burrell, the Earl's son-in-law, was responsible for emigrants from his area of mid-Sussex.

On the other hand, the rector could apply pressure on the local landowner. Sockett spent much time writing to local gentry and landowners, outlining his scheme and asking for money for emigrants from their parish. Before 1834 such money might be an outright gift or perhaps a loan to the vestry to be repaid out of the rates — or repaid by the vestry rescinding the rates until the value of the loan was paid back, a procedure that was illegal, as auditors of the parish accounts pointed out. Sockett did not have an easy task persuading men of substance to part with their money. 'It is very easy for Mr R[idsdale] to sit on his Brussells carpet and give opinions — but to act upon them is another matter'.[333] Nevertheless some landowners, anxious about their poor rates and their poor labourers, and frightened by the actuality and implications of the very recent Swing Riots and more revolutions in Europe, did lend money, usually at five per cent interest, which they did not always get back.

Sometimes it was the poor people themselves who put pressure on Sockett, or their local vestries, to help them emigrate, and the rector as chairman of the vestry could be their advocate; in some cases, he might actually lend the money himself, as the rector of West Grinstead was to do for Henry Heasman.[334] Sockett was to say in later years: 'many told me they had been thinking long of going but had not before had a chance'.[335]

Some 1,800 men, women, and children did snap their ties and go to Canada on PEC ships — from Sussex, the fringes of neighbouring counties, further west from Wiltshire, and east from Cambridgeshire. The largest number were young single men, some of whom were the 'beer shop boys' — a constant annoyance to Sockett and doubtless, at times, to their parents and neighbours. Humanitarian feelings certainly played a large part in the organising of emigration, but sponsors and clergy were not always inspired by Christian charity; emigration was a useful way of siphoning off potential local discontent and rebellion — 'the scum that came to the top'. Sockett and the Earl, for example, were quick to name Shepherd and Vinson as possible emigrants.

After the success of the first two PEC ships in 1832, the scheme gathered momentum as people wished to join their relatives or friends, or were spurred into action by letters sent home. Sockett provided his emigrants with writing paper and suggestions as to the content of letters, and he was relieved when encouraging missives began to arrive. He was quick to realise their propaganda value and had them printed in local newspapers or little, cheap booklets. After the introduction of the harsh details of the new Poor Law and union workhouses from 1834 onwards, many emigrants were driven by anger and despair. 'What would have become of my children if they had been in England and I had been put in some poorhouse?'[336] wrote Ann Mann from Canada in 1837. Some would-be travellers turned up on the quayside at Portsmouth at the last minute asking to be taken, and if there was room they embarked. Sockett later said this last-minute embarkation required a

> good deal of delicate management, and a discretionary power vested somewhere, to act at the <u>last moment</u> — to have any berths vacant is a waste of money and effort: therefore as I have before observed, when a ship is once engaged she should be filled by <u>any who will pay it so greatly lightens the outlay</u> ...[337]

It was at this last moment that 'the scum' floated to the top and were accepted for matters of economic efficiency, after the solid and respectable had already embarked. In the practical matters of hiring a ship and organising the terms of the passage, Sockett had the advantage of being a frequent visitor to London and knowing the area around Leadenhall Street where Carter and Bonus, the shipping agents, had their offices. He was also within easy distance of Portsmouth and, each April for six years from 1832 to 1837, he took up residence there in Penny Street for several days before the Petworth ships departed. He also cultivated the approbation and help of his neighbour the Duke of Richmond at Goodwood. The Duke had authority at Portsmouth dockyard as Vice-Admiral for the County of Sussex, and held land and sway in a large number of parishes.

One could organise funding and ships, but how to persuade people to go? Some were ready and waiting; nevertheless, it was a decisive and traumatic thing to do. Malthus acknowledged the qualified value of emigration as a short-term measure — not upsetting his overall thesis, as colonized countries would inevitably succumb at some distant date — for easing the economic stringencies of a surplus population. Contrary to Hawley's disdain of Sussex babies unwilling to budge, Malthus was outspoken on the trauma of people driven to leave their home and country:

Is it then a fault for a man to feel an attachment to his native soil, to love the parents that nurtured him, his kindred, his friends, and the companions of his early years? Or is it no evil that he suffers, because he consents to bear it rather than snap those cords which nature has wound in close and intricate folds round the human heart?[338]

Sockett ruefully acknowledged the reluctance of many Sussex people to leave their natal smoke,[339] and it was a powerful indicator of the grim climate of the time that many did so.

A number of single men came from the Isle of Wight. Single men and boys imbued with a spirit of adventure and enterprise could often hardly wait to get away. Adolphus Grafenstein in Brighton begged the Earl of Chichester to send him, and George, Sockett's son, was another young man desperate to get to Canada. The Isle of Wight boys, many of whom had been in the stringent care of the House of Industry, thoroughly enjoyed the food on the voyage. These single men, isolated at night in their own quarters were noisy — gambling, drinking and smoking. For some boys and men, it was a chance to get away from problems at home. Some skipped ship before the Petworth vessel reached its designated port of Montreal. From Sockett and their sponsors' point of view, they were nevertheless well worth funding as emigrants; they would not make early, imprudent marriages in England and have numbers of children; whereas Canada welcomed young strong men and their potential families, provided that some young women went too, for women were in short supply.

From the emigrants' point of view, single men had more realistic expectations of being able to come home again if they wished. Indeed, some did so straightaway; James Gates and Thomas Grinyer were two young men who very quickly came back,* as William Shepherd had done. Sockett had a clause written into the contract with the shipping agents providing that ships taking out emigrants would be fined if they brought any back on the return journey. Many emigrant ships, the Petworth ships among them, did not put into Plymouth on their way down the English Channel for fear that their passengers, once on land, would not set sail again. Sponsors and vestries that had paid the passage for emigrants were not pleased to see them coming back up the road. Some authorities

---

* Sarah Jackman, another emigrant from their home village of Goring, wrote of Gates and Grinyer: 'If they should come home don't believe what they say.' *English Immigrant Voices,* letter 124.

wanted the right of settlement taken away from sponsored emigrants, but Sockett argued against this threat saying that it would deter some potential emigrants from embarking and enhance their feeling that they were being got rid of.[340] Nevertheless, by 1838 he was to say to George Wyndham:

> In considering the relative advantages of the upper or lower province, as places for sending emigrants to, it must always be remembered (altho it need not be spoken of) that the greater, or less facility, of returning, shd be taken into account.[341]

A second group to emigrate was old soldiers and sailors who had already seen something of the world and were not easily settling back into their old life. Old soldiers had a financial pull in that they could claim one hundred acres of land, instead of the five given to other emigrants, and, if necessary, have their pension transferred to Canada. Old soldiers and sailors often acquired an ambivalent attitude towards authority and were labelled troublemakers, and indeed they did give Sockett especial trouble in 1833 and 1837.

We do not easily discern who it was in a family who initiated emigration. Parents did so for the sake of their children; growing sons and daughters may have persuaded their parents. Letters from those families who emigrated give glimpses of factors that kept others at home. The breaking of family ties and the knowledge that the parting was probably forever were extremely painful to contemplate.

Sockett would have to endure criticism from relations left at home whose kith and kin had left them, from whom they might not have news, or news they did not wish to hear. Many emigrants on the first two ships in 1832 died of cholera after reaching Canada. Sockett kept a book in which he entered year by year the name of every person who sailed on a Petworth ship. As news filtered home, he recorded any scraps of information he had received, and people would come from near and far to enquire if he had news of a son or daughter or of a family.*

Besides family ties, other less traumatic but nevertheless strong reasons for staying at home were the sea, the climate in Canada, the bears, the Indians. Sussex has a long seaboard and many potential emigrants were well accustomed to the ocean — which may or may not have encouraged them to embark. Other emigrants from the north of the county and elsewhere had possibly never seen the sea and did not care for it when they did. Some would-be emigrants on reaching Portsmouth

---

* Unfortunately, it is not known if this book still exists; it is not to be found in the Petworth House Archives.

harbour and seeing the tiny sailing brig and their cramped conditions in the steerage, turned around and went home. As well as the danger, descriptions of wretched seasickness figured large in letters home. Sockett must have had mixed feelings as he waved the ships goodbye as they left Portsmouth for a month on the North Atlantic.

Between January and March 1832, he worked hard to have two ships ready to sail for Canada in April; to equip his emigrants with useful information as to what opportunities they might find overseas; to make the sea journey as bearable as possible; to look after his emigrants down the St Lawrence; and to see them settled in a home and work before winter came. This was partly for the emigrants' own sake, partly to ensure the reputation of his committee, and partly to safeguard the approbation and reputation of the Earl. He wrote countless letters, gathering numbers from interested sponsors and vestries; negotiating for ships — the Petworth Committee did not use commercial emigrant ships but hired its own — arranging superintendents for the journey; providing food and water on shipboard; sorting out the government regulations with regard to the provision of a surgeon and a medicine chest; and negotiating special rates for a party from Dorking who wished to travel on a PEC ship.

The would-be emigrants were supplied with a list of desirable clothes to meet the rigours of a Canadian winter, and pressure was applied to their local vestry to fund this outfit where necessary. The emigrants from Petworth itself were given a clothing grant of £10 per head, with £5 for children; other vestries trimmed this amount down. Emigrants were advised to take bedding and cooking utensils and other useful items to ease conditions on shipboard. Amongst all the practical concerns, the spiritual well-being of the pilgrims was not forgotten. The rector of Kirdford took little George Shepherd down to Portsmouth and bought him supplies for the journey. Henry Wagner, the vicar of St Nicholas's Church, Brighton, gave the emigrants from his parish in 1834 a good send off with a supper of 'good old English fare', roast beef and beer. He handed out gifts of tea as well as Bibles, prayer books, and other useful books and addressed them in an 'impressive manner', giving 'excellent advice as to their future conduct'.[342] The party from Hellingly, bound for the same ship, was also given Bibles, although one man, Samuel Richardson, had already sold his for one shilling and sixpence before he reached Portsmouth.

Sockett's former curate, James Knight Greetham, took a large party from his parish of Kirdford down to Portsmouth in 1832 and saw them safely stowed on board, a kindness that earned him a warm thank-you letter from Canada. In Greetham's case it was kind, but one could inject a cynical note by saying all the kind concern to see people safely stowed on board was out of anxiety to see that their charges, in whom time and money had been invested, actually sailed away. For all the seven ships that went under the Petworth scheme, Sockett organised a £5 box of suitable tracts and books from the Society for Promoting Christian Knowledge (SPCK), the Anglican publishing house. The SPCK put together an Emigrants' Library of fifty-five books, especially for emigrant ships, saying:

> it is fearful to contemplate the growth of states, such as we are founding both in North America and Australian dominions, likely to lead to such a height of physical well-being in conjunction with so great a degree of religious destitution.[343]

The Emigrants' Library, to mitigate such religious destitution, consisted almost wholly of theological and highly moral works, ranging from *Paley's Natural Theology* to *Learn to Die* — the latter not an entirely happy choice for people embarking on the passage across the Atlantic. Emigrants did die on shipboard. The Petworth Committee was thankful that few did so on their ships, those who did being several babies and children, but many emigrants later died of cholera up the St Lawrence, or of accidents up the country.

On Sundays there was a service on shipboard, and Sockett wrote a sermon for the 1832 ships which was perhaps repeated on later voyages.* Captain J. C. Hale, the superintendent of the 1833 ship, the *England*, wrote in his log of a 'very gratifying course of devotions' he organised on Sunday 5th May as the ship left the Lizard (the most southerly point of Cornwall). The girls and boys from the Isle of Wight came on deck and sang a hymn, and presumably Hale read Sockett's sermon: 'The Reverend Rector of Petworth himself had he been present would not have been ashamed of his congregation'.[344]

A real and vital consolation to families parting, never to meet again because of geographical distance and very possible untoward death, was the sure hope of meeting in another country and on another shore. Such firm belief was a relief to the painful homesickness that many of the first generation of emigrants suffered. Mrs Pullen writing to her son, daughter-in-law, and grandchildren, who had gone to Canada in 1837, echoed the sentiments of many separated families when she said:

---

* We are sorry not to have a copy of this.

The Earl of Egremont

has signified his intention of continuing his liberal assistance to persons wishing to emigrate to

UPPER CANADA.

The COMMITTEE will therefore engage a vessel to sail from PORTS-MOUTH, *early in April next,* under similar arrangements as those of 1832 and 1833.

Applications for Passages should be made as early as possible to

J. PHILLIPS,

LIBRARY, PETWORTH.

Petworth, Feb. 14th. 1834.

Phillips, Printer, Petworth.

38. Emigration poster, by courtesy of the Trustees of the Goodwood Collections.

now my dear children I must conclude with my blessing to you and the dear children; tell them I hope they read their Bibles. Poor dears, how I should like to see them and the dear little Stranger, But I hope we shall meet in that Blessed abode where sin and sorrow never comes, where the Lamb shall wipe all tears from our eyes.[345]

This was doubtless a hope that Sockett entertained too — to sweeten the bitter things in his life.

Not every year was smooth sailing, and in 1833 there was trouble with the *England.* Captain Hale was recommended to the PEC by Carter and Bonus. He had a troublesome voyage to superintend; the weather was wet and stormy, and provisions stowed on board on a wet day at Portsmouth went mouldy in the damp hold. Two babies were born en route, one of whom died after two days. The single men and boys were noisy and refractory, and the journey up the St Lawrence was trying as the Rideau Canal, built to avoid the rapids on the river, was out of order. Hale kept himself and many of the emigrants reasonably alive and free from seasickness with the contents of his brandy cask, and supplemented the diminishing rations by selling goodies of his own. Special purchasers were a party of young men and boys from the Isle of Wight, who landed with little left of the guinea they had been given to ease their early days in Canada. News came home, via the Canadian and English press in October 1833, of the dissatisfaction of some of the *England* passengers. Sockett was upset at this and at the vexation of the Earl. Captain Hale was not appointed to any more PEC ships, and it was at this point that Sockett thought of his old friend, James Brydone, and, with some persuasion, enrolled him in 1834 as surgeon superintendent of the *British Tar* and of the next three PEC ships.

Another source of trouble after 1834 was the clause in the new Poor Law Amendment Act which allowed vestries to borrow money for emigration on the strength of their poor rates. They could do so by borrowing from a local sponsor, and the newly appointed Poor Law Commission would underwrite the loan, or they could borrow the money from the Exchequer itself. In some ways this method was a relief to Sockett in that he did not have to persuade local sponsors or vestries to raise the money, but in other ways it was an added complication. The bureaucracy in London now entered the picture and, as in other areas of his life, power began to slip from Sockett's hands into other agencies. To raise a loan through the Poor Law Commission, local vestries now had to cope with forms A, B, C and D sent down from London to be returned in the correct order and correct time. Forms A, B, C and D gave many parishes and Sockett great trouble.

Many vestry members and parish officers were barely literate. Sockett spent much time helping small parishes to fill in their forms. Forms did not arrive, were lost or not filled in correctly, were sent back to be redone, or were not returned in time. It often fell to the local rector, or Sockett, to expostulate, apologise and wrestle with the bureaucracy in London as the date for the sailing of the ship drew ever nearer. It took Yapton vestry from February to the end of September 1835 to negotiate approval for a loan from the Poor Law Commissioners for emigrants who had sailed in April, financed by a short-term loan from a local landowner.[346] The Poor Law Commission also began to interfere in the emigration itself, refusing to allow loans for Petworth Committee emigrants — they cited the Petworth scheme as too expensive. Humanitarian, well organised, and well respected it may have been, but other agencies offered to send people more cheaply. The relationship between Sockett and the Poor Law Commission was rapidly soured by this, and by the arrival of the Assistant Poor Law Commissioner in Sussex.

The Winged Thunderbolt:
William Henry Toovey Hawley

After the new Poor Law Amendment Act was passed in 1834, assistant poor law commissioners went out into the field to explain and implement the provisions of the Act. Sockett was, with reservations, in favour of the Bill and hoped that the Earl of Egremont would be too. His hopes were short-lived when the first assistant poor law commissioner for West Sussex, Henry Pilkington, took up residence at the Swan Inn at Chichester with his pair of compasses. His mandate was to supervise the establishment of the new Poor Law unions in West Sussex and specify the parishes to be put in each:

> [H]e had a map with him and stuck a pair of compasses into it, and swung them round; he formed his unions with a pair of compasses; he knew nothing whatever of the localities of the neighbourhood; he never asked for information; he took a parish that belonged exclusively to Lord Egremont, called Up Waltham, and because it came into the ring fence he worked it into the Westhampnett Union; the parish belonged exclusively to Lord Egremont. Lord Egremont in my presence spoke to him about it and said, 'It was a very extraordinary thing you should take Up Waltham and join that with a parish nobody knows where, of which I know nothing; you might at least have consulted me about it'. He was very sorry, and begged his Lordship a thousand pardons, but he did not know that Up Waltham belonged to him. Lord Egremont was very much annoyed at the manner in which this was done, and he would never hear a word about the New Poor Law after that — I had myself formed the plan of a union; I do not know that it was a good one, but I believed it was, and I submitted it to Lord Egremont. He said 'If you think you can manage it well and good; let me hear about it and I will think about it' But from the moment this act was done there was no hope of doing anything.[347]

For the Earl the overriding issue was that of territory. Up Waltham was his parish, as was Tillington, the parish next door to Petworth. Tillington was put into the Midhurst Union with Northchapel — another sore point for the Earl — and with territory went influence. Pilkington could ride around the unions in his territory sitting in on guardians' meetings with instructions from London to tell them — not consult with them — how to administer their poor relief and what they might or might not do. Pilkington's thousand pardons rang hollow to the Earl and probably to Sockett, although in his evidence to a Select Committee of 1844 he maintained Pilkington's action was mere carelessness, 'not taking the trouble to make inquiries', which was annoying enough. Mr Colville, a member of the Select Committee, suggested, however, that in reality Pilkington's object was to destroy local influence; the principle of the Act was to take away from all local authorities the power of thwarting the will of the general legislature,[348] and the Earl realised it. Yet, it was not all pique on his part. The bill, the assistant poor law commissioners, the large, amorphous unions, all were anathema to the paternalistic, philanthropic autocrat, and the actuality of the new union workhouse buildings was an affront to his sensibilities. The Earl was not going to change his values and opinion that the new law, 'unless it is administered with great caution and moderation [is to] be one of the most tyrannical that was ever passed'.[349] He was a pattern for the desirable paterfamilias extolled by the Reverend Dr Folliott at the after-dinner debate on the current enthusiasm for political economy, at Crochet Castle:

> In the family there is a *paterfamilias* who regulates the distribution, and takes care that there shall be no such thing in the household as one dying of hunger, while another dies of surfeit. In the state it is all hunger at one end and all surfeit at the other.[350]

Sockett stood with a foot in either camp. A capable and experienced administrator, one of an up-and-coming sector of English political and economic life, he deplored the muddle and inadequacy of the old system; guardians and overseers who could neither read nor write; farmers who did not, or could not, pay adequate wages; and a poor law system which removed an increasing sum at source from his tithes. The implacable opposition of the Earl was possibly one reason why, in 1835, Sockett refused to work with the newly established Petworth Union. He was asked to act as guardian for Petworth but refused, begging people not to nominate him. Perhaps he wanted a rest after twenty years of dealing with the dilatory Petworth vestry. Perhaps he was annoyed at having his plans for a union come to nothing; he may have had great plans based on his experience with the Sutton Union. Perhaps he, like the Earl, did not want to have his previous authority and power over poor relief administration set aside by poor law commissioners such as Pilkington. He was to say in 1844, when asked if he had changed his mind: 'I do not feel at all disposed to come under the dominion of the Poor Law Commissioners'.[351] Perhaps he felt he already had sufficient avenues for his energy and administrative skills with Sutton Union, which as an existing Gilbert Union comprising fifteen parishes chose not to come under the aegis of the Poor Law Commission, and he was by 1834 in the midst of the work of the PEC.

The guardians of the Sutton Union would not defer to the poor law commissioners but claimed they administered a more humane and sensible policy than that of the Commission at no greater cost, and that their diet was generous compared to that enforced by Poor Law rules. A further issue stiffening the backbones of the Sutton Union was the fact that the workhouse was leased from the Earl of Egremont. Although Petworth, as a single-parish Gilbert Union, had to succumb to the new Poor Law Commission, it did not easily submit to the yoke and kicked against the Commissioners' rule from its inception. How much was it influenced by the powerful if unseen presence of the Earl and Sockett as rector of the parish? William Hawley, the assistant poor law commissioner in East Sussex, was early aware of this influence. Writing to the commissioners at Somerset House in 1834, he expanded at length on the misplaced actions of 'munificent noblemen possessing great Power and Influence' who created 'immense charities' which contributed to habits of improvidence,[352] and on ministers of religion who

> to their shame be it spoken, have endeavoured to embarrass the parochial Boards by working on the feelings of the poor, and sowing the seeds of discontent and resistance amongst the flocks to whom it was their duty to have preached peace and submission to lawful authority.[353]

Pilkington lasted only a year in West Sussex. He had the gift of upsetting other people besides the Earl; Tyler spoke tartly of 'this Mr Pilkington who is riding rough shoed over this part of the county'.[354] He upset the Sutton Union by telling one guardian, the Reverend Mr Eadle, to 'hold your tongue, Sir'. Mr Eadle was said to be so unnerved he did not speak for the rest of the meeting, during which, it was claimed, Pilkington talked a 'parcel of rigmarole nonsense'.[355] He was moved to Lincoln in October 1835 and dismissed soon after.

William Henry Toovey Hawley took over West Sussex in September 1835. He had already supervised the setting up of thirteen unions and suitable workhouses all over the eastern side of the county and was more than ready to tackle the problems of West Sussex where the Gilbert Unions of Sutton and East Preston covered forty parishes between them. These, with the recalcitrant Earl at Petworth, formed a solid geographical and administrative barrier to his aspirations. Hawley used the image of the family very differently to that of the Earl. Hawley and his wife, Elizabeth, had no children but the new unions he created were to be his children: 'the numerous family I have had born to me in this county'.[356] He was a hard father, who would not hesitate to enforce and correct with 'a rod in pickle';[357] there is 'no flinching in me.'[358]

He hired a 'sort of phaeton drawn by two horses' — appropriately enough for a Winged Thunderbolt, the Hawley coat of arms.* This carried him, his books, and his papers — the real weight of bureaucracy — to guardians' meetings, 'the nurseries of the infant unions',[359] including those of the Petworth Union at Wisborough Green. He sat in at their meetings, challenging their decisions, and sprang surprise visits on workhouses to ensure they were not exceeding the dietary rules, nor allowing smoking. The guardians must have dreaded seeing his carriage coming down the road. When he couldn't visit, he wrote numerous letters, sent copies of rules, and regulations, as well as tabular returns to be filled in at length, which he calculated would tire rebellious ardour. From the beginning, he and Sockett were at crossed swords.

William Hawley was an odd man. He was born in 1793, the son of Catherine Jepson, who the next year married Lieutenant-Colonel Henry Toovey Hawley of the 1st King's Dragoon Guards, described in Hawley's own words as 'my reputed father'.† Hawley certainly conformed to Melbourne's strictures on illegitimacy — 'which seems to distort the mind and feelings and render them incapable of justice or contentment'.[360] Hawley's reputed great-grandfather, Lieutenant-General Henry Hawley, was a harsh disciplinarian: 'the troops dread his severity, hate the man and hold his military knowledge in contempt'.[361] These are characteristics that may have been inherited by his reputed grandson.[362]

Hawley was a justice of the peace and deputy lieutenant for Hampshire; the family home was West Green House, Winchfield. He received £700 a year as an assistant poor law commissioner plus

---

* The winged thunderbolt, the Hawley family crest, from Fairbairn's *Book of Crests of the Families of Great Britain and Ireland*, 19th Century, Vol 2.

† In his will, Hawley also mentions two 'reputed' brothers and a 'reputed' deceased sister.

a guinea a day when he was out in the field, as well as his travelling expenses; in 1835 they came to about £182 to £190 a quarter. In 1837 he was cross when the Commission pruned his claim for his carriage and horses, maintaining he had travelled over 1,000 miles for the Poor Law Commission.[363] He was equally cross with the guardians of Petworth Union when they asked to claim travelling expenses to union board meetings: 'I have generally answered that their expenses were amply paid by the reduction of the poor rates.[364]

He lost no time in visiting Petworth House in October 1835 (Tyler had recently died). He was received by the 'exceedingly polite and courteous' Earl who, nevertheless, did not hesitate to denounce the new poor law as 'one of the worst measures that could have been devised'. Hawley was courteously asked to stay, but his engagements would not permit and he left vowing to 'persuade the Earl of the advantages of the new system by pen and ink'.[365] The Earl probably took little notice of the pen and ink campaign, but it was largely in pen and ink that Sockett and Hawley came to metaphorical blows, although much of Hawley's passionate and extensive writing passed Sockett by. Asked if he had not read the Reports of the Poor Law Commissioners, Sockett replied, 'I have read one or two of them'. — 'Do not they send them to you?' — 'Sending and reading are different things'.[366] In his second annual report, in June 1836, Hawley spoke with approval of Sockett's work with the PEC. He, nevertheless, was reluctant to attribute the fall in Petworth's poor rate to anything but the effects of the poor law administration and had sharp comments to make about the disinclination of the Sussex people to migrate overseas or within the UK, quoting a Lewes pauper who went to New York and tried in vain to get father and friends to join him: 'I don't expect to see any of the Lewes Bricklayers out here for they won't come unless they can bring the <u>Hills</u> and the <u>Parish</u> along with them'.[367]

In the summer of 1836, Hawley moved house from Lewes to Chichester. He and Sockett had spoken on the issue of emigration and in May 1836 exchanged letters. Hawley requested material for his midsummer annual report, and Sockett sent him papers on the subject with a lengthy letter, copied I presume by one of the Sockett household:

Petworth May 17, 1836,

My dear Sir — There needs no apology with respect to the subject of your letter, as if aught that I can say, write or do, shall contribute in any way, towards bettering the condition of our population, of all classes, my satisfaction will be great. With respect to emigration, I am not aware that I possess any sources of information, excepting as to our own operations, that are not equally open to yourself. I enclose, however, some papers on the subject, and only regret that owing to many engagements, I have been so tardy in doing so. I cannot bring myself to agree with those who deny the existence of a surplus population; all my experience is on the other side: in this parish of Petworth, which I have known for 40 years, the population has increased, within the last 30 from 2000 to 3000, and not a single additional acre of land has been brought into cultivation nor can be, unless we cut down the few patches of wood that remain, and run to Canada for sticks to light our fires with and heat our ovens ... The emigration of this present year from this neighbourhood is clearly traceable to the operations of the Poor Law Amendment Act. From Tillington via the Midhurst Union 50 individuals have departed; the expense of their victualling, conveyance etc etc being defrayed by Lord Egremont, and an equal proportion would have emigrated from every parish in that union had there been a Lord Egremont in each to defray the expense. The applications I received were numerous and bitter were the complaints of the poor people, that they could neither obtain work nor relief, nor the means of flying to a distant country from that starvation which threatened them in this. You may depend upon it, my dear sir, that there is a class of persons who will take advantage of the new law to grind down the really deserving labourer to the lowest possible rate of wages — to a rate at which it is impossible that he can support a family and at the same time afford himself sufficient sustenance to keep up his strength for his daily labour. In the parish of Tillington, one individual complained that so many were enabled to emigrate. And why? Because he feared lest he should not be able to get a man (with a wife and five or six children to maintain) to work for him at 5s or 6s a week.

The parish of Petworth ... is at present very peculiarly situated, and therefore does not afford any fair criterion of the working of the new law; Lord Egremont ... is possessed of such perfect rigour of mind, and so large a portion of bodily energy, that he is very quick to see what things will be for the good of the neighbourhood, and very prompt in forwarding every useful scheme. He is employing a most unusual number of men in lowering hills, turning roads, erecting various buildings, and in short, performing all such works as he thinks likely to be useful to the public at large, as well as his own property. In addition to this, a gas company has been formed here, which is now in full operation. Lord E has also this year cut an unusual quantity of timber. All these circumstances combined (to say nothing of a portion of our people having emigrated) to cause such a demand for labour in this neighbourhood as has not existed since the close of the war. And if these very peculiar circumstances are not taken into consideration, any reasoning upon the fact of our just now having no people out of employ — whereas in 1832 we paid 1400£ for the single item of want of employ — would lead to false results, which if acted upon might cause much mischief. We should at this moment be dreadfully oppressed by surplus-labour, were it not for the extraordinary demand created by Lord Egremont, not only by the works he actually performs with his own funds, but by the great stimulus he causes to expenditure by others.

As I stated to you ... my mind was entirely made up to a conviction of the necessity of some strong legislative measure, to control the demands of a constantly increasing pauperism; but an evil so inveterate cannot be cured at once, or by hasty and violent remedies, and I much fear that the commissioners, anxious as they are to do right, will be misled by incorrect or interested reports (unless they exercise a caution almost more than human) into the commissions of much wrong. The order which I am informed has been issued to the Petworth Union to discontinue all relief out of the poor-house to the families of all able bodied paupers, after the 21st of June next, causes me strongly to feel this apprehension. What is a man with six, seven or eight small children to do? The farmer's pay cannot enable him to keep them. The farmer cannot increase his payments, the man must starve or steal. I already know cases where the father of the family is dwindling away, from the lack of sufficient sustenance. However fine a column of figures this system may produce, it cannot do in practice. But I will close this long scrawl; it is because I wish well to the system generally, that I object to some of its details.

I am dear sir, very faithfully yours,

P.S. One moral effect of the new law I in vain inquire for; a diminution in the number of our beer shops.

Sockett may well have stressed the errors to be made from incorrect or interested reports, for Hawley took no notice; he quoted only part of Sockett's letter, making 'highly coloured and incorrect' statements about Petworth and the PEC, mistakes that were to lead to angry comment from the Petworth Union Board, angry letters from Sockett in the national press, and embarrassing moments for Hawley at the Select Committee of 1837. He was foolishly slapdash at best — if not knowingly untruthful — in his desire to attack Petworth. Sockett did not outright accuse him of lying but remarked that there were ways of colouring the truth.

Eager to show the mismanagement of the Petworth Union and the degree of habitual pauperism, Hawley attributed the 1,456 PEC emigrants, sent out between 1832 to 1836, to the Petworth area alone, where he maintained there was still ingrained pauperism. These emigrants, in fact, came from a wide area reaching from Wiltshire to East Sussex and far-flung areas of Cambridgeshire. Sockett was particularly incensed as he had painstakingly put together a chart giving detailed numbers and figures which Hawley had ignored (perhaps he received it but had not read it, or read it with little attention), quoting inaccurate figures for many of the parishes involved, or failing to point out the important extenuating factors Sockett had outlined in his letter. Sockett accused Hawley at best of carelessness, at worst of 'the far more criminal intention of distorting fact and mis-stating figures in order to support a favourite theory'.[368]

Sockett was angry at the inaccuracies in the report and also at the language Hawley chose to use. In February 1837 he wrote a refutation of both and sent it, with a copy of his original letter, to his friend from Oxford days, John Walter. Walter was now MP for Berkshire and chief proprietor of *The Times,* which had attacked the new poor law from its inception with a great deal of public support. Walter sent Sockett's letter to the evening paper, *The Standard,* newly established in 1827, a Tory paper concomitant to the morning *Times.* It printed the correspondence in full. *The Standard* had attacked the new law, and not long before had published a long quotation from Dickens's *Oliver Twist* — including Oliver asking for more — the first two chapters of which had just appeared in *Bentley's Miscellany.*

Petworth people were incensed by Hawley's comments that 'a moral rather than a pecuniary effect has been produced by removing those vicious characters who, steeped in vice and habitual pauperism have preferred the uncertain advantages of expatriation to honest industry at home'. Sockett took exception as he was currently publishing letters from Petworth emigrants, now in Canada, who were neither vicious, nor willingly paupers. Hawley wrote a placatory letter back, saying that some parochial authorities had indeed described emigrants as 'scum of the population' and 'the great rogues in the parish', and reiterated that Petworth and the Poor Law Commission 'differ so much'.[369]

One significant issue, as Sockett wrote, was the granting of out-relief. Neither money nor food was now to be given as out-relief to unemployed able-bodied labourers nor their families. If in dire need, the family was to be offered the workhouse, but children were not to be taken in without their parents. The Gilbert Unions could continue to give out-relief, the new poor law unions could not, or rather should not. Hawley grumbled to the Commissioners that Petworth Union was very resistant to only 'offering the house' (the workhouse), that 'wholesome regulation' they call 'shameful'.[370] The ratepayers of the Petworth Union declared they would not be made 'the instruments of such a system'.[371] As a result of their refusal to act, a deputation of guardians was requested to attend the Central Board in London to discuss the matter. Equally distressing was the removal of a regular parish allowance of money or flour for families with young children. Hawley insisted this was another wholesome regulation; children were not now kept at home in idleness and looked upon with pity by the relieving officer but put to work. Fathers would chasten their sons if their behaviour was likely to lose them work, and mothers could take the babies with them to the harvest fields.[372]

These fights with the Petworth guardians and the correspondence and publicity engendered by Sockett were used by Walter in a speech to the House of Commons, in which he quoted evidence from 'a highly respectable gentleman, a clergyman and magistrate in the county of Sussex'. Walter was encouraged to call Sockett and the Petworth guardians as first witnesses to a Select Committee he initiated in 1837. The committee was mandated to enquire into the working of the new poor law. Lord John Russell, the Home Secretary; 'was prepared to resist any motion which would go to the repeal of the Act, or to any extensive change in its machinery or details'. He was willing to have an inquiry into the working of the law, although 'he had no doubt that it would be found that the commissioners had acted on sound principles throughout — If, in the result of the inquiry, any amendments could be suggested for the working of the Bill, he would not object to them'.[373]

The Select Committee was appointed on 27th February 1837 with twenty-one members, including Lord John Russell, and John Walter. Attendance by just five of the committee could make a quorum, but Walter claimed that only he and three other members were against the new poor law bill. Sockett, with members of the Petworth Union, went to London for the first meeting of the committee on 9th March 1837. The weather had been chilly and wet, and a nationwide epidemic of influenza was said to have visited Petworth very generally, 'scarcely a single person has escaped attack'; the Earl had been one victim.[374] The King had decided to stay in Brighton, and fashionable soirées were very much curtailed. Hawley himself had succumbed to the 'baleful epidemic', although he had managed to go pheasant shooting.[375] The winter had been severe with heavy falls of snow and consequent unemployment for the men who worked at coppicing in the Sussex woods, engendering conflict between the Petworth Union and the poor law commissioners over the giving of poor relief or the taking of individual children into the workhouse. Sockett, being independent of the commissioners, had been able to help many through the 'immense' Petworth charities.

Such charity was forcibly attacked by Hawley as destroying 'the instinctive faculties of forethought and self reliance, and [degrading] reasonable beings below the level of some of the most insignificant reptiles of the creation'.[376] He claimed he was too busy to come to the committee's sessions; he had by this time relinquished his position in East Sussex but had acquired east Hampshire, which gave him trouble.[377]

He passed scathing comment on the Petworth Union witnesses. Edward Butt and Mr Ellis were humanity mongers. John Napper, the chairman of the Board and a magistrate, was one of the most obstinate and perverse characters you ever met. Mrs Napper had asked permission to give the children in the workhouse a Christmas dinner but Hawley would not allow it on the principle that governed the ethos of the workhouse system — that conditions inside should always be less attractive than the life a labourer could earn for himself and his family outside.

The appearance of the Petworth people at the committee was reported in national and local papers and Petworth was proud of its fame and its rector. The *Hampshire Telegraph* — one of the newspapers taken by the Earl of Egremont — reprinted at length the heroes' welcome given to the party on its return:

> The esteem in which the benevolent and worthy Rector of Petworth, the Rev. Thomas Sockett, has long been held, is well known; he has for some years assiduously attended to the comfort of the emigrants who are annually sent to Canada by the munificence of the Earl of Egremont, and has latterly been distinguished by his very clear and intelligent evidence on the working of the New Poor Law, before a Committee of the House of Commons.

To the Rev. Thomas Sockett, Rector of Petworth,

Rev. Sir, — the manifestation of reciprocal good feeling which has so long existed between yourself, as Rector, & us, your parishioners has been so often and so strongly expressed (particularly on a recent occasion) that it would seem superfluous now to renew it. The truly Christian and benevolent steps, however, which you have taken to stem the rapid progress of a torrent, which was destroying not only the comforts, but risking the very existence of our poor and helpless, but deserving neighbours, calls forth at this crisis an especial token of regard. Many of us are aware how much the Parishioners of Petworth are indebted to you for the assiduous and unremitting attention and labor which you bestowed on their behalf, as Visitor and Chairman of the Vestry during a long period, and not a few of us regretted that you declined being chosen a guardian under the present system. We now, however, all see that you were right in that determination, as your efforts and watchful care of the vital interests of the poor would have been in a great degree shackled and paralyzed.

Be assured, Sir, that we feel truly gratified by the correct views which you have taken of the working of the New Poor Law Act, and of the manner of your substantiating these views by indisputable facts before a Committee of the House of Commons. We esteem it honorable to the Parish of Petworth that our Rector should have been the first witness called on so important an enquiry — an enquiry which will (if the partial efforts of a hostile majority in that Committee do not stifle the truth) be productive of such an amelioration of this severe law, as humanity would dictate; and it must at least show to posterity that those of us who are rate-payers have taken no part with those jobbing and unfeeling calculators, who with a reckless regard of economy in a machinery enormously expensive, at the same time insist on the most rigid saving of money, where the wants of the poor are concerned, rather than allay the heart-rending sufferings of an honest unoffending fellow creature ... We therefore, your parishioners, the inhabitants of Petworth, with the utmost respect beg leave to subscribe ourselves your obliged and faithful servants. March 31st 1837. Signed by 100 rate payers.[378]

Sockett's evidence was clear and intelligent. He was first witness on the first day when fifteen members of the Select Committee were present. He was circumspect in his answers, refusing to be drawn into quoting figures or information that he did not have at his finger tips. He dealt calmly with John Barneby who was rude, and with Sir James Graham who was aggressive, and took the opportunity to pick up and enlarge on the leading questions on medical and outdoor relief fed to him by Walter. Towards the end of a lengthy examination, he grew more confident and exchanged sharp words with Sir James Graham over the provision of meat puddings in and out of the workhouse, and with George Paulett Scrope over the desirability of gratuitous medical relief for the labouring population at the 'discretion of some proper person'. 'Where a labourer is receiving high wages, say 11s.6d a week do not you think that is one of the cases in which the parish is not bound to provide gratuitous medical relief?' he was asked. Sockett had the last terse words: 'I do not consider 11s.6d. a week high wages at the present price of corn'.[379]

In spite of being so busy, Hawley had to appear before the Select Committee on 14th March and again on 16th. He was questioned about his troubles with the Petworth Union and was on the defensive, reluctantly admitting he had been careless over the use of material in his report.

The Committee's work was cut short with the dissolution of Parliament on the death of William IV and the accession of Queen Victoria. It reported it did not have enough evidence to come to any conclusion, for it had examined only Petworth, Fareham and Droxford and begun to look at Somerset. It proposed doing more work during the next session of Parliament. Meanwhile, it noted that in the Petworth area the aged and infirm were well relieved — perhaps better than before. The morals and conduct of the poor were improved; people were anxious to get and keep a job and were respectful to their employers. However, the new poor law was severely felt in the loss of allowances for children; rents had not fallen enough to compensate, and wages had not risen nor food prices fallen. Nevertheless, the Committee was largely against any system of allowances.*

Given his discomfiture at the Select Committee and the increasingly stringent pruning by the Commissioners of his annual reports, Hawley acknowledged the advice of Poor Law Commissioner George Nicholls to tone down his strong and immoderate language. He had planned to visit Petworth again but had a sore throat — perhaps

---

* It was to be over one hundred years before this opinion was rescinded in the UK in favour of family allowances.

rough justice — and was confined to the house. He was sent to Ireland at the end of 1838. 'I am very glad of it, if he deserves it', was Sockett's dry comment. From Ireland, Hawley went to Cumbria in 1842, where he had a 'natural' son, William Hawley, with Margaret Graham of Rockcliffe, near Carlisle.[380] It is to be hoped he did not force her to wear a yellow striped gown, as the women with illegitimate children were made to do in the Westhampnett Union with his approbation.[381]

Sockett was by this time in his sixties. He and Hawley had had a confrontation in July 1837 when Hawley attended a meeting of the Sutton Union in view of the coming legislation affecting Gilbert Unions. He pointed out that, although Sockett had hitherto been both visitor and auditor to the union, under the new rulings he could not be so. The Poor Law Commission had the right to appoint the auditor, with duties totally distinct to those of visitor, who was now not automatically chairman of the board. Hawley reported there was no sign of any compliance on the part of the Sutton guardians, the commission would have to resort to coercion 'to suppress that Spirit of Opposition to the proceedings of the Commission so prevalent in many parts of the District'.

After 1838 Sockett was spared contact with Hawley, but his role as visitor to the Sutton Union was increasingly a trial and irritation; he threatened to resign over the new regulations but was persuaded to stay. In 1841 George Wyndham, now owner of the Petworth estate, wrote to his erstwhile tutor:

> I would certainly recommend your leaving the Sutton Union — We must always have poor people and many idle persons, and these People bother you without doing themselves any good, nor do I see what possible good can be done for them, until they make up their minds to go to new countries — this is an advantage which the Poor of this country have over the Poor of other nations, on account of our colonies.[382]

It was not so much the poor and idle that fretted Sockett but the relatively rich and idle. The Board of the Gilbert Union could recommend giving out-relief but it had no power to force the guardians and overseers of the individual parishes in the union to do so. Petitioners who applied for relief to the overseer of their parish and were refused could go, in person, to the next meeting of the Sutton Board and ask the Board to grant them relief. The Board might well do so and Sockett, in theory, had the authority to compel it; but when the petitioners returned home to their parish the local guardian and overseer still 'shuffled out of it', for such relief would come out of their pockets or their local rates to the anger of the ratepayers, and Sockett lacked the power to compel it. He wanted the Gilbert Unions to adopt a policy of having an official whose duty it should be to administer the relief which the Board ordered, and to see that it was done:

> So many instances of the oppression of the poor under the Gilbert Act have come under my knowledge and which I have had no means of preventing, I have become tired of the office of visitor, and have requested to be released from it ... I would not be made a tool or cat's paw in aiding to oppress the poor.[383]

It may have given Hawley very delayed gratification to report on the eventual dissolution of the Sutton Union in 1869.[384]

THE YEARS ROLL SWIFTLY BY, 1837

I hardly think, whatever
You dissenters choose to say,
She's an honest woman
That wed another way.[385]

Sockett might have felt pleased with himself after receiving the acclamation of his fellow townsfolk following his appearance at the Select Committee, but his pleasure and triumph, if it was such, was short-lived for 1837 brought great changes in his personal life, in Petworth, and in the nation in general.

The Church of England received considerable attention from the Whig ministries of the Reform government after 1832, and the secular power and authority of the church were challenged and diminished. In July 1837 the registrar of births, deaths and marriages, set up by the Marriage Act and the Births and Deaths Registration Act of 1836,[386] began his work. The registrar was responsible for a network of registry offices embracing the whole of England and Wales at which births, marriages and deaths were to be entered. Hitherto the Church of England had, with the exception of Jewish or Quaker congregations, been legally responsible for the registration of births, marriages and deaths in its parishes, comprehensively covering England and Wales. Nonconformist churches and chapels, such as the two in Petworth, could now, with the concurrence of at least twenty of their regular members and a fee of £3, register as a legal place for marriages; or, with the attendance of the registrar of the district, perform marriages in unregistered churches and chapels. There was also the purely secular alternative of being married by a civil ceremony at a registry office.* The effect of these changes was slow to be seen, but they had made an impact before Sockett died, as the table on marriages over the following years indicates.[387]

Year	Marriages		
	Church of England	Nonconformist	Registrar
1838	107,201	2,976	1,093
1848	121,469	11,718	4,790
1855	127,751	16,640	7,441

* The Revd Francis Kilvert referred to registry office weddings as 'a gypsy "jump the broom" marriage'. *Kilvert's Diary* 11th November 1871.

183

As well as losing a legal monopoly for taking and recording marriages, the rector or curate suffered financially with the loss of marriage fees.

In 1809 Nonconformists acquired the right to burial in the parish churchyard. From the 1840s onwards, there sprang up new cemeteries designed to relieve the pressure for space in the unpleasantly overcrowded city churchyards and crypts. These new cemetery companies set ground aside for Dissenters with their own chapel and unconsecrated ground (ground not consecrated by an Anglican bishop).[388] Petworth was not without its problems. In August 1843 Sockett called a meeting to discuss the question of overcrowding in the parish burying-ground. He reported a record sixty-nine burials between January and August 1843; some of these were buried two or three deep in a single grave. He suggested that no person outside the parish should be buried in Petworth without payment, above the usual burial fees, of an extra guinea for a common grave and two guineas for a vault or brick grave. Although he was entitled to these extra fees, he proposed to save this money towards the purchase of extra ground.[389] This rule was not without unspoken implications, for Sockett was incensed at having to bury paupers from Petworth Workhouse who did not belong to Petworth parish. The humane argument was that paupers were entitled to be interred in their own parish churchyard where their kith and kin were. The extra payment in Petworth might now encourage authorities to take a pauper home for burial.

In September 1852 the Bishop of Chichester consecrated the new Petworth burying-ground, part of the glebe given by Sockett, for the ground in the Barton, consecrated in 1805, was almost full.[390] By 1854 the parish had to reluctantly conform to the Burial Act of 1852.[391] Sockett told the vestry meeting of April 1854 that henceforth there could be no more burials in the old churchyard, and, apart from vaults and family graves in the Barton and the new graveyard, there was to be only one body in each grave. He had, perhaps as rector, imagined himself buried in the churchyard but that was not to be.

The secular registration of births gave all churches problems, since some parents, as a matter of principle or through indifference or ignorance, felt they had done their duty by registering the child and eschewed further ceremonies in church or chapel. Sockett and his fellow clergy needed increasingly to stress the spiritual vocation of the church and its ceremonies as its legal and secular function decreased, but Sockett had not embarked on his ministry as above all a spiritual mission. The SPCK, the publishing house of the Church of England, issued tracts urging baptism as well as secular registration. Other tracts, printed and sold for 1d. each in the 1840s, had a stark message: 'Children That Have Been "Registered" without Having Been Baptized Are Not Entitled to Christian Burial'.[392] Charlotte M. Yonge, daughter of the rector of nearby Otterbourne in Hampshire and a contemporary of Sockett, was at pains to introduce into her best-selling book, *The Daisy Chain*, poor Mrs Taylor, the mother of twins, who felt uneasily she had done her duty when 'they was set down in the gentleman's register book'. She was persuaded by kindness and practical help to bring the babies to church to be baptised.[393]

Another facet of diminished links between Sockett and his parishioners — albeit one he may have appreciated — was the commutation of tithes.[394] Nonconformists resented the payment of tithes, in money or kind, to the local rector. In January 1837 Sockett met with the Commissioners at the Half Moon Inn in Petworth to come to an agreement on the value of his tithes. These were based on a sum drawn from the average of the seven years preceding Christmas 1835, and were now commuted into an annual money payment, a tithe rent charge, based on the price of corn, included in the tenants' rent, and payable by the landlord. Sockett's average tithe for Petworth was given as £917.4s.0d. for which he was offered £850 in lieu of tithes. Tithes for Duncton averaged £379.9s.4d. for which he accepted £350. At his tithe audit dinner for eighty tithe payers in 1840, Socket stressed that he had had no power nor control over the management of the tithe commutation: 'he thought the tithe payers were generally well satisfied, there had been no reluctance in the payment of the different portions; the sum that was left unpaid, he had no doubt was so from some trivial causes, the whole of the arrears due to him at that moment was 25s'.[395]

He also had £252 from North Scarle. Sockett's three-pronged income was threatened by the 1838 Act of Parliament[396] regulating pluralism. The right to hold the living of more than one parish was now severely restricted. Such parishes had to be within four miles of each other by the nearest road, footpath, or ferry, with an annual value not to exceed £400; exceptions could only be granted by the Archbishop of Canterbury or the Bishop of the Diocese. This same 1838 Act also reinforced the growing antagonism to Anglican clergy having secular interests and income. Restrictions were introduced into the extent of farming that an incumbent could do for himself on his glebe. If he farmed more than eighty acres, he again needed permission from his Bishop, and any 'spiritual person' farming more than eighty acres without such permission forfeited forty shillings a year for each acre. Nor was he to engage in trade.

Sockett's own farming of his glebe did not exceed eighty acres, but by the 1850s he came under increasing pressure to cease farming for himself.* He was allowed to keep his three livings intact during his lifetime and made shrewd public relations of his good fortune; at the same tithe audit dinner of 1840, spent with 'much hilarity and good humour', he said

> that as regarded the next rector, when it pleased God to remove him (Mr Sockett) from the livings he now held, he would be able to hold only one of the livings, he might therefore be unable to invite them to a dinner, but as regarded himself he would say thus much, that so long as it pleased God for him to remain along with them, he should be happy year by year to meet them all to partake of a dinner at his cost (immense cheering).[397]

His parish of North Scarle missed out on this kind of celebration, and from this time on Sockett was to come under increased pressure from the Bishop of Lincoln, John Kay, to provide a suitable house as residence for a curate who would be a presence in the parish and take regular services.

The average pay for a curate in the Lincoln diocese in 1835 was £77 a year, and Sockett probably paid around the average; by 1846 he offered £90 a year with morning and evening service, and the possibility of quiet, comfortable lodgings in the village. Nevertheless, none of the curates before 1849 lived in North Scarle itself. In 1844 the curate, Milnes Townsend, wrote to Sockett suggesting that the old rectory on the glebe, occupied by a small farmer, be made suitable for at least a curate's residence, at an estimated cost of £330. Townsend suggested the money should be borrowed from Queen Anne's Bounty and the interest deducted from his stipend — which, he pointed out, Sockett had lately generously increased. Sockett replied that it would be hard to turn out the existing tenant farmer, who had lived there for many years, and, although Townsend might be willing to pay the interest on the loan out of his stipend, any future curate might not wish to do so. Sockett was right in his arguments but it does seem his perpetual anxiety and carefulness over money also played a part.[398] As he had stressed to the Bishop in 1829, he was very anxious to do his best for North Scarle but asked that his Lordship not 'call upon me to incur expences which I cannot afford'.[399]

Most of the curates for North Scarle served several parishes, and it is hard to see how they provided Sunday services in parishes at some

---

* In 1855, partly as a result of such pressure and partly because of old age, he was to give up the fields and stock he had farmed for himself. WSRO, PHA 1113.

distance from each other. Thomas Galland, curate from 1827 to 1843, had been living in the next village of Eagle, but on becoming rector of Laneham in Nottinghamshire, he had to cross the Trent by ferry and travel by horseback eight miles to North Scarle, nine miles if the river was flooded and he had to cross by Dunham Bridge. Some curates had other problems. Mr Bounsfield was grateful to Sockett for agreeing to take him as curate in 1850, for he had left his last parish under a cloud because of his addiction to 'strong drink'. Sockett wrote to the Bishop of Lincoln to

> offer my sincere thanks for your kindness in granting to Mr Bounsfield, an opportunity of recovering himself from the painful conditions into which he had fallen ... and earnestly hope, that he may be enabled to persevere in that better course on which he has now entered.[400]

It may be that his experience with his own son coloured Sockett's kindly attitude towards Mr Bounsfield. He did live in the village, for North Scarle was felt to be a quiet, retired place in which he could pursue a better course with the help of his wife, but he did not stay long. Between 1851 and 1853 Jonathan Shortt was curate but he found the village did not agree with him for health reasons.

The presence of Roman Catholics was increasingly noticeable nationwide. Having gained the franchise in 1829, they were also gaining ground in number and influence in the country at large. Sockett seems to have been on civil terms with the Biddulphs in the parish of Burton, hard by Duncton, but in 1838 he reported to George Wyndham that Biddulph had offered to give land and £399 towards the building of a new church for Burton. Sockett suspected that Biddulph wanted the old church for the Roman Catholics — the Arundel Roman Catholic priest 'has been moving in it'. The Bishop of Chichester had appointed Sockett and, ironically, Henry Manning at Graffham as neighbouring rural deans to make the arrangements — 'but', as he wrote to Wyndham, 'we look at the matter with suspicion', and they feared the Bishop has been taken in.*

This example of paranoia over the issue of 'popery' was intensified when the Roman Catholic hierarchy was re-established in England in 1850. Petworth joined in the national outcry, and in November 1850 sent a petition to the Queen signed by 'numerous inhabitants of the parish' protesting against the establishment of the Papal hierarchy.[401] A month later, at Sockett's tithe dinner at the Swan Inn, Ellis congratulated

---

* Henry Manning was to 'go over to Rome' in 1851 and became Cardinal Manning by 1875. WSRO, PHA 734.

Sockett and Klanert for 'not allowing any of the new fangled forms to be introduced into the sacred edifice of the parish' and 'for maintaining the even tenor of its simple form of worship'. Presumably referring to the spread of High Church ceremony and doctrine which came dangerously near to 'popery'.

Sockett had been praised in the local press over his appearance at the Select Committee but he appeared in less laudatory terms in the autumn of 1837. *The Brighton Patriot*,* a radical newspaper, largely agreed with him and the Earl over the administration of the new poor law, missing no opportunity to attack the Duke of Richmond — 'Duky' — and his Westhampnett Union. In 1836 the paper printed a long account of the hanging of a portrait of the Earl of Egremont, painted by George Clint, in Brighton Town Hall, stressing that they did not admire the Earl 'because he is a nobleman, ... not because he is one of the magistrates of the land ... but above all because he is a <u>friend</u> of the poor'.[402]

In November 1837, however, the same newspaper published a copy of a letter from an emigrant on the *Diana*, which had sailed in April with Brydone as superintendent as usual. It was a rough, uncomfortable passage. This was Brydone's fourth journey with a Petworth ship and perhaps he was getting tired. There were seventy-eight emigrants from the Isle of Wight among the party, outweighing those from West Sussex. The Isle of Wight men and boys were cited as being particularly troublesome. There were also the usual problems over the rations and the distribution of alcohol.

The anonymous letter described employment conditions in Canada as falsely represented: 'If the people knew what poor emigrants have to go through, there would not be so many come to Canada'. It described Brydone as mean, stopping several passengers' porter rations but bottling off several dozen for the use of the cabin passengers. Brydone was cited as getting drunk and fighting on board the steamer on the St Lawrence, and kicking a 'poor friendless boy who came out with us', for which he was fined £2. 'In fact instead of being treated like respectable passengers we were treated like convicts. His (the superintendent's) conduct enraged the men that were sent out by the parish to such a degree — and some of them were the greatest blackguards on earth — that they kept the ship in state of mutiny all the way over.' There was apparently little love lost between this Sussex writer and the party from the Isle of Wight. It would also appear the emigrants knew that Brydone had indeed in the past taken a party of convicts to Australia. Sockett appeared now in the paper in unflattering scarcely concealed anonymity: 'The book that old S— gave me was full of lies'.[403]

---

* Called the *Brighton Patriot and Lewes Free Press* 1835–36; the *Brighton Patriot and South of England Free Press* 1836–39.

Having gone to town one week in its attack, the *Brighton Patriot* two weeks later printed two letters contradicting the accusations. Frances Pullen, from Northchapel, who had sailed on the *Diana* with her husband Richard, wrote one. Although for her the voyage had been one of great trouble and misery for 'dear Ann', her first-born, had died, nevertheless, she had never wanted for attendance. The second letter was from Edward Lane, the master of the ship, who said that he had valued Brydone's help in keeping order on the ship and his attention, 'Both by night and day, gained the respect of the elder and more sensible part of passengers'.[404] This trouble and bad publicity with the *Diana*, the rebellions in Canada, the emphasis beginning to be placed on emigration to Australia, and above all the death of Egremont were responsible for this being the last ship to be commissioned by the PEC for its own use.

Nevertheless, there were celebratory days in 1837. In May the Petworth Friendly Society celebrated its forty-third anniversary. The Earl of Egremont gave £100 to the funds of which Sockett was treasurer. The money was gratefully received. The president, Mr Ellis, giving evidence earlier in the year to the Select Committee on the Poor Law, had said that the society's members consisted mainly of mechanics rather than labourers, as the latter had no money to pay two or three shillings in monthly contributions, in spite of their dire need of the benefits the society offered in times of sickness or bereavement. Indeed, in 1832, citing a reduced income and higher demands on funds with the stringent times, benefits had been reduced, and the Society had circulated all the nobility, clergy and gentry in the Petworth area asking them for help and hoping they would also 'induce Persons they may be acquainted with to become Members'.[405] In spite of its financial difficulties, the Society's members enjoyed themselves on this anniversary. After a service in church, the company retired to the Angel Inn where, by evening, the spirits of all were 'very buoyant', the revellers ended the day by marching to Petworth House and in front of the house played 'The Old English Gentleman', cheered, and retired.[406] At midsummer the Earl gave his annual fête for the poor women and children of Petworth and surrounding villages, seven hundred stones of beef,* sixty stones of potatoes, quantities of salad and 1,600 plum puddings were provided for a feast for five thousand people, followed by sports and fireworks. Arrangements were in the hands of Klanert, and Sockett proposed the health of the Earl, who was ill in Brighton. The assembled crowds, led by Sockett, sang once again 'The Old English Gentleman'.

---

* A stone weighs fourteen pounds.

THE FINE OLD ENGLISH GENTLEMAN.

39. 'The Fine Old English Gentleman', melody and text by Henry Russell (1812–1900).

I'll sing you a good old song that was made by an old pate
Of a fine old English Gentleman who had an old estate
And who kept up his old mansion at a bountiful old rate,
With a good old porter to relieve the old poor at his gate.
Like a fine old English gentleman, one of the olden time.

His hall so old, was hung about with pikes, and guns and bows,
And swords and good old bucklers which had seen some good old blows.
'Twas there his Worship sat in state in doublet, and trunk-hose,
And quaffed his cup of good old sack to warm his good old nose.
Like a fine old English Gentleman, one of the olden time.

When Christmas old brought frost and cold, he opened house to all,
And, spite of three score years and ten, he featly led the ball;
But though, he feasted all the rich, he ne'er forgot the small
Nor was the house-less wanderer e'er driven from the hall
Of a dear old English gentleman, one of the olden time.

But time, though sweet, is strong in flight and years roll swiftly by,
And autumn's fading leaf proclaimed this fine old man must die!
He laid him down right tranquilly, gave up his latest sigh
While mournful friends stood round his bed, and tears bedimmed each eye
For the fine old English gentleman all of the olden time.[407]

It may be that the last verse was tactfully left out at these performances during the summer of 1837, but it was all too soon to be entirely appropriate. The Earl was ill intermittently during 1837, in spite of a few better interludes — he went to a cricket match in Brighton and later was seen at Egdean colt fair. By November, the reports on his health, coming from Petworth House, were increasingly grim. His physician, Sir Matthew Tierney, was summoned from Brighton, to little avail, and the Earl's sons and daughters gathered at Petworth House. He died at 11:15 p.m. on Saturday, 11th November 1837.

Flank.	Mutes.	Flank.
Six Gamekeepers in single file.	Churchwardens.	Six Gamekeepers in single file.
	Household (two abreast) :—	
	Comptroller, Groom of the Chamber.	
	Two Valets, two Cooks, Confectioner, Butler.	
	Cellarman, Master of the Stables.	
	Master Gardener, two Bailiffs.	
	Surveyor, Master Builder.	
Six Porters of the Lodges (singly).	Artists, Phillips, R. A., Turner, R. A. Leslie, R. A., Clint, A. Carew and Son (Sculptors).	Six Porters of the Lodges (singly).
	Mr. Murray (Steward), Mr. E. Murray. Two Clerks. The Earl's Coronet.	
Ten Grooms, in file.	Two Clerks. Fourteen Clergymen (in canonicals), two abreast. Officiating Clergymen, Rev. T. Sockett, Rector; Rev. C. Klanert, Curate. The Funeral Car,	Ten Grooms, in file.
Eight men to draw the Car. Mutes. Four Footmen.	(entirely covered with black velvet, and surmounted by two tiers of black plumes,) containing the Coffin, which was covered with purple velvet, the handles, &c. of silver gilt.	Eight men to draw the Car. Mutes. Four Footmen.
Six Footmen singly.	Chief Mourners, his three sons, Col. Wyndham, Gen. Wyndham, Col. C. Wyndham; his three sons in law, Sir Charles Burrell, Bart., Earl of Munster, John King, Esq.; his two grandsons, Percy and Walter Burrell, Esqs.; Sir Walter Riddell, Bart., —— Blount, Esq.; and two other Gentlemen.	Six Footmen singly.
Ten Grooms as before.	Master King (grandson); Mr. Mellish (his tutor), Mr. Klanert, sen.	Ten Grooms as before.
Two hundred Labourers at equal distances, in their white frocks, with black gloves, crape hatbands, and crape round their left arms.	One hundred and twenty Gentlemen, two abreast, consisting of the Magistrates of the county of Sussex, private Gentlemen, and Professional Men. Three hundred and eighty Tenants, Tradesmen, and Inhabitants of Petworth and the neighbourhood, also two abreast. The late Earl's Endowed Schools : Two Mistresses—Forty Girls. Two Masters—Forty Boys. Every person was in the deepest mourning.	Two hundred Labourers at equal distances, in their white frocks, with black gloves, crape hatbands, and crape round their left arms.

40. Funeral procession of the 3rd Earl of Egremont, 21st November 1837.

A Very Grand Funeral and Afterwards

'His Lordship is dead and Colonel George has got the estate — your brother John have drawn him to church; we had a very grand funeral; there was hundreds of people; your brother had a sut of clothes', wrote Elizabeth Pullen and Ann and John Summersell to relatives in Canada.[408]

It was indeed a grand funeral, as the *Gentleman's Magazine* reported at length, including a plan of the funeral procession [see facing page].[409] John, who drew his Lordship to church, was evidently one of the men chosen to pull the funeral car, which was covered with black velvet and surmounted by two tiers of black plumes. The coffin itself was covered with purple velvet and ornamented with brass nails and handles of silver gilt. John's new suit was one of the many sets of mourning clothes distributed by George Wyndham, now the owner of Petworth.

The death of the Earl and the turn-round whereby Sockett's erstwhile pupil, George, now became his master brought traumatic and hectic times. The Earl died without the ministrations of his chaplain and long-time rector, for Sockett was forbidden the house. The Earl was almost eighty-six, and in the last months of his life had been sporadically in poor health, fretful, and upset. He accused Sockett of being partly responsible for the defeat of Henry Wyndham in the national election called in the summer of 1837 after the accession of Queen Victoria to the throne. It was taken for granted that the two candidates, Lord George Lennox and the Earl of Surrey, both of whom supported Melbourne's Whig ministry, would be returned unopposed for the two West Sussex county seats and therefore there would be no need of a poll. To everyone's surprise, including apparently Henry's, William Holmes, at the last moment, proposed Henry as a third candidate supporting the Conservative cause. There was suddenly 'much personal feeling and debate' at the meeting from speakers who were 'more or less heated' over the issue.[410] An unexpected and hasty poll was called in a matter of days amongst the electorate of West Sussex and Henry came third with just over a 1,049 votes, compared to 1,247 for Surrey and 1,291 for Lennox.

It was a near thing; if the poll had not been so hasty and if Henry had had time to canvass a few more voters, he might have overtaken Surrey. Sockett was accused of abstaining from voting himself and encouraging others not to vote for Henry. It was true he had not voted, but he strenuously denied that he had influenced others not to do so and he claimed that Lord Egremont's mind had been poisoned by lying reports.[411]; He does not specifically name Henry as the perpetrator but doubtless had him in mind. Egremont and Henry took this defeat to heart, and the Earl, perhaps at Henry's insistence, called Sockett ungrateful and forbade him to come to Petworth House. His action caused Sockett much pain, for his pleasure at being offered the Petworth living in 1806 was first of all that it was 'convincing proof' that the Earl was pleased with his conduct and wished to settle him close to his own door'.[412] This trouble renewed the long-time antipathy between Sockett and Henry and was to be part of the maelstrom of recriminations and animosity between the Earl's sons in the months after his death. Much dirty linen was washed in public and feelings ran high. Gossip also said that the Earl was upset at finding at an inspection of the weekly bills that his servants had been cheating him and stealing his money. He was said to have embarked on a frenzy of dismissing servants and taking on others before fatigue and vexation made him ill and led to his death.[413] There may well have been a discrepancy in the accounts, for Tyler had died in 1835. He had kept an eagle eye over the staff and the household expenditure, and his successor, Murray, was less efficient, with an eye less searching.

The Earl was prone to chest infections, which were the immediate cause of his death. At the end of October he went to Brighton to pay his respects to Victoria, the new Queen. Colds were rife in the town — the Queen herself had recently been indisposed with one — and Egremont brought a cold back to Petworth with him and died of inflammation of the lungs. His death certificate was signed by Henry Jackson, surgeon, of Pound Street, Petworth. Sockett learned of the Earl's death at midnight in a brief note sent by Charles Klanert, the curate. Sockett was to be accused, by Henry, of being back in Petworth House before the Earl's body was cold, but if so it was at the insistence of George Wyndham, now owner of the estate, who, harried and overwrought, looked immediately to Sockett for help and advice.

He had a myriad tasks to do, and a myriad letters to write in answer to the many that arrived from friends, acquaintances, clergy, tenant farmers, local magistrates and landowners. Smith, in the estate office, was drafted to help write the great many copies of a stock letter sent in reply. The funeral was to be a private walking funeral, and the custom of the well-to-do of sending their carriages, if not themselves, to a funeral was declined. These arrangements may have been the wish of the Earl, who was known for his dislike of pomp and ceremony, but in practice the logistics of manoeuvring numbers of carriages in procession around the narrow streets of Petworth would have been difficult if not impossible. Attendance at the house was limited to near relatives and clergymen presented to their livings by the Earl.

On the Sunday before the funeral, St Mary's was hung with black cloth, and the congregation heard 'solemn and effective voluntaries' from the organist; a metrical version of Psalm 90, 'Thou dost sweep men away; they are like a dream', sung by the children of the free schools; and two sombre sermons from the chaplain of Petworth House of Correction, the Reverend T. W. Langshaw.[414] At half-past two on Tuesday, 21st November, a dreary, late-autumn afternoon, the long procession with mutes and black plumes left the house out of the lodge by the stable yard. The children of the village schools, forty girls and forty boys, brought up the rear and behind them streamed a multitude of friends and members of the public who wished to pay their respects. They walked around the town and back to the church door, where Sockett took his place at the head of the procession and began to read the funeral service for the dead; 'I am the Resurrection and the life said the Lord; he that believeth in me, though he were dead yet shall he live ... We brought nothing into this world, and it is certain we can carry nothing out'.[415] After the church service, he then took the service in the burying-ground where the third Earl of Egremont was interred in a vault he had had built for himself. The occasion must have been very painful for Sockett, who, until the last few days, had been close to the Earl for over forty years.

Clad in white satin with a white satin cap, the Earl had been on show in his bedroom until 14th November, when all persons, rich or poor, were allowed to take a parting view. Everyone at the funeral was in deepest mourning. George Wyndham, with Sockett's help, was responsible for providing black mourning cloaks, black beaver or kid gloves, and black crêpe or silk hatbands for the gentlemen. All the domestic servants and many of the outdoor staff were given mourning clothes. Mary Wyndham, George's wife, undertook to see to the black outfits for the female servants; she, perhaps wisely, opted to give them the money; £8 for the lower, and £10 for the upper servants, and left them to buy their own. All these clothes had to be hastily made by toiling seamstresses in the ten days between the Earl's death and his funeral.

As always with arrangements for large occasions, there were problems. Charlotte Green, the head groom's wife, thought she should be given mourning clothes, as well as her husband, but was not on the official list and was refused. Mr Bartellot had a bad cold and sore throat and doubted whether he was well enough to join the procession; Sockett suggested he go only to the church. Emma Bartellot hoped Mrs Sockett was tolerably well — the usual content of brief remarks about Sarah. Mr Biddulph was certainly unwell and would have liked to send his carriage, but the no carriages rule was strictly enforced. No hatchment — a diamond-shaped tablet with the Earl's armorial bearings, denoting the owner's death — had been hung at the London house, and Mr Chrippes needed to hurry and take one up.

It was a very grand funeral and, as a unifying occasion for rich and poor, was probably greatly appreciated in sad fashion by the people of Petworth and the neighbouring villages, and the 147 tenant farmers who were said to have attended. Afterwards came the changes in the house and estate, which were divisive and troublesome and tiring and difficult for Sockett. He took parting with the Earl on bad terms very much to heart and as a personal sorrow, and was upset about the gossip and scandal that was engendered in the town. George Wyndham wrote to him in February 1838, saying he had noticed that Sockett was sensitive to the opinion of the Petworth people and what they might say. George accused his father, the Earl, of being too fond of popularity and of siding with public feeling at times over that of his children. He, George, had had great affection for his father, mixed with a degree of fear, but he personally was not looking right and left for popularity but intended to follow a straightforward course. He hated being flattered and puffed by newspapers and indeed at times would almost prefer abuse to praise.[416]

The Earl's will was read on Sunday afternoon, the day after his death, at the wish of his family. The 188 folios took Murray an hour to read, and he reported that afterwards there was little said as the family went their separate ways. Fortunately for George Wyndham, the Petworth estate was not entailed and, although illegitimate, he could and did inherit both it and lands in Surrey, Yorkshire, and Ireland. Henry inherited the Cumberland estates, and Charles, the youngest son, had the very newly acquired manor at Rogate and some money. The entailed west country estates and the title passed to the Earl's nephew, also named George Wyndham. He became the fourth and last Earl of Egremont.* Born in 1785, he was the son of the Earl's younger brother, Hon. William Wyndham, who had died in 1828. Although married, George had no children and when he died in 1845 the title died with him.

In 1839 it was announced that the name of Ayliffe/Iliffe/Ilive was to be dropped in favour of the usual plain Wyndham for the children

---

*Although the earldom became extinct, in 1963 the Egremont title was revived for (the eight Earl's son) George Wyndham's great-great-grandson John Wyndham, who was created Baron Egremont of Petworth.

of the third Earl and Elizabeth. In 1815 George had married Mary Blunt, the only daughter of the Reverend William Blunt of Crabbet Park near Worth in mid-Sussex, and by 1837 they had six children. George had neither the wish nor the means, having lost the Cumberland estates with their profitable mines to Henry, to maintain Petworth in its former state, and a new regime was quickly initiated. Elizabeth Pullen described it to her family in Canada:

> Your sister, Martha, is come down to the Lodge in the Tillington Road to live where the poultry is kept. She has got a good house but Sarah's husband have nothing to do they have been in view of a place several times but it is all a blank and she have been very poorly, and the children have all had the hoping coff [whooping cough].[417]

Sarah's husband was Charles Dilloway, the third Earl's former gamekeeper, now out of work. George Wyndham consulted Sockett over his finances, saying he was spending £6,000 beyond his annual budget. Sockett, after some thought, suggested the two most expensive items were the Brighton house and the maintenance of outlying areas of the Petworth Park for shooting. He suggested selling or letting the house at Brighton, giving up the outlying shooting areas, and cutting back on the number of horses. George had asked for advice but the answer he received was certainly not what he wanted to hear. He said he would rather burn down the Brighton house than sell it or let it, and he certainly could not give up his horses.[418]

Petworth House was not open for show for three months after the Earl's death.[419] Sockett had a letter from George Wyndham saying that all the servants on yearly wages were to be on board wages — wages that included an allowance for the servants to provide their own food — from the day of the Earl's death for three months. At the end of that time, those who were discharged would be expected to leave straightaway. Those who had found other positions and left before the three months were up would still receive their three months' wages. Wyndham wished his communication to be taken in 'the spirit and manner of kindness': 'that is why I ask you to have the goodness to arrange it for me', he wrote to Sockett. It may be that Sockett protested at having to do this, or perhaps George thought he had asked too much of him, for a second letter suggested that Murray should do the unpleasant task, 'for I find that servants and common People are more difficult to please than Lords and Gentlemen and Ladies and I should not wish you to run the risk of offending them'.[420]

George was willing to send to Canada any of these people who thought they could do well there, and James and Sarah Lannaway and their children were one family who went. James had been a groom and coachman to the Earl. They sailed on a ship organised by Carter and Bonus from London in April 1838 with Sockett making the necessary arrangements. He was still giving lectures on emigration in the spring of 1838. He was aware of the rebellion in Canada and the encouragement the government scheme was giving to farm labourers and their families to emigrate to Australia, but he felt that Australia was not the right place for redundant stable-boys and housemaids from Petworth House. Although the PEC ceased hiring ships, between 1837 and 1850 around 170 men, women and children went to Canada on Carter and Bonus ships under arrangements made for them by the Petworth Committee.[421]

One family for which Australia was considered very right was the Ayliffes, Elizabeth Ilive's relations. George was eager to get his mother's kin out of England as soon as possible; they were perhaps undesirable reminders of his illegitimate birth and a potential drain on his resources.

In May 1838 Sockett arranged the manifold details of their despatch and settlement at the other ends of the earth for, as he pointed out, if they were sent to Canada they might come back very soon.[422] Frederick Mitchell of Haslemere was appointed superintendent of the party. He could take his own family and assist the Ayliffes to 'establish themselves comfortably'. Mr Ayliffe senior and his three sons, George with his wife and family, Thomas, and Henry, made a party of around twenty in all.

The Australian Commission granted a free steerage passage for the party, and George paid the extra for them to be upgraded to intermediate or second-class cabins.[423] The Mitchells were to proceed by the ship *Pestonjee Bomangee*, which was to sail mid-May from London, picking up the Ayliffes in Plymouth with their baggage. They shopped extensively before they left, spending £239 at the drapers, the collar and shoemakers, and the ironmakers. Colonel Wyndham paid for the shipping of houses (flat-packed one presumes), implements of husbandry, twelve sheep, one stallion and a bull with the party. Sockett records in his account book for 22nd May: 'I was this day backwards and forwards to the Docks attending the embarkation of cattle and other matters from 6.am to 8.30pm'. A colt had been kept in a stable near St Katherine's dock, and Sockett assisted a man to take the colt's shoes off before it went on board, accompanied with its own medicine supplied 'by Mr Tattersall's advice'. Batley, the chemist, provided a medicine chest for the passengers. Sockett tipped the man who helped him, the labourers at the dock, and, by Mary Wyndham's desire, the servants on the *Pestonjee*.[424]

Arriving in South Australia, Mitchell was to erect the houses, secure the stores, and look around for suitable farming land for settlement. Brydone recommended the land around Adelaide and, once this was chosen, Mitchell could buy stock. Ayliffe senior and George were to receive £70 a year each and Thomas and Henry £30 each, to be paid on their arrival. George Wyndham stipulated that the Ayliffes should have 160 acres of land and Mitchell 40 acres for himself and an annual salary of £150. George Wyndham retained total property rights over the land and wanted a rent of 1s. an acre to be paid half yearly.

The party arrived at Adelaide in October 1838. The Ayliffes had ideas of their own and were a trial to George Wyndham and Sockett from the beginning. Bills left unpaid in England followed the family out, although Sockett did say that, if they were properly accounted for, Wyndham would pay them. Thomas soon opted out of the undertaking and went his own way to work as a carpenter. The rest of the family were not pleased and George Wyndham cut off his allowance. Mr Ayliffe wrote that they were unhappy with Mitchell's management, and their sheep were being killed by wild dogs. Would George Wyndham pay for a horse so that he could ride to church? Sockett sent out £1,960.16s. in July 1838 and a further £600 in December and gave permission for George to go to Adelaide to practise as a medical man. Mitchell had much difficulty in pleasing all parties, and the money from England was slow in coming. By 1840 he was threatening to resign and Sockett pleaded with him not to do so. Mitchell agreed to stay if he had an increase in salary. By 1841, following complaints about his dilatory and scrappy accounts, he did resign. By this time George Wyndham had spent £3,821.1s.4d. on the project. By 1842 he feared the Ayliffes were 'incapable and unwilling of exerting themselves' and demanded Mitchell's farm be handed over to repay a loan of £200 and a £140 deficiency in Mitchell's accounts. The remaining Ayliffes were to have an allowance and a small amount of land to rent and nothing more. George Ayliffe died in 1844, leaving a wife and six children. He seemingly did not do well in medical practice for £10 was sent from Petworth for his funeral expenses.[425] George Wyndham and his siblings were spared having the embarrassing and demanding Ayliffes hanging around them in England but their exile cost George dear.

The upheaval among the servants and their rehousing had given Sockett problems nearer home, including the plight of poor Bat Nevatt. One catches a glimpse of Sockett's pastoral care as visitor and go-between in his parish when he wrote to Mary Wyndham about him. The oldest servant in the Petworth establishment, Nevatt had been receiving a pension of 7s. a week and £10 a year, clothes and boots. He and his wife had lived rent free in one of the lodges before a man called Puttick said his Lordship had promised it to him:

> Poor Bat Nevatt is very uncomfortable in his new abode — he has not I believe ascended a pair of stairs for the last fifty years and he says that doing so makes him very ill — it is a cramped up place where he is but we could not get a better. I tried yesterday to comfort him saying we would look out for him ... Old Dibble is likely to die and then there will be a vacancy in Lord E's almshouses and I do not think the Colonel can find a more fit person to put in than Old Bat.[426]

Mary Wyndham was in Ireland at the time with her husband and Brydone. George Wyndham went in the summer of 1838 to inspect his inheritance in County Clare and Limerick and to distribute largesse to such deserving local institutions as infirmaries, dispensaries, the House of Industry, and the Protestant Orphan Asylum.[427] It was a considerable family expedition with children, nursemaids, governesses and servants — seventeen in all. One excitement of the journey was that after two days' coach journey to Birmingham they then travelled on the recently opened Birmingham to Liverpool Railway at a cost of £15 for the whole party and completing the journey in five hours.[428] The link from London opened later in the year.

Sockett had been asked if he would care to go along but regretfully declined; he felt he would be 'mere live lumber'.[429] Perhaps he did not wish to be part of such a diverse retinue, but he said he could not afford a trip with the expense of 'my boy's Oxford education'. He recommended Brydone, who was not going to Canada with a PEC ship that year and needed to eke out his pension and half pay to enable him to bring up 'his very nice family'. He was a gentleman who could ride any distance, look at farms, copy papers, keep accounts (most accurately), and be useful in case of accident; put broken limbs to rights; and, as a medical man, he could be useful on the sea-crossing — although he was a member of the old school and might not look with a favourable eye on the homeopathic doctrine favoured by Mrs Wyndham.*

Sockett's assessment of Brydone's abilities was accurate as Mary Wyndham agreed when she wrote to Sockett from Ireland:

---

* Mary Wyndham used the homeopathic system for her children and favoured Dr Dunsford of 28 Somerset Street, Portman Square. WSRO, PHA 729.

My dear Sir,   George St, Limerick, June 14th (1838)

I was much obliged to you for your letter, which was full of interest to us in these foreign parts. Mr. Dowbiggin* has not yet begun, but in a few days I mean to hint at our departure from hence, and that his Designs will not travel after me, but be returned, if not in time. Col Wyndham is going on I must say to all appearance admirably, it seems to have been of great use — his coming, and there is plenty still to do. Mr. Brydone will I hope one day give you every particular of the business they transact, and also his own impressions altogether. I cannot tell you how admirably he suits, and works; nothing could have been better in every way. You know him however, and thought it would be what it is, so I need not describe, while he seems quite at his ease, and very chearful and comfortable, not to say often exceedingly amused, as we all are. When Col Wyndham visits a farm or I might say an Estate with several, he is followed as he walks by a crowd of a hundred or two who press on him, and Mr. Brydone drops behind amongst them, and picks up a deal of little information quietly, and disseminates Emigration where he can. They are a very loyal set to their Landlord, but you cannot believe any intelligence or opinion they give, for the character of them is that they never speak truth, but by accident.

And now about Petworth, in which I long to be settled comfortably, and to feel at home. I would just give a hint or two for you to work upon if you see any occasion. I may be quite mistaken, but I have not the highest opinion of the Petworth [workmen — deleted] Painters for anything more than common, and anything like a hint to them of modern improvements in their art, might produce a very overstrained result. I daresay however the Brighton Painters as more in practise have already been chosen to paint the best rooms. I have no doubt it will look very nice, and probably had I been on the spot to give an opinion I should have given a great deal of what might in fact be unnecessary trouble and much more expense but (and perhaps you know it) there is such a thing as consulting the colours

---

* Thomas Dowbiggen and Co. were furnishers and decorators at 23 Mount Street, Grosvenor Square, London.

of the furniture, even in tinting the white paint, and yet when you see the whole, it only looks white, but this had better not be meddled with except by an experienced Artiste for obvious reasons. Mr. Upton said to Col. Charles that when the white and gold room was painted, the Gilding would require to be newly done. Dowbiggen looked all over, of course, with a longing eye as to a commission, and told me that it would not require new Gilding for years, but only to be carefully painted with a proper tint, and I did not ask him for his opinion at all. He made one other observation, which was of great regret at the little modern Chimney pieces in some of the best rooms, saying he thought there must have been formerly some of the style of the White and Gold, for which he said he should be happy to give 150gs [guineas] I merely mention this mere gossip, to ask whether there are anywhere about old fashioned chimneypieces put away, supposing these to have been substituted which may not have been the case. On one more subject in as few words as possible — In a fit of thinking that you had too much trouble perhaps, I begged Mr. Murray to have a Visitors' bell put from the back door of the house (near the fountain; to be heard in the footmen's room below, I think I mentioned it to you also:) and also a large strong bell at the front door (till another entrance is made) notwithstanding the entry of wind. I have heard so much of the inconvenience to ladies calling, (and I think it myself troublesome to take that long walk from the stables as the only way,) that I wish to have for Visitors a bell at the front door for the present. I think the wire might descend immediately below, and be carried thro' below to as near the waiting room door as would ensure the footmen's hearing a large "sonorous" bell. We had a London bellhanger to make the house comfortable at Drove, because we found that the Chichester man could not manage a long pull without it soon getting out of sorts, Mr. Murray however, said that he thought the Petworth bell-hanger was a clever one — The choice I would leave to your judgement however — [430]

Sockett's relationship with Mary Wyndham was a friendly one, but it is evident from her letter just how much he was undertaking on the Wyndhams' behalf at Petworth, as well as despatching the Ayliffes to Australia and looking after his parishioners. No detail of the renovation of Petworth House and the re-ordering of the estate seemed too small for his attention and he spent a good deal of his time in the big house.

The local painters did not fare too well as the scaffolding fell down and one of them broke his leg.[431] There was also the question of the disposal of the donkeys. George wanted to keep the larger and darker-coated donkeys for his own use, but charged Sockett with the task of finding good homes for the others. He had a letter from one local man, addressed delightfully to 'Kernal G Windom', offering a good home to a donkey who would act as step-mother to his recently orphaned colt. George agreed he should have one.[432]

A more taxing request was that Sockett should, in as kind a way as possible, dismiss Murray. George was anxious and fretful about him, plying Sockett with letters and stressing that his father had said before he died that Murray 'required to be looked after sharply'. He had been ordered to do up all the accounts until Egremont's death, and was taking a long time to do so. Sockett reverted a little to his old role as tutor urging George not to act hastily and repent at leisure. He drew a graphic account of the aged Murray and his son toiling away in the office over the intractable accounts, saying how distressed Murray would be to be dismissed; he earned him some leeway for he was still at Petworth in 1847 when he died aged seventy-nine and Henry Upton took over as steward.[433] Many staff were dismissed at this time, but some new ones were appointed, including Burgess who, George Wyndham said, already had 'the peculiar smell belonging to a game-keeper'.[434]

Rather than the lordly patronage of his father, George's policy was to favour a money-based economy, but he did still dispense charity on suitable occasions. The children of Petworth were given a feast day in June 1838 to celebrate the coronation of Queen Victoria. There was a dinner of beef, followed by plum pudding, for 400 poor children at the Swan Inn and for the grown-ups there was a ball in the evening. The children did less well for Victoria's wedding to Prince Albert in February 1840, as the weather was poor and their medals had not arrived; nevertheless, they did have tea and a plum-bun. Two years later was the occasion of the christening of the Prince of Wales in January 1842 — 'Nothing could have been done better and little Albert ... behaved so well' —[435] and the children processed around the town and were each presented with a bun by Mrs Sockett.[436] Four years later, on a frosty morning in December 1846, the Queen and Prince Albert drove from Arundel Castle to view the Earl's pictures. As they approached, the Royal Standard was raised from the church steeple. The Queen expressed the 'highest gratification with her visit'. Back at Arundel Castle Mr Young, the 'Wizard of the North', performed before the august party, and later went to Petworth to perform before lesser but appreciative audiences.[437]

It wasn't only Queen Victoria who occasioned celebration. When George and Mary Wyndham's eldest daughter, Fanny Charlotte, married Alfred Montgomery in the autumn of 1842, seventy-four girls from the Petworth school gathered at the rectory where they were presented with prayer books from Mary Wyndham and, dressed in new pink frocks — doubtless made by themselves at sewing lessons in school — and straw bonnets trimmed with blue, they lined the path from the south gate of Petworth House to the church door. Sockett officiated at this marriage himself, as he did in 1848 when Blanche Wyndham married Robert Bourke, the MP for Cockermouth. On this occasion, the girls from Petworth school had another new dress, given by the bride. After a sumptuous déjeuner for thirty guests at Petworth House, a ball was given for the domestics in which 'the quality' joined.[438] Fanny Burrell, writing from Knepp Castle, was pleased that Blanche was to be married in a manner 'so satisfactory to you all' — 'if an Irish man is really a gentleman he is generally a very good-humoured pleasant person'.*

Brydone did so well in Ireland in 1838 that George offered him work as his secretary during the winter of 1838–39 if he would go back to Ireland in 1839 to organise the proposed emigration from the Wyndham estates to Canada. Brydone wrote to Sockett in the summer of 1838, looking forward to being again in Sockett's 'snuggery' recounting all that had happened. He had 180 applications for emigration, although most of the applicants wished to go to Australia. He was pleased to hear good accounts of the health of Mrs Sockett, Caroline and Henry and supposed that Fanny was housekeeper as Sockett was in Brighton. He looked forward to being reunited with Eliza, 'her whom I love' and 'all our dear children', and was glad Sockett had been busy for his friends 'because I know it is not only agreeable to you but conduces to your health which is never better than when over-whelmed with business, I often wish I was possessed of half your mental energy'. The Wyndhams all say 'they did not know what they should have done without you'.[439] Brydone did go back to Ireland in 1839 and helped to organise on the spot the emigration of 183 people from Limerick, who sailed on the *Waterloo* from the River Shannon at the end of May 1839. Charles Rubidge, the superintendent, was glad of Brydone's help for the departure of the ship was not without trouble — husbands and fathers of families disappeared and whole families did not appear at all. In all, sixteen ships went with tenants from the Wyndham Irish estates to Canada between 1839 and 1847.[440]

---

* Fanny had an ulcerated ear and was to die later in 1848; Robert Bourke became Earl of Mayo in 1867. WSRO, PHA 11092.

George Wyndham asked Sockett to perform yet another difficult task. George was pleased with Brydone's work but, as they were often thrown together, he would like Brydone cured of his habit of 'constant sniffling and snorting and making all sorts of noises with his nose, throat and lips — it may be his habit or it may be nerves'; 'we would all give a great deal to cure him of a most unnecessary trick', but, he added, Mary Wyndham 'begs me to say that she is the only Person of the Party, who is not put out'.[441] Sockett, faced with an embarrassing task, wrote to Brydone:

> My Dear Sir, I know you are so well satisfied of my anxious wish to serve you that you pardon a liberty I am about to take. It often happens that truly valuable qualities in those with whom we associate are rendered less pleasant to us by some habit or peculiarity of no real moment and that some kind of coldness and distance arises and for want of candour — no one can guess why. After this long and perhaps you will say quite unnecessary preface I will send you an extract from a letter Colonel Wyndham sent to me but which you must not appear to have seen ...[442]

BITTERNESS AND HEARTBURNING:
THE WYNDHAM BROTHERS

Perhaps George and Henry Wyndham had fought as children. Although Sockett said he loved Henry — while he deplored his faults — Henry may have had little love for Sockett after his tutor's few words with him over his behaviour as a boy, and later as a man over the 1837 election. When their father died, George was fifty-one and Henry forty-seven, but Sockett was still in the delicate position of acting as go-between and negotiator in their quarrels. They were all their father's children, inheriting his temper.

One fight began on a morning in December 1838 as George was about to leave for London.[443] Before he went, he hastily instructed his huntsman to take the hounds out the next Saturday to nearby Flexham Park. George had been in charge of the Petworth hunt since 1817 when his father bought Drove, a house near Singleton, for George and Mary, and established a pack of hounds for the 'Petworth country'. George hunted largely over the southern territory, especially after Henry, living at Sladelands to the north of Petworth House, hunted in the northern territory. When Henry had returned from Canning's expeditionary army in Portugal, his father set him up with a pack, encouraged him to hunt, and promised the loan of his horses, Rushlight or Cockatoo, any time he needed more mounts. Henry was proud of his hunt. The local papers regularly reported the details of the chase and the proud fact that they killed fifty foxes in one season.

Unfortunately, when George's hunt went north to Flexham Park on that Saturday morning, they came face to face with Henry's pack, which had come south, and chaos ensued before George's hunt-master gave way and drew off his hounds. All might have been well if Mr Napper, who hunted with Henry, had not arrived at Petworth, and 'remonstrated' with George, who was leaving for Brighton, for drawing coverts in Flexham woods. These woods, part of the Petworth estate, now belonged to George, who was indignant at being told by a third person that 'he could not draw in his own coverts'. Nevertheless, on the way to Brighton, he stopped at Steyning and wrote a conciliatory letter to Henry, saying he would alter his hunting days so that this need not happen, but adding he would not allow interference by any third party. From this moment on, the two men spent the Christmas season writing increasingly acrimonious letters to each other, and words such as 'bitter estrangement', 'indignant', 'injured', 'barbarity', 'cold disdain', were flung around, largely by Henry, in letters that were then signed by both sides as 'your affectionate brother'.

Foxes were sidelined over deeper issues of family estrangement — behaviour at the deathbed of their father, the Earl, and veiled hints as to Henry's 'peculiar position'. Writing more in sorrow than in anger Sockett was brought into the uproar when Henry referred to his 'deadly insult to me' over the election, and claimed that, although Sockett was forbidden the house, he was back 'before the body of his benefactor was cold'. Sockett, from the time of the election onwards, had insisted that, although he did not vote for Henry — which was perhaps insult enough — he did not urge others not to do so. George did not help by pointing out that Sockett's only fault was one of omission in that he did not vote; other friends and acquaintances had positively voted against Henry.

This was only part of the trouble. Henry was estranged from his family. It may be he was jealous of George's having inherited Petworth House and lands; even though he had been given the Cockermouth estates in 1834 at George's expense. Henry was angry that Charles Burrell, his brother-in-law, was an executor with George of the Earl's will and not himself. Perhaps above all the problem was Letitia de la Beche. She was the cause of Henry's 'peculiar position' over which George, as a husband and father, had taken a decided line. Henry and his wife, Elizabeth Somerset, had parted, and Letitia, after a notorious legal separation from her husband, Sir Henry Thomas de la Beche, had moved into Sladelands as Henry's mistress. A 'most unhappy tempered and vindictive woman', she was said to have Henry in 'most unhappy thraldom'[444] and was the voice behind his letters, exerting a 'fatal influence' over him and encouraging his propensity to take matters to extremes. Henry claimed it was only his father who had remained on good terms with him; perhaps the Earl had no strong moral grounds to do otherwise. Sockett said in 1838 that he had not been to Henry's home for ten years and when he had been there last Henry's wife was there.

Henry and Letitia spent part of Christmas Day 1838 composing another letter to George reiterating their attack on Sockett, for the Rev Mr Sockett's 'intriguing acts' were proverbial, and accusing George of blatantly sending his hounds on four successive occasions to Flexham Park. The letter taken over to Petworth did not engender Christmas goodwill. George replied: 'your hints and insinuations are unworthy of you and insulting to me, therefore our intercourse ceases'. Another letter arrived on 28th December which George sent back unopened.

On 30th December, Henry wrote to the Reverend J. Hurst, the rector of Thakeham and a member of Henry's hunt. Henry confirmed that he was not speaking to George over the issue of the hunt and also in consequence of 'my disapproval of every part of his conduct in the administration of my father's will and affairs'. Hurst replied in the New Year saying he was sorry for the rift between the brothers, which 'will be bitterness and heart burning to you both for the rest of your lives'. He went further and said that Henry's answer to George's conciliatory letter was uncalled for; they should forgive and forget and 'not rip up old sores'. He concluded: 'This letter of mine may not please you, but it is my honest and independent opinion'. He then wrote to George, saying that 'Henry asked for my advice but did not follow it'.

By April 1839, George decided to keep 'all coverts, my own property for myself'. Henry could not hunt on the Petworth country any more. Both brothers then spent a considerable time recruiting evidence from friends and supporters and issuing pamphlets stating their side of the quarrel. In the autumn the *Brighton Guardian*, 'that most worthless, low, radical paper',[445] had a field-day printing up whole pages of one point of view or the other.[446] Burrell was incensed at Henry's accusation that he had not properly fulfilled his duties as an executor of the Earl's will: 'I did not abandon my trust nor any of my duties', and Murray was called upon to confirm this. There were letters attacking hunting parsons, and much debate as to whether George could stop Henry hunting on his land; was Henry doing so on the sufferance of the owner of the Petworth country, or had the Earl by his actions given Henry rights to the north of the county? Opinion was sought from hunting experts hither and thither. The *Sporting Review* entered the fray on Henry's behalf, saying that the Earl had certainly intended Henry to have hunting rights and had indeed purchased two farms for him 'with good coverts'. It pointed out that Colonel Wyndham had no right to contest Henry's claim; he 'is not the heir of Lord Egremont only by the especial will of his father — he had no more claim to the broad lands of Petworth than the wandering piper or wandering jew',[447] and gossip had it that George had committed the most heinous acts of the whole controversy — he was slaughtering foxes by other means, 'an indecorous and indefensible outrage'.[448] Another source claimed he was poisoning them.[449]

The eloquent remarks as to George's inheritance of Petworth struck a sore spot. He could get the Ilive removed from his name and get his troublesome Ayliffe relations removed to Australia, but these did not alter the fact of his illegitimate birth, and in Victorian England this would matter far more than it had in Georgian times. In November 1839 George wrote to Sockett of the whole conflict: 'I hope to hear no more about it, and beg you will not speak, or write about it'. From this time onwards, Sockett protected George, urging kith and kin to 'keep that perfect guard' on their tongue which is necessary for that gentleman's tranquillity.[450] Sockett spent a considerable amount of time fending off threats to George's tranquillity. Now only George's hounds hunted the Petworth country.

Charles took little part in this quarrel, but the repercussions of his elder brothers' animosity to each other rebounded on him. In June 1839 George was approached by the local Conservative Association asking him to stand as a candidate for West Sussex at the next general election. George did not want to do so but urged the association's representative, Charles Shirley, to ask Charles, for he, George, would back Charles and oppose General Henry Wyndham with 'all in my power' for 'he has behaved very ill'. Charles reluctantly agreed to stand as a candidate,* but he would need a considerable amount of grooming for the part. Sockett took the minutes at a meeting of the local Conservatives in July 1839 and told Charles that he needed to do some intensive personal canvassing over the whole of West Sussex for the 'scurvey radical' had already done so. Charles was not keen at this prospect but was to be supported by a local gentleman of note in every district. A draft of Charles's election address was supervised by Sockett, and George told Charles what charities it would be politic to support.

Apart from encouraging Charles, there was the problem of mollifying Henry. He might have expected to have been asked after his narrow defeat in 1837. Shirley and Sockett decided it would be prudent to encourage Henry to turn his attention away from Sussex towards his inheritance at Cockermouth. Shirley would have gone to talk with Henry but for Letitia: 'I could not call upon him as I know that odious woman watched him as a Cat does a mouse, and I will never see her, so I had to write'.[†] [451]

Wyndham men seemed to have a penchant for spending the Christmas season writing angry letters to each other. Over Christmas 1846 and New Year of 1847, a very snowy and cold festival, Sockett

---

* Colonel Charles Wyndham went into the army when he was fifteen and served in France, Spain, Portugal and India. He married Elizabeth Ann Scott, daughter of the sixth Lord Polwarth, in 1835.

† Henry was to have two unsuccessful election campaigns before he was elected as MP in 1842 for Cockermouth, a burgage borough in which as landlord he owned a considerable number of the votes (Elie Halevy, *A History of the English People in 1815*, 1: Political Institutions [Penguin, 1937], 178). Henry was MP for the County of Cumberland from 1857 to 1860. Charles was Conservative MP for West Sussex from 1841 to 1847.

again was third party to a quarrel, this time between George and Charles. In December 1846 George wrote to Charles that he wanted the deeds of Charles's home, Rogate Lodge, housed for safe keeping in the Petworth Estate Office. Charles did not want to give the deeds and was further incensed by Murray's assertion that Charles owed him money for services rendered in the past. Again the issue of the Earl's will was brought forward. On Christmas Eve, Charles wrote to George pointing out that 'everyone consoled with him how badly off he was left by his father's will'. He had no money to spare and would not be drawn into litigation nor leave his 'poor children' with a threat of litigation. 'It is unfeeling of George to let his attorney hurt my feelings'. George responded by once again refusing to read any letters — this time from Charles — and Sockett spent the Christmas season acting as arbitrator between the two.

Charles's wife, Elizabeth Ann Wyndham, came to see Sockett. One can sense their mutual goodwill was based on an unspoken but agreed knowledge of the tempers of the two men. If Charles would admit that he owed Murray money, then George would pay the debt. Sockett said that it was best not to enquire why the money had not been paid long ago; the question should be left to sink into oblivion. Elizabeth went back to Rogate Lodge as a skilled negotiator, for on 13th January 1847 Murray's account was sent to Charles, who accepted it. On 13th February Elizabeth wrote to Sockett saying that George, having won his point, had paid Murray £200 and the deeds for Rogate Lodge were housed in the Petworth Estate Office.[452]

Bitterness and Heartburning: The Sockett Children

> Your kindness almost overwhelms me, I am relieved of a weight of corroding care that has pressed upon me for nearly twenty years and will give me more comfort and tranquillity than I had ever hoped for, my embarrassments are my last thoughts at night and my first in the morning; I cannot hesitate but will accept the munificent offer.*

George Wyndham wrote in April 1838 offering Sockett a gift of as much money as he felt he needed. He had, perhaps, hoped to benefit from the Earl's will and had been disappointed, or possibly Wyndham thought that Sockett deserved some payment for all the work he had done for him since the Earl's death. Sockett answered that £400 paid into Stoveld's bank would keep him going until Christmas, and £1,000 'when I get to London' would enable him to pay his debts to Phillips — if Phillips wished; repay Mrs Sockett's sisters, who had lent the money to send Henry to Oxford, and repay Brydone the £100 owing to him for paying George's debts.

If Sockett was hoping for comfort and tranquillity in the years to come it was not to be. Henry, who had now been two years at Oxford, had perhaps in traditional fashion cost his father far more than he had expected, but certainly George had already cost his father a great deal. On George's arrival in Canada in 1833 Sockett sent him £400 to buy a hundred-acre farm at Eramosa Township, in the Gore district of Upper Canada.[453] George had no experience of farming and by 1835 was largely in debt; amongst his creditors was William Bulmer Nicol, newly arrived in Canada with Brydone after the voyage of the 1835 PEC ship. Brydone paid George's debts on Sockett's behalf, and bought the farm back from George, again on Sockett's behalf, at an annual payment of £30 — presumably to give George some income. At the same time his father bought, for him, another hundred acres of land on a clergy reserve, to be paid for by ten instalments. In September 1836 the farm was let for one year to Arthur Carnie.

In July 1838 George exacerbated his situation by marrying sixteen-year-old Ruth Griffin, who had emigrated in 1837 with her

---

* The phrase 'corroding care' was an accepted literary phrase in the eighteenth and nineteenth centuries. Pope, for example, used it in his translation of the Odyssey in 1725, (vol. III, 63) 'steal from corroding care one transient day'; it is to be found in Wesley's letter to his brother in 1726; and was later used by Robert Burns and others. WSRO, PHA 684.

mother and step-father from Shoreditch in London. Sockett's twelve grandchildren then began to arrive at regular intervals. Sockett sent another urgent letter of credit for George in April 1840, which may have given him some technological pleasure in that it went by Brunel's latest innovation, the steam ship *Great Western* from Bristol to New York, taking only fifteen days for the crossing.[454]

There was also trouble at home in Petworth Rectory. Fanny and her father were both unwell at the end of 1839 and into the early days of 1840. Adelaide O'Keeffe wrote in June 1840 urging Sockett to do 'all in your power to keep up Good Spirits and Cheering Hope' and offering condolences 'on the illness of your Daughter, and I hope early to hear of some amendment'.[455] It may be Frances who had been at least part of Sockett's 'corroding care' during the past twenty years. We have slight glimpses of her; when she was baptised, at the age of almost two, at Northchapel; when she returned to school, seemingly in London, when she was fifteen; was away in the Isle of Wight when she was twenty four; was housekeeping during her father's absence in Brighton in 1838; and was organising the Petworth Ladies' Society in 1839.[456] She may have inherited her father's mental energy and was never in such good health as when she was mentally well occupied, and life at the rectory gave her little opportunity to exercise her active mind and talents, whereas Henry, her half-brother, had recently finished three years at Oxford; perhaps she did not get on well with her step-mother.

In July 1840, when she was twenty-eight, Frances became severely ill and was taken by her father, on the official legal recommendation of two Petworth surgeons, to Lea Pale Asylum, near Guildford, where she was to remain for a year.[457] Lea Pale had been an asylum since 1774. There were three other patients in residence with Frances and the asylum had therefore to be licensed and visited, at least four times a year, by local magistrates and a medical practitioner. They paid such a visit on 11th July and found Frances in the Ladies' Day Room in a 'state of religious melancholy'. In November they found her in the garden, with an attendant, still in a 'disponding state of mind' and asking to see her father. She showed no improvement in January 1841, and was said to be still in a 'state of distressing mental excitement' in April 1841. A surgeon of Guildford visited regularly, the patients were said to be under apparent proper care and treatment and the house was reported to be warm, clean and comfortable. None of the patients could be prevailed upon to attend prayers or enter into any amusement or occupation but they did take regular exercise in the garden.[458]

It seems unlikely that Frances contracted religious melancholy from her father. Sockett in all his manifest correspondence and churchmanship shows no evidence of any sense of damnation and despair but one does not know what belief and practise was to be found amongst the other family members at the rectory. Mary Wyndham, herself an avowed Evangelical, wrote to Sockett:

> I do sympathise truly with you upon the subject of your dear excellent Daughter's establishment in — I hope — a comfortable home, and I am very thankful that you have found one that appears so suitable. I shall always remember her <u>Christian</u> character as it appeared to me during my short acquaintance with her, and which struck me the more from total absence from profession which accompanied it to us — I am sure you feel that her life and responsibility are ended, while she is carefully watched over by her Heavenly Father who we cannot doubt is overruling all for her good. I hope you feel quite recover'd from the attack of illness a fortnight ago altho' weakened I fear by the treatment of it.*

Frances's care was more expense for Sockett.† The care of the mentally ill in the 1840s was still largely provided in private households, private asylums or public mad-houses. In 1826 Charles Lamb recommended a private asylum at twenty-eight shillings a week with board at Mr Warburton's Private Asylum in Hoxton, beer and washing extra, for a lady who 'requires restraint'.[459] He and his sister, Mary, had years of personal experiences of mad-houses in and around London after Mary murdered her mother in a frenzied attack in 1796. The building of county lunatic asylums was only being legally enforced by 1840. John Clare, the poet, ended his days in the Northampton General Asylum in May 1864 but it is very doubtful that Sockett would have sent his daughter to one had there been one available; Sussex was noticeably dilatory in the establishment of a county asylum; the first one was to be built in 1858.

Frances was discharged 'uncured' from Lea Pale House on 8th June 1841 and the same day set out, with Brydone, apparently en route to another asylum. He wrote a brief note to Sockett in the evening from Swindon:

---

* The reference to Sockett's treatment may be occasioned by Mary Wyndham's preference for homeopathic medicine. WSRO, PHA 1664.

† In July 1841 he borrowed £22.1s.3d at 4 percent over twenty years on the strength of his Duncton living to pay his share of his tithe commutation expenses (WSRO, PAR 69/6/4); and in 1846 borrowed £400 from George Wyndham at 3.5 per cent.

Here we are arrived most comfortably — Fanny wished herself to get on this far and does not feel over fatigued. She has been most agreeably rational all the way. I have not time to say more as the post leaves this [box] in a quarter of an hour.[460]

Brydone was a surgeon, and presumably capable of dealing with Fanny's condition — if she was suicidal or a danger to others — as well as being her half-uncle by marriage. It is possible they were en route for Cheltenham.*

Whilst Frances was thus away, Sockett received a disturbing New Year letter from Canada. Ruth's step-father, John Thomas Leslie, wrote on George's behalf to say that George was ill in bed with suspected kidney disease:

his wife, as evils rarely come alone, had been confined about three weeks — and on this occasion had to go a distance of half a mile or more, at this bitter season of the year in the night to call a neighbour to go for a Doctor 7 miles distant.[461]

Ruth begins to emerge as a sturdy character. Leslie, in his long letter, drew a dire picture of George and Ruth's situation. The farm was not paying and Leslie described how difficult it was to make a farm pay in Canada, and presented a very different picture of emigrant hired helps, as 'idle dissolute blaggards', to that promoted by Sockett and the PEC. He suggested George must again let the farm; a suggestion squashed in a second letter a fortnight later when Ruth's mother, Elizabeth, and Leslie had taken George, Ruth and the children into their home, so that George could receive proper attention. We may pity the first Sarah Sockett, George's mother, coming from Westminster to primitive Northchapel in 1811, but Ruth came from London to even more primitive conditions at Eramosa for Leslie described the present house as falling to bits, wanting a chimney, roof and hearth.

George's weakness was whisky. He possibly started to drink heavily in the army; soldiers had reputations for so doing. He now got drunk, especially when Ruth was confined with a new baby, and when he received those carefully written joint letters from Petworth. Leslie

---

* Castleton House, an asylum at Charlton Kings, near Cheltenham was run by Dr William Conolly MD. William was the brother of the notable John Conolly, who had practised in Lewes and Chichester in the 1820s. By 1839 John was Resident Physic at Hanwell Asylum in London, where he introduced a policy of no physical restraint. In June 1842 George Wyndham, Sockett and Mrs and Mrs Ladbroke went to Cheltenham. Wyndham and the Ladbrokes were possibly going to the races, and perhaps Sockett went to see Frances. *Sussex Agricultural Express*, 9 July 1842.

suggested care should be exercised over the content, which should not make George sadly compare his present lot to that at home. Apart from home-sickness, he was doubtless distressed over the news of Frances. Brother and sister may have helped to make each other and their father ill. I am 'sorry you give me such a bad account of yourself',[462] Charles Wyndham wrote to Sockett in May 1841.

Their father sent £150 to pay for the building of a new stone house, with the promise of curtains and carpets to help furnish it. It was finished inside and out by 1845 and was 'the best house in this part of the province'.[463] George was given a yearly allowance of £53, and boxes of clothes went out to Canada each time there was a new baby, containing not only clothes and shoes for the children, but clothes for George and Ruth, 'including under-clothing and all ready made up'. Caroline, and later Frances, had plenty to occupy them during the long winter evenings at Petworth. Money also went out for the infant Canadian church. In June 1846 Bishop Strachan thanked Sockett for one donation of £35 and proposed giving a portion of this to the church at Eramosa, 'where your son lives'.[464]

George was described, by his father-in-law to his friend, Thomas Williamson in London, as 'the most good natured and likeable man I ever knew'. He had not been drunk for the past six months but then she (Ruth) is his companion everywhere so that he has not a chance of escape:

> She with her infant and him went to Town for a ton of lime & when they were ready to start home just before dark he gave her the slip and got drunk in a trice — she had the gentleman when he was found placed by her side for he was insensible — and the child in her lap — mounted on a load of lime & drove him as far as our house 3 miles after dark with a span of horses ... but his good nature to the children when sober makes her forget it all soon.[465]

'His father, the Rev Mr Sockett — is I think the kindest old gentleman I ever heard of'.* [466] This was true, for George was 'his dear boy', his first-born son by his beloved first wife, but Sarah, his second wife, may have resented all this money going to Canada. John Leslie was a little resentful; he accused Ruth and George of getting uppity. Their seventh child was born just before Christmas 1850, but the family was not invited this year to Christmas dinner with the Leslies:

---

* Sockett's experiences with George may account for his kindly attitude to Mr Bounsfield, his curate at North Scarle.

41. Eramosa, the home of George and Ruth Sockett near Guelph, Ontario, Canada, in 1991.

I intend to show my resentment by not asking her to a Christmas dinner which we have provided for her for 9 or 10 yrs at least — we mean on this occasion to eat the turkey ourselves — and all the good things we can get.[467]

Frances celebrated Christmas 1850 as the new wife of the Reverend Thomas Wall Langshaw. Mary Wyndham may have written as though Frances was permanently removed from this world but her 'life and responsibility' were not ended. She was back in Petworth by the late 1840s when she was efficiently organising the spending of the £80 that George Wyndham gave annually for the poor. Some of this was spent on wine for the sick and other 'small things' but the bulk of it was spent on clothes and shoes, 'as the girls could not in many instances be got out at all without such assistance'.* Frances rendered an account to Colonel Wyndham in February 1849 but soon turned her attention away from Petworth towards West Grinstead. On 7th November 1850 in Petworth Church she married the Reverend Thomas Wall Langshaw, rector of West Grinstead. Henry, her half-brother, now rector of Sutton and Bignor, officiated, and her father and Eliza Brydone signed as witnesses. Frances was thirty-eight and Thomas was forty-three, and a widower.

Frances met Thomas when he was chaplain of Petworth House of Correction from 1836 — with a brief intermission from July 1838 to 1841 — until 1849. Langshaw had been a young man climbing the clerical ladder and not pausing long at each step.† He was a notable preacher, his name appeared frequently in accounts of services and occasions in Petworth, including that of preaching on the Sunday between the Earl of Egremont's death and his funeral. Sockett gave Langshaw a reference on his second application for the post of chaplain in 1841[468] and Langshaw was on sociable terms with the Socketts at the rectory, being invited to dine with them and attending Sockett's tithe dinners.[469] Langshaw must have known of Frances's illness.

---

* In 1848 she bought from Mr Halliday, the mercer in Petworth, (employing seven men in the 1851 census); 175 yards of flannel, 164 yards of calico, 23 blankets, 46 pair of sheets, 42 pair of trousers, 60 round frocks, 33 gowns, 6 bed tickings, 10 shawls, 5 pairs of stockings, 4 pairs of shoes and 4 upper petticoats. WSRO, PHA 1104.
† J.A. Venn, *Alumni Cantabrigienses*, Part 11 from 1752 to 1900, Vol IV, 96; He was born in Bristol in 1807; graduated from St John's College, Cambridge in 1828; ordained deacon for Llandaff in 1830; priest in Llandaff in 1831; curate of Malpass Monmouth 1830–1832; curate of Woollas, Newport, 1832–1833; and moving steadily eastward was curate of Warminster 1833-4; curate of Midhurst 1834–6 and from thence to Petworth by 1836. The entry is incorrect when it says Langshaw was chaplain of Petworth House of Correction only from 1836 to 1838; he was also to be so from 1841 to 1849 at the same time as he was rector of Bepton 1840–49. WSRO, QAP5/W5.

There were three Houses of Correction in Sussex: one at Lewes, another at Battle and the third at Petworth. Langshaw's flock at the Petworth house contained men and women awaiting trial, or serving sentences of hard labour. The house had been erected in the 1770s as a result of the Act regarding Houses of Correction,[470] passed largely to cope with the problem of what to do with law breakers after the American War of Independence precluded them being shipped across the Atlantic. By the time Langshaw arrived in 1836 the house was committed to the fashionable reformation regime of solitary confinement and silence for all prisoners serving sentences of hard labour for theft, felony or larceny. There were ninety seven cells for male prisoners, and nine for female.

Langshaw's duties, as chaplain, consisted in reading prayers and portions of scripture every morning at 8:30. and taking two services in the chapel on Sunday, one of which was to include a sermon. He should visit each prisoner at least once a week in his cell to give religious and moral instruction and supply copies of the Bible and prayer book. Each House of Correction was also to have a schoolmaster to teach prisoners to read and write and learn their catechism. Literacy was seen primarily as a means to spiritual enlightenment through study of the Bible but it was also regarded as conferring moral and social virtues.[471] A navvy gave testimony to the benefits of being taught to read in Lewes Gaol:

42. Petworth House of Correction, 1860.

There they taught me to spin mops, and it was there that I got hold of most of my scholarship. I learned to read from the turnkey — a very nice man. He come and stand by my cell door and helped me to a word whenever I asked him, and a church parson used to preach to us every morning of the week — and very good it was! It did me a deal of good going to prison, that time. [472]

The navvy, however, did remark, 'we were kept rather short of victuals'.

In January 1842 the schoolmaster to Petworth House of Correction resigned and Langshaw suggested he should combine the two posts in one. He doubtless had an interest in combining the two salaries to supplement the £127 a year he had as rector of Bepton. There were only one hundred and sixty-six souls in Bepton parish and he had time to spare. He was successful and was awarded £150 as chaplain and £50 as schoolmaster.[473] He might have been glad of the money as he had a rapidly growing family.

Langshaw did not exemplify Malthus's creed of 'prudential marriage'. He married at twenty-five, and was to have three wives and eighteen children. When he came as chaplain to Petworth House of Correction, in 1836, he had been married to Mary Anne Maria Reynolds for four years and they had two of the eighteen children that Langshaw was eventually to father. By the time Langshaw married Frances in 1850 there were eight children and one baby that had died as a 'blue baby' of cyanosis. Mary Anne, aged thirty-three, died in childbirth in August 1848. The next year Langshaw resigned as chaplain to the House of Correction to become, for the next forty years, rector of West Grinstead, a living in the hands of George Wyndham.

Frances thus became the step-mother of eight children ranging in age from seventeen-year-old Susanna to William, who was four. As well as the children, there were in the household Mary Matthews the governess, Eliza Downer the cook, Martha Burmingham the parlour maid, Mary Reen the housemaid and Samuel Stiles, an indoor servant.[474] Frances had experience of step-mothers for she had one herself. She and Thomas had no children and perhaps Frances regretted this. Thomas was certainly fertile and she might have wished for children of her own, or was perhaps expected to fill the gaps left by the children who were to die.

Seven years after her marriage, on 7th April 1857, she 'cut her own throat when in an unsound state of mind'.[475] It was to be the end of September before the coroner at Petworth issued her death certificate, suggesting there may have been trouble over this. There was no mention of her suicide in the local newspapers. The *Sussex Agricultural Express* carried only a formal notice of her death: 'On the 7th inst at West Grinstead Rectory, Sussex, Frances, beloved wife of the Rev. T. W. Langshaw'. She was buried on April 14th.[476] Local newspapers were usually quick to report unexpected deaths, accidents or suicides; perhaps enough pressure was applied to persuade editors to hush up any details.

There were three other deaths at West Grinstead Rectory before Frances's and another six months later. Mary Ann Georgiana, aged seventeen, died in May 1852 of phthisis — in nineteenth-century terms consumption, or pulmonary tuberculosis (TB); Harriet Catherine, aged eleven, died of an 'effusion of the brain' at Petworth Rectory in August 1852, possibly as the result of an accident or fall; Caroline Sockett is given as the person present at the death;[477] Jane Eliza, aged nine, died of pulmonary TB and pneumonia in June 1854; William, aged eleven, died eight months after Frances, of pulmonary TB in November 1857 having been ill for six months. Six of Langshaw's children were recorded as dying of pulmonary TB.

TB, then called consumption, was the scourge of the nineteenth century. Every year it killed more people in Britain than smallpox, scarlet fever, measles, whooping cough and typhus fever put together.[478] It was not confined to overcrowded urban areas, but flourished equally well in primitive country cottages and gracious Georgian rectories. Deaths from TB at West Grinstead rectory began after Frances came in 1850. This may have been coincidence; perhaps in 1850 the rectory changed its milk supplier and the children contracted bovine TB from the dairy herd. Pulmonary TB, however, is more likely to be contracted by contact with droplet infection in coughs and sneezes, which quickly spread throughout a family. One of the servants, or the governess, could have been the original carrier or perhaps Frances was a carrier herself; but neither her father nor siblings appear to have had TB. One potent source of infection was the House of Correction. Tuberculosis was widespread in prisons and the surgeon of the Petworth house reported both scrofula —TB of the lymph glands — and pulmonary TB amongst the prisoners and the staff. William Bowlding, a porter and watchman, was one who retired in January 1843 with pulmonary consumption.[479] Langshaw, who had quarters at the house, may have carried the infection home.

Frances may have felt responsible for the children that died under her care. Perhaps she was afraid she had caught TB from the children and did not mean to wait for death as they had to do. It may be that she was unhappy for other reasons and the atmosphere at the rectory of sickness and death was more than she could bear and her old mental illness re-asserted itself. Her death would have been a bitter blow to her father and sister, and neither of them outlived her long. She was buried in West Grinstead churchyard. On the Langshaw family monument, erected after Langshaw's death in 1889, she is given as the beloved wife of Rev. T. W. Langshaw and the 'daughter of the late Thomas Sockett, Rector of Petworth'; her husband and her father conferring her status in life.[480]

Sockett disappears from view for the rest of 1857. In the summer George and Ruth left their ten children and came to England to see him and Caroline, twenty-four years after George and his father had parted at Gravesend. It would have been an emotional meeting with Frances's death fresh in their minds. Ruth and George also visited the Williamsons at 53 Park Street, London, old friends of the Griffin and Leslie families, especially Thomas Williamson, with whom Ruth's step-father had kept up a lengthy correspondence.* Thomas remembered Ruth as a little girl, and was careful to note that her husband, George, even after twenty four years, was a military man.[481] Their departure meant another sad parting, for Sockett was eighty and they were not likely to meet again in this world. He was said by Wyndham to be 'out of spirits' in September,[482] and was not present at his tithe dinner at the Swan Inn in December, when his place was taken by his curate.

Langshaw did not appear crushed by Frances's death. Two months later he officiated at the annual feast day of the West Grinstead Burrell Arms Friendly Society. The festivities included a service in the parish church, where Langshaw greeted members with criticism of the club for holding its meeting in a public house, and went on to give an 'extempore' sermon from 1 Peter, 4 verses 2 and 3: 'For the time past of our life may suffice us to have wrought the will of the Gentiles when we walked in lasciviousness, lusts, excess of wine, revellings, banquetings and abominable idolatries'.[483] A sermon which he may easily have given 'extempore', having probably given it on many occasions to his flock in the House of Correction. The Friendly Society may have felt they did not need to be so harangued on their one feast day. Langshaw's influence may have been one cause of Frances's religious melancholia.

His reputation appears to have suffered in local opinion and gossip: 'I think poor Langshaw has been somewhat misrepresented to you', Sockett wrote to George Wyndham in January 1858, claiming that Langshaw was behaving well towards Caroline in that he was

---

* The two men had been steel engravers and may have worked for the same employer.

relinquishing his prospective share 'in right of his wife' in Sockett's life insurance of £3,000. 'I consider this to be very liberal conduct and have been the more anxious that <u>you</u> should know it'.* This may have been liberal conduct on Langshaw's part but he was to leave an estate eventually valued at over £21,000 compared to that of under £800 left by Caroline.†

One year after Frances's death Langshaw married Mary Ecclesia Lyne Glubb, the daughter of the rector of nearby Shermanbury. Thomas and Mary had nine children. Half of Langshaw's eighteen children, and his three wives, died before him; Mary Ecclesia died just after Christmas in December 1876 of pulmonary TB, which she was said to have had for two years.[484] Thomas Langshaw died in March 1889, aged eighty two, of 'natural decay and congestion of the lungs'.[485] Perhaps he did not drink milk. Perhaps he did but acquired immunity from bovine TB before coming into contact with human bacillus. Perhaps he had a genetically acquired 'familial resistance'; if so he did not pass it on to all of his offspring.[486]

When Langshaw died the fight against tuberculosis had scarcely begun, but by the end of the century alternatives to Malthus's grim checks to over-population were becoming possible; family size and infant death rates, especially among the middle classes, began slowly to decline.

---

* WSRO, PHA 1113.
† The late Cecil Longhurst, of Partridge Green, near West Grinstead, wrote in 2003, 'My grandmother, Jane Turnell, talked quite a bit about Mrs Langshaw. Grannie was born in 1875 but as her father was Sexton of St George's West Grinstead her parents would have known both Mrs Langshaw and the Rector ... Mrs Langshaw's suicide was still a matter of interest in the parish ... it would seem Mrs Langshaw was very depressed by the deaths of the babies and finally unable to cope with it drowned herself...the impression I got even in the early 1920's was that there was much sympathy for Mrs L but not for her husband'. Letter from Cecil Longhurst to Leigh Lawson, December 2003. It is interesting that Frances's manner of dying was altered in the parish memory over the years. Perhaps drowning was felt to be a less horrific manner of suicide, and a tributary of the River Adur runs through the village.

'His Study From When He Was Twelve Years'

Sockett may not have seen his grandchildren but he had taken pleasure in George and Mary Wyndham's children. In 1839 he took 'part of Col W's family' to the Royal Polytechnic Institution, and Fanny and Blanche to the Adelaide Gallery to see the exhibition of devices and scientific models.* In 1840 he took a party of thirteen young ladies to the Tower of London, where they paid £1.3s. to see the jewel room and more for books, buns for the menagerie, and a 'plate of armour' — possibly a cut-out book — for Miss Blanche.[487]

Sockett was apparently asked for, or proffered, advice on the children; 'I thank you very much for good advice respecting her' wrote Mary Wyndham of one of her daughters, but in the way of despairing mothers of indolent children, went on to say; 'but I have ever failed in impressing the same upon her mind, or at least persuading her to follow it. In London, however, she is diverted from her usual sedentary pursuits and therefore sleeps better.'[488]

Amongst all his trouble and anguish Sockett's great pleasure and recreation was the Literary and Scientific Institution, formed in 1838, of which he was president. He obviously enjoyed the meetings greatly and became one of their regular speakers. Charles Klanert was vice-president, Messrs Sanders and Death were secretaries, and by 1839 there were forty members. They had a balance in the bank of £17.14s.10d and 150 volumes in circulation from their library. Meetings were held weekly, with a lecture by a member one week and a conversazione the next. In the first year there were lectures on subjects as varied as 'The History of the Ancient Britons' by Klanert; 'Physiology of Digestion' by T. H. Hale (the Petworth surgeon), and 'Electricity' by T. Sockett. The members conversed on the Mole Cricket, the Upas Tree, the Origin and Antiquity of Letters, Trigonometry, and the Steam Engine.[489]

During the winter of 1839/40 Sockett gave six lectures accompanied by illustrations, which called forth 'much applause'. Young Henry Sockett came to help, 'taking as much pains and delight as his respected father to make them prove interesting and instructive'. One imagines Henry greatly enjoyed tinkering about with the apparatus and amazing the people of Petworth. The reporter to the *Sussex Agricultural Express*[490] was impressed with the apparatus, which must have put the

---

* The Polytechnic opened in Regent Street in 1838 as a rival to the Adelaide Gallery, or 'National Gallery of Practical Science blending Instruction with Amusement' in the Lowther Arcade. It contained some 250 machines, devices and scientific models; a precursor of the Science Museum. *The London Encyclopaedia*, ed. Ben Weinreb and Christopher Hibbert, 6.

lecturer to great expense, 'he having bought several of the instruments for the sole purpose of making his subject clear to his hearers'. The reporter was especially taken with the electric telegraph and sceptical of its possibility, until by demonstration Sockett showed with what rapidity an electric current might flow between Petworth and South Australia by means of a connecting earthed wire; with the implication that by intermittently switching this current off and on, one could send coded messages and even designate letters. Sockett's skill as a tutor came forth here and the expensive instruments, obviously dear to his heart, were another drain on his finances. At another time, science, rather than the classics and the church, may have been his career; although he might not then have had the pleasure of his great love of Horace.

The use and development of galvanism/electricity was Sockett's interest and forte, as it had been in the days in Weston Underwood, and presumably before that with his father, who was said to have made the electrical machine that introduced young Tom to Hayley and Sussex. Sockett admitted he had lost touch with many of the rapid developments in the subject in the interim, but had enjoyed picking up the subject again, reading the work of Humphrey Davy and his assistant, Michael Faraday. Sockett's contemporary Faraday (1791–1867) published his 'Experimental Researches in Electricity' in *Philosophical Transactions of 1831–1838*, where Sockett may well have encountered them, before they were published in book form between 1839 and 1855.

Sockett may have been interested in Faraday not only for his work but for his family background. He was the son of a blacksmith at Newington Butts, south of the river near the Elephant and Castle, a district of London. Apprenticed as a bookbinder his spare time was devoted to science; he too had built an electrical machine as a young lad, and went to chemical lectures at the Royal Institution, where Davy took him on as an assistant in 1813. Sockett gave his Petworth audience outlines of the development of the magneto-electric machine and the galvanometer; showed them examples of soft iron, rendered magnetic by surrounding it with a coil and passing a strong electric current round it — the iron magnet could then lift a weight of several pounds 'calling forth loud approbation from the audience', 'a box made by a turning lathe powered by Galvanism', Ritchie's rotary magnet from which shocks were given, and more.[*] [491]

---

[*] On 22nd Jan 1842 the *Sussex Agricultural Express* reported that Sockett's electrical machine had been again used for medical purposes when he tried to resuscitate, without success, two eleven-year old boys, Robert Austin and William Garland, who had drowned whilst sliding on the frozen lake in Petworth Park in January 1842. They had been told not to venture to the area of the lake around the statue of the dog, for the ice was thin there, having been cut for the ice-house; but, in the way of young boys, did so.

Sockett was enthusiastic about the railways. As he spoke, the line between London and Brighton was being built, to be followed by a network of railways over Sussex. In 1839 he took the recently completed railway from London Bridge down to Deptford[492] to see the *Waterloo*, the ship that took Irish emigrants from George Wyndham's estates to Canada.

In July 1840 at a dinner at the Half Moon, Sockett was presented with a book as thank you for his 'kind exertions during the late season in affording them amusement and instruction'. After toasts to the Queen; her new husband Prince Albert; the greatest warrior of the age — the Duke of Wellington; Colonel and Mrs Wyndham; and prosperity to the Literary and Scientific Institution, Sockett rose to speak:

> ...when however the Institution was formed, being conversant with the ordinary experiments, and being possessed of an excellent apparatus he was induced to offer a lecture, and when he began that one he found he must give another, and so on till he had concluded the sixth, and still he had left many subjects untouched. But he hoped, if it pleased God to grant him life and health, to bring before them winter after winter many more phenomena of this beautiful science.[493]

At the conclusion of his lecture in May 1840 he had

> laid before his hearers the motives for pious adoration to Him by 'whom all things are so fearfully and wonderfully made' reminding them 'that if the Creator pleased, he could by taking away one, the smallest link in the great machine, destroy the whole, and return this beautiful world to its original chaos.' [494]

This image of the world as 'the great machine' was very much an eighteenth-century idea of the universe. God was the marvellous clock-maker, far from an evangelical personal saviour, but a marvellous creator of a beautifully planned, rational world and one that Sockett could dimly appreciate. Nevertheless, the institution was not above ending their presentation to Sockett in a very human fashion with plenty of toasts to be drunk, interspersed with songs, so that 'the day passed off with much harmony'.

Prince Albert would have been pleased with this institution; Queen Victoria less so. Lord Melbourne was to say at the beginning of 1841:

> The Prince is bored with the sameness of his chess every evening. He would like to bring literary and scientific people about the

Court, vary the society, and infuse a more useful tendency into it. The Queen, however, has no fancy to encourage such people. This arises from a feeling on her part that her education has not fitted her to take part in such conversation; she would not like conversation to be going on in which she could not take her fair share.[495]

This dedicated little group in Petworth was an example of that urge to self-improvement and earnest education that was one important characteristic, much encouraged by Prince Albert, of the Victorian age just beginning.

By 13th March 1858, the year before Sockett died, the Scientific and Literary Institution had metamorphosed into the Mutual Improvement Society and had the unprecedented experience of a woman lecturer. Mrs Balfour came to speak on 'The Female Sovereigns of Europe'. The *Sussex Agricultural Express* reported it as a great treat and it was certainly hoped that she would come again.[496] This was most probably Clara Lucas Balfour, a staunch advocate of women's emancipation and supporter of the temperance movement. In the second half of the nineteenth century there would be an increasing number of women, like Clara, who would feel able and willing to stand up in public and speak on subjects dear to their hearts.[497]

In the year that Sockett died, Darwin published *On The Origin of Species by means of Natural Selection*, a work that had already been preceded by other academic theses pointing towards evolutionary theories. These would probably have interested but not greatly troubled Sockett, the man with the interest in new scientific ideas; for one could always move the marvellous creator back in incalculable time and acknowledge even more intricate and unfathomable details of his works.

I Go Hence and Be No More Seen, 1859

On the 17th inst. at the Rectory, Petworth, the Rev. Thomas Sockett, in his 82nd year. The Rev gentleman had held the Rectory nearly 43 years, having been inducted April, 1816.

PETWORTH

THE LATE REV. THOMAS SOCKETT — The funeral of this gentleman took place on Tuesday. As a last testimony of respect nearly the whole of the tradesmen closed their shops, and many of the gentry and farmers of the neighbourhood attended the mournful ceremony of interment. Among those in attendance were the Revs. C. Klanert, R. Ridsdale, T. W. Langshaw, Latham, W. Sinclair, T. Brown, New, Oswell, Witherby, J. F. Cole, Randall, L. Clarke, Hunter, Colonel Wyndham, W. T. Mitford, Esq., Captain Wyndham, M. P., Percy Wyndham, Esq., J. M. Brydone, Esq., H. Brydone, Esq., R. Turner, Esq., J.H. Robinson, Esq., R. Blagden, Esq., H. Upton, Esq., A. Daintry, Esq., Captain Montgomerie, &c, &c. On entering the church the coffin was placed immediately in front of the reading desk, and the pall taken off. A dirge was played on the organ during the entrance of the procession. The Rev. Mr Daltry read the Psalm and Lesson. On leaving the church the organ again played, and on reaching the place of interment, the "Old Barton's", the pall was again removed before that portion of the service used at the grave. In this part the Rev. W. W. Godden officiated. The coffin was made of elm, waxed polished, the lid being in the shape of a cross, roof shaped, with a trefoil on each side of the cross piece and on the head and foot. The inscription was in gold and colours (the missal style); at each side of the head of the cross was —

"Thomas Sockett
Fell asleep
March 17th, 1859."

Lengthways of the foot of the cross, on one side, was —

"Thy loving kindness hath followed me all the days of my life,"

a text repeated by the deceased not long before his death, and on the other —

"Lord say unto my soul, I am thy salvation:"

the words last spoken by him, before his soul took its flight to the unseen world. The coffin was placed on a bier, with the inscription on either side —

"Blessed are the dead which die in the Lord:"

also in the same style of printing. The whole of the arrangements was entrusted to Mr. B. Dawes, of the firm of Dawes and Hammond, and were most efficiently carried out. The church was thronged during the service, a great many ladies being present. In the churchyard and burial ground were also a great number of persons, but the whole was conducted with the greatest decorum and respect. Mr. Superintendent Kemmish, with a body of police, was in attendance to keep the passage clear for the melancholy *cortege ... Requiescat in pace!*[498]

His death certificate states that Thomas Sockett died of old age and paralysis. The Petworth surgeon, Roger Turner, was present at the death.[499]

Sockett's funeral service was led by his curate, William Godden, accompanied by a cluster of local clergy. One clerical outsider was Henry Lloyd Oswell. He had been born in Shropshire in 1813 and was now rector of Leighton, Shropshire. He provides a tentative link between the west country, London, and Sussex Socketts. He had married at Petworth, in December 1850, Catherine, the daughter of Charles Murray,* George Wyndham's steward, and Caroline Sockett was godmother to their daughter, Emily Dorothy.[500]

Caroline was among the ladies present at her father's funeral, but Sarah, Sockett's wife, was not. She was an old lady but lived on another thirteen years to die in 1872, aged ninety-four, at Sutton Rectory, her son Henry's home. Two of the Wyndham brothers, George and Charles, came to the funeral with their sons, but Sir Henry Wyndham KCB did not.

---

* Ten of the Murray family signed as witnesses.

Later the same year George lost his plain Wyndham to become the Right Honourable the Lord Leconfield, after his Yorkshire estates, a title granted by Queen Victoria. After the debacle of the Crimean War in the mid-1850s, affairs were slowly to change in the army. By the 1870s it would no longer be possible to buy commissions, George, Henry and Charles Wyndham, and George Sockett, would then have had to earn their promotions by merit. Superintendent Kemmish and his body of police were a recent addition to the Petworth scene and another sign of changing times. The Police in Counties and Boroughs Act of 1856 tightened up the legislation calling for the establishment of a paid police force, many of whom were ex-army men, in every county and borough — another adversary for Petworth poachers.*

The dreaded day had come, and the Sockett home at Petworth Rectory was broken up. Sarah went to Sutton, and Caroline to lodgings at the home of schoolmistresses Harriet and Elizabeth Holt in North Street.[501] They were perhaps friends of Caroline if she had helped in the school. Much of the rectory household and garden furniture was sold at auction [see page 109].

Henry, Sockett's son, and Henry Gray, Brydone's son, were executors of Sockett's will, in which he left under £3,000.[502] His potential estate was diminished the year before his death by a trust fund of £2,000, set up jointly by himself and Caroline, on behalf of George and Ruth in Canada for their joint lives or the life of the survivor. Sockett and Caroline were anxious about the Canadian family right up until the day they died — and beyond. In his will Sockett left another £500 to be invested as an annuity for George and Ruth or the life of the survivor. Sarah, Sockett's second wife, had nothing but she may have benefited from a life insurance taken out by her husband.

Caroline also inherited nothing beyond all the printed books that had belonged to her mother, but she presumably benefited from the life insurance Sockett had taken out for his daughters' benefit, which now included Frances's share.[503] Caroline died, aged forty-eight, only three years after her father. Her death certificate states the cause of death as 'atony', a rather vague term for weakness.

She left under £800, out of which she gave £200 to Ruth, her sister-in-law; £20 to Mary Cooper, the daughter of Sockett's bailiff; and £20 for the benefit of Emily Dorothy Oswell.[504] The remainder went to Henry, her brother, who also inherited the remainder of his father's

* John Kemmish, b. c1827 at Beaulieu, Hants; lived with his family in a house in the prison yard, Petworth.

estate. Presumably some of this was intended for the benefit of his mother, Sarah.

George did not live long to benefit from the trust fund set up by Caroline and Sockett; he died in November 1860, twenty months after his father. He was forty-nine. Nevertheless, Ruth and their children were beneficiaries for another forty years. Ruth proved a good steward of the money. The boys were sent to school, the girls had a governess, and when the eldest daughter, Fanny Ruth, was married in 1864 there was a celebration of some style on the farm at Eramosa.[505] When Ruth eventually died in 1906, she had a considerable amount of land, houses, goods and money to leave to her children and grandchildren.[506] In his will Sockett had left George an oil painting representing himself and Colonel Charles in his youth, and there were other likenesses and photographs which made their way to Canada over the years. Ruth eventually shared out among her children precious likenesses of George, Fanny and Mrs Sockett, pictures of Petworth and West Grinstead rectories, and more. These, sadly, seem to have been lost over the intervening century.

Sockett left his Petworth and Duncton livings in reasonably good order. The religious census of 1851, taken on 30th March at the same time as the population census, caused heart-burning nationally for, on average, it revealed that less than half of the population had been to church or chapel that day.[507] The population of Petworth numbered 3,439 and out of these 2,084 had been to church or chapel, 1,672 to St Mary's, 300 to the Congregational Chapel, and 112 to the Calvinist Providence Chapel. This was better than the national average, but these figures may well include adults and Sunday scholars who went twice to service. Little Duncton was said to have had between sixty and seventy in the congregation in the morning and 100 to 120 in the afternoon; some of these may have attended both services, but the actual numbers are high for the little church.

North Scarle still maintained its large Wesleyan Methodist presence. The chapel recorded 300 adults and Sunday scholars in its congregations on census Sunday. All Saints' had a congregation of 175 adults and Sunday scholars. It might seem invidious that the Wesleyan Chapel had 120 free sittings but also 100 private sittings, but by the 1850s the Wesleyans were becoming very respectable chapel folk. Wesley would have been dismayed about the private sittings, but otherwise pleased if he had come back to North Scarle in 1859.

When in 1850 Ellis had congratulated and thanked Sockett and Klanert for not letting any 'new fangled forms' to be introduced into the parish and maintaining the even tenor of its simple form of worship',[508] he was referring in part, to the national hysteria at the time over the reinstatement of the Roman Catholic hierarchy in England, but even more immediately to the anguish with which the erstwhile evangelical Wilberforces and Manning, on Petworth's southern doorsteps at Lavington and Graffham, were figuratively crossing the road from west to east into the Roman Catholic church at Burton Park. Coupled with the fear of Roman Catholicism was the more immediate dislike and distrust of new-fangled High Church ritual: the introduction of confessions, perhaps incense, candles, sung responses, and priestly attire. All of these practices were causing notorious trauma and trouble in towns such as Brighton. At the same time evangelical fervour could be as fervently disliked. There was a striking difference between an evangelical conception of district visiting as an opportunity to admonish, correct, and wrestle with a soul for God, to that of Sockett's concern that his parishioners should have a bellyful at home, or failing that overseas.

He had had little grounds for personal anguish in the great debates of the early-nineteenth century over the supremacy of secular versus spiritual authority. When he had the advowsons of Petworth and Duncton in 1815 and 1816, they were gifts from the Earl of Egremont, who had secular authority over the livings in his hand. We know of no conflict between the Earl and his clergy over doctrinal or other practices and none between George Wyndham and Sockett, but after 1859 the living of Petworth went to Charles Holland, an avowed evangelical and presumably George Wyndham's choice, or the influence of his evangelical wife, Mary.

Sockett maintained a course between the Scylla and Charybdis of the contemporary High and Low Church. He did, for example, accept the new emphasis on confirmation and presumably with it the frequent service of Holy Communion, but had to fend off contemporary criticism of his three livings, livings that were rapidly separated after his death. Charles Holland came from Shipley to Petworth; Henry Inman was appointed to North Scarle in August 1859, where an Anglican rectory was built on part of the glebe land; the Duncton living went to the curate, John New.

Sockett seems always to have had a soft spot for 'my little parish of Duncton', in which he had endeavoured to benefit 'the spiritual and temporal concerns' in every way.[509] Writing to George Wyndham one Sunday afternoon in February 1855 — it not being prudent to venture to church — he spoke with approval of George's destruction of the Duncton paper mill. The village was now once again a purely agricultural community, not having more labourers than was fairly required. His reaction is an interesting one in its dislike of an industrial element in a rural area. There may have been economic considerations. The paper makers were a possible source of unwanted population growth with settlement rights in the parish, and also increasingly potential poor law recipients as a displaced labour force suffering from the introduction of mechanized production and the use of wood pulp rather than rags in the second half of the nineteenth century. Another source of distrust may have been that, out of the handful of workers at the paper mill cited in the 1841 census of Duncton, there were several young women. These relatively independent women posited an alternative to the accepted occupations of rural women and were perhaps a threat to traditional roles and values.

There was to be a new Duncton Church on a new site by 1876, and a new rectory, the 'decent parsonage' that Sockett, in his letter, had suggested for Duncton 'for the new Rector must be in residence'. One of the last marriages at which Sockett officiated was the marriage of John New to Henrietta Jane Brydone, James and Elizabeth's daughter, on 27th July 1854. Family history has it that a prized ancient 'Flodden' sword had descended through the family to William Brydone, and when he was at sea it hung over Henrietta Jane's bed at Duncton Rectory (it is to be hoped on a sturdy piece of string).[510]

43. Revd Henry Sockett.

Henry Sockett married Evelyn Maria Campbell Godden at Sutton in September 1889. He was seventy-one; she was twenty-nine. They had no children and after Henry's death, in 1900, his wife married the curate, Henry Louis Newman; one feels there is a Trollopian novel hiding here. The immediate Sockett line died out in Sussex, but as Sockett himself was to say in 1853, on hearing of the birth of his fifth Canadian grandson 'the name therefore, does not seem likely to go out in that part of the world'.[511] George and Ruth in Canada had certainly gone forth and multiplied, and it is there that many later histories of the Socketts are to be found.

THE SOCKETT FAMILY AT ERAMOSA
BY GARY WILSON

One can only imagine the poignancy of the moment, when George said goodbye to his father as he and Ruth prepared to return across the Atlantic, after their visit back to England in the summer of 1857. It would have been much different than in 1833 when George first set sail for Upper Canada filled with the dreams, hopes and aspirations of a young man about to establish himself in the new world. This time he knew with certainty that he would never see his father again, for Thomas was in declining health and indeed had but a year and a half to live. George himself was not in much better shape, and although he would father two more children, he would only survive his father by fourteen months. His own health had been precarious as far back as 1835 when the ownership of his Eramosa farm had been put in the name of his uncle, James Marr Brydone, and in the following year into Thomas Sockett's name. It was not transferred back to George until 1858.

How much of this was due to a true physical ailment or induced by his alcoholism we can only speculate. Letters written by Ruth's stepfather, J. T. Leslie, indicate that George was near death in 1842 and 1843, but by 1847 Leslie's letters appear to indicate that George had conquered his demons with the bottle and perhaps he was able to enjoy a decade of reasonable health before it began to fail again for the final time.[512] On 6 November 1860 George passed away aged only forty-nine. We have no knowledge of the exact cause of death, but when his sister, Caroline, died eighteen months later aged only forty-eight, her death registration gave the cause as atony (debility or organ weakness).[513] There has been a lengthy history of Bright's disease in every subsequent Sockett generation right up to the present day, and perhaps this affliction was already genetically well rooted in the family at this time.

Letters preserved in the Mary Leslie fonds at the Archives of Ontario enable us to share in the family's grief over George's death. Mary Leslie, known to the family as Polly (1842–1920) achieved a small measure of note as an early Canadian writer and was a younger half-sister of Ruth. Her brother John Leslie, a dentist, was living in Mount Forest with their sister, Elizabeth.

John wrote home on hearing of George's death:

Canadian Sockett Family Tree

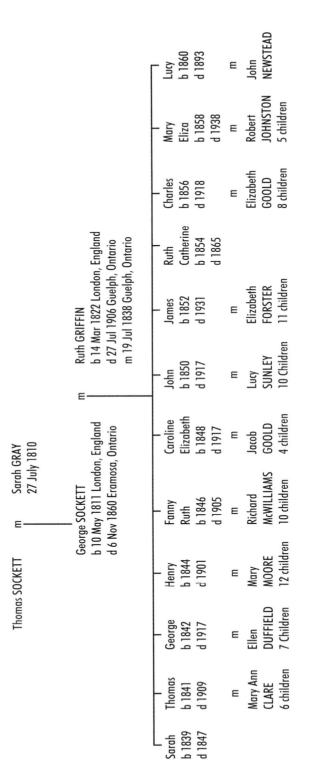

Thomas SOCKETT   m   Sarah GRAY
27 July 1810

George SOCKETT
b 10 May 1811 London, England
d 6 Nov 1860 Eramosa, Ontario

m

Ruth GRIFFIN
b 14 Mar 1822 London, England
d 27 Jul 1906 Guelph, Ontario
m 19 Jul 1838 Guelph, Ontario

Sarah b 1839 d 1847	Thomas b 1841 d 1909	George b 1842 d 1917	Henry b 1844 d 1901	Fanny Ruth b 1846 d 1905	Caroline Elizabeth b 1848 d 1917	John b 1850 d 1917	James b 1852 d 1931	Ruth Catherine b 1854 d 1865	Charles b 1856 d 1918	Mary Eliza b 1858 d 1938	Lucy b 1860 d 1893
m	m	m	m	m	m	m	m		m	m	m
Mary Ann CLARE 6 children		Ellen DUFFIELD 7 Children	Mary MOORE 12 children	Richard McWILLIAMS 10 children	Jacob GOOLD 4 children	Lucy SUNLEY 10 Children	Elizabeth FORSTER 11 children		Elizabeth GOOLD 8 children	Robert JOHNSTON 5 children	John NEWSTEAD

Dear Mother   Mt Forest, Nov. 8 1860

I am truly sorry to hear of your having cause to lament the loss of
a son — but as he has left this world of trouble disappointment
and sorrow — let us hope that he is better off where he has gone
— and that we shall yet have the felicity of meeting him again
face to face — where bodily pain, sickness and grief are unknown
— And if he has departed this life in peace with his maker —
we ought to rejoice rather than grieve — as the last year of his
life must have been a living death — his bodily feelings — (but
especially the state of his mind at times) must I think have been
terrible in the extreme. I hope you have not worn yourself out
watching — or injured your own health as I am afraid you have
— as Lizzie mentioned your looking rather unwell when she was
at home — And I am sure you could not make free with yourself
in the nursing him — I suppose that Ruth is staying with you
at present — we should be glad to see her here — if she can
possibly come — the roads are all but impassable for the last
five miles — Lizzie is now writing to her ... I suppose that I shall
see you at Christmas — hoping that this may find you in good
health — give my love to Ruth — Fanny — Cal and the boys
— and now good bye — And believe me ever your affectionate
son, J. T. H. Leslie.

Dear Father,

We was so very sorry to hear of Poor Sockett's death, which we
did by the arrival of Polly's note this afternoon — I suppose
that you are all very much grieved — and should think that Ruth
and the children would be terribly cut up — And as it would be
best for her to leave home for a while — tell her that she will be
welcome here — And if she can get here in the present state of
the roads — that we should be glad to see her And will make her
as comfortable as possible — it would be something new and in
all likelyhood would divert her mind from her present feelings
and sorrows — As Polly gave us to understand that he will have
been buried today — I thought it would be useless my coming as
in all probability it would be all over before I could start — even
if I started at once and traveled all night — so I determined on
not coming — from Polly's note it would seem his death was a
painless one, which is so far good — the next time you write, tell
us where you have laid him ...[514]

Although the Socketts belonged to the Church of England, George was buried in the Stone Church Methodist Cemetery, located on lot 12, concession 3, just across the road from the homestead. It was where their eldest daughter, Sarah, had been buried in 1847. In the early years of the settlement when the roads were poor, and the church of one's faith could be many miles away, it was quite common for the settlers to worship in the nearest church, no matter the denomination.

On 16 October 1860 George made out his last will and testament naming his wife, Ruth, and her stepfather, John Thomas Leslie, as the executors of his estate. In 1848 he had received a crown grant of 300 acres in Normanby Township from the government, for services in the army during the winter of 1833–34. George left these 300 acres to his three eldest sons. Upon attaining the age of twenty-one, Thomas was to receive lot 61, George lot 62, and Henry lot 63, all in the third concession. These lands were about five miles northwest of Mount Forest where the hamlet of Gleneden was about to spring up. The west half of lot 12, concession 4, Eramosa, was to be split between the next two sons when they reached the age of twenty-one, with John getting the westerly 50 acres and James the easterly 50 acres. When they took possession of their lots, Ruth was to furnish each of the boys with one yoke of oxen, one cow, one logging chain, and one axe. Charles, the youngest son, was to receive the 100 acre homestead lot — namely the west half of lot 13, concession 4, Eramosa —but not until after the death of his mother. Charles would then be required to share with all his brothers and sisters the value of the farming stock and farm implements from the homestead. If any of the boys left the farm before the age of twenty-one, they would be required to pay their mother £25 currency 'for each year that they shall be absent themselves.' The daughters were each to receive £50 currency and a cow upon attaining the age of twenty-one or when they got married. [515]

To be left widowed with eleven children in the middle of the nineteenth century would have meant significant hardship for most women. Ruth, however, had dealt with adversity all her life, and with her strength of character formed by her experiences, together with the generous financial assistance given them by George's father, she was able to pull through. She had been born in the parish of St Leonard's, Shoreditch, in the East End of London on 14 March 1822 to Elizabeth and Thomas Griffin. Her father must have died when Ruth was very young for her mother re-married, at least as early as 1831, John Thomas Leslie (1794–1871). He was a steel engraver by trade in London but retired and emigrated to Guelph Township in 1837, settling on lot 5, concession 7, four miles east of Guelph.

---

* It is possible Elizabeth and Thomas were cousins; Elizabeth was born 21 July 1800 in the parish of Avebury, Wiltshire to John and Mary Griffin.

Ruth and George were married 19 July 1838 at St George's Anglican church in Guelph. Ruth was barely sixteen years of age and was to be the mother of three children by the time she was twenty. She also had the challenge of coping with a husband prone to bouts of depression and drinking. In a letter, dated November 1843, from Ruth's stepfather to Thomas Williamson, an old family friend in London, we are given a picture of her early married life:

> Your friend Ruth has three children — two boys and 1 girl & has a fourth in its passage — she is very well & quite fitted for the country having a great taste for pigs, poultry, horses and cattle of all kinds —is fond of hauling brats & all over our roads without being particular whether it is pitch dark or no & occasionally gets an upset which is looked for as a matter in course — her Husband who I think I told you was a Drunkard & a Gentleman was nearly dying this time Twelvemonths but has from necessity become sober for his state of health & he has many attractive qualities.[516]

Twelve children arrived over a span of twenty-one years, the last being only eight months old when George died. Two children did not survive childhood; Sarah died in 1847 aged seven; and Ruth in 1865 aged ten. Fortunately, Ruth seems to have been amply provided for. In 1858 the Reverend Thomas Sockett had set up a trust fund of £2,000 sterling for the benefit of George and Ruth. This was initially administered by George's cousin, Henry Gray Brydone, a Petworth solicitor, and George's brother, the Reverend Henry Sockett. By 1877 they both asked to be relieved of their role as trustees and Ruth and her eldest son, Thomas, were appointed as co-trustees of the fund.[517]

At the time of Ruth's death in 1906 the fund still contained $9,512.27. In addition after the death of Thomas Sockett in March 1859 another trust fund containing £500 was set up by the terms of his will, the money to be invested by the trustees as they saw fit, to provide an annuity of £50 a year to George, or to Ruth if she should survive him. If one calculates an assumed investment return of say 5 per cent this fund would have produced an annual income of £50 for about fourteen years. Furthermore, Ruth inherited another £200 from her sister-in-law, Caroline Sockett who died in 1862. These moneys would have allowed Ruth to employ farm help if needed; the 1861 census shows one hired hand, and with the older boys approaching manhood, aged nineteen, eighteen and sixteen, she must have been able to carry on without the worry of financial distress.

An account of her daughter Fanny Sockett's wedding to Richard McWilliams in October 1864 illustrates how the money from the family at Petworth, and Ruth's competence, had brought much better times — at least financially — at Eramosa. Mary Leslie, Fanny's half-sister, is writing to her sister, Elizabeth Leslie:

Dear Lizzie,

... Poor Fanny Sockett was married on the only fine day last week and that but partially fine. The children enjoyed the affair, and so did mother who looked very bonnie in her new dress and white bibs but I don't think Fanny has made the match for herself, or if she has it has been helped on a great deal by Ruth and Richard, our new nephew, altogether I am inclined to think she was the only person who did not rejoice — Mr Thackeray seemed to think that crying a fortnight after marriage was rather early, what would he say to crying on the wedding day and positively refusing to leave the house as Fanny did? I don't like this new nephew of ours (though I have never seen him) he may be a good hearted fellow enough, but he's awfully coarse and vulgar. If I can believe mother's account, and if she has coloured matters it is unintentionally, for she admires him.

I think the governess they have must be a nice little body, with some fun in her. I saw the wedding cortege pass. It consisted of four vehicles and there was a great fluttering of white and pink and (strange to say) yellow ribbons. The bride wore a white bonnet and veil trimmed (the bonnet) with lilies of the valley instead of orange blossom (and looking pretty so far as I could judge with my short sight) and a blue plaid silk dress, and black cape, and Cal who was bridesmaid was arrayed in white, and had a bonnet adorned I believe with pink and yellow and blue roses ... Mr Palmer performed the service and George gave the bride away. Had I been there I might give you some idea of the splendour of the entertainment in the evening, and how many turkey, geese, ducks and chicken, (not to mention noble rounds of beef, splendid hams and fragrant tongues) partridges, pheasants, prairie hens, and other delicacies, were consumed by the admiring and enchanted guests, but I was not there, therefore you must be contented when I tell you that the entertainment was perfect in its way and has never been surpassed in Eramosa... * [518]

---

* Their mother was Fanny's grandmother. It should perhaps be said that relations between Mary and her half-sister Ruth were not always amiable and this may account for Mary's absence from the wedding.

By the time of the 1881 census, Ruth was living in the city of Guelph with her two youngest daughters, the rest of the children by now having all married. Charles, the youngest son, had done so in 1878 and this was likely the occasion for Ruth to leave the farm and move to the city where she invested heavily in real estate. The 1901 census shows her to be the owner of eleven lots and nine houses, although in her will we are able to identify only nine lots and eight houses, including the homestead. Ruth lived in a double house, 209 Dublin Street, at the south-east corner of Dublin and Green Street. Her daughter, Mary Eliza, and son-in-law, Robert Johnston, lived at number 211. Ruth was eighty-four when she died. She had outlived George by forty-six years and survived longer than five of her twelve children and ten of her seventy-three grandchildren. Although she is remembered in the family as a very domineering, strong-willed woman, her children must have held her in high esteem for she had nine granddaughters named Ruth. There were also seven grandsons named George. Interestingly, although only thirteen out of a possible sixty-three grandchildren received a direct inheritance from their grandmother, all nine granddaughters bearing the name Ruth received a bequest of money.

Ruth made her last will on 29 January 1900, with added codicils in March 1902 and December 1903. The details of her will not only specify the money and properties that were bequeathed to her children and grandchildren but also give a vivid picture of the household at 209 Dublin Street. One can, for example, furnish the parlour, picture details of Ruth's wardrobe, and gather a sense of the links with Sussex that had been maintained over the years by the photographs and pictures of the Petworth rectory family and their English homes, that she left to be distributed to kith and kin after her death.[519] (See appendix.)

When the will went to probate on 7 September 1906 the estate was valued at $21,335.25, comprising personal assets worth $15,385.25 and real estate assets of $5,950.00. This did not include the homestead on the west half of lot 13, concession 4, Eramosa Township, which by the terms of George's will of 1860 was to go to Charles at the time of his mother's death. As soon as he was free to sell the property, he promptly sold the farm on 3 November 1906 to his neighbour James Oakes, who owned the adjoining farm to the north.

Allowing for the $11,500 and the real estate already spoken for by the terms of Ruth's will and the payment of funeral fees, legal fees, court fees, and other sundry expenses totalling $442.45, there remained a residue of $3,442.80 to be divided among the nine living children. Although Henry and Fanny Ruth had recently died, their spouses, Mary Louisa Sockett and Richard McWilliams, were entitled to their shares of $382.53.

There was also the trust fund set up by Thomas Sockett in 1858 and now containing $9,512.27 to be dispersed. This was to be divided into ten equal shares as John Newstead, widower of Lucy who had died in 1893, was entitled to her share, worth $951.23. The final tally on the estate can be summarized as follows:

Personal assets	$15,385.25
Real estate	$5,950.00
Trust fund	$9,512.27
	$30,847.52
Less	
Expenses	$442.45
Gift to Stone Church	$200.00
Total left	$30,205.07

After adding each child's share of the residue, plus the share of the trust fund, to what had been bequeathed to them in Ruth's will, and assuming an equal division by the children of the $200 worth of household goods, the value of assets, both cash and real estate included, each family would receive was;

Thomas Sockett	$3,055.98
George Sockett	$2,605.98
Mary Louisa Sockett widow of Henry	$2,455.98
Richard McWilliams widower of Fanny Ruth	$3,805.98
Caroline Elizabeth Goold	$4,305.98
John Sockett	$2,505.98
James Sockett	$2,605.98
Charles Sockett	$3,005.98
Mary Eliza Johnston	$4,905.98
John Newstead widower of Lucy	$951.23

To put these figures in context: $500 to $600 was a good yearly wage; Houses could be rented for $7 a month and an average city home could be bought for $1,000.

George and Ruth's last grandchild passed away in 1992 at the age of 101. Tom and Sarah Sockett's and George and Ruth's descendants, numbering at least 600, may be found across Canada from Montreal to Vancouver as well as in the United States.

44. George and Ellen Sockett with their family, 1880.

45. Thomas and Mary Ann Sockett, married 19 January 1865.

The Children of George and Ruth
by Gary Wilson

SARAH SOCKETT b 1 Sept 1839, d 1 Apr 1847 | she was buried across the road in the Stone Church Methodist Cemetery | the cause of her early death is unknown

THOMAS SOCKETT b 3 Mar 1841, d 26 May 1909 | as a child he attended the Rockwood Academy, a private school, as did his next two brothers George & Henry, but any thoughts of further education were probably abandoned with the early death of their father | marr 19 Jan 1865 in Guelph to Mary Ann Clare b 24 Nov 1841 in Ireland, daughter of Robert Clare & Hannah Bailey who had settled in Eramosa in 1851 | Thomas & Mary Ann then moved up to Lot 61, Concession 3, Normanby Township. Grey Co. to farm the lot left to him by his father | here were born their 6 children | in 1892 Thomas sold his farm to his brother George and moved to Amabel Township. Bruce Co. farming on Lot 19, Concession 12 until his death from Bright's disease | he was buried in Cochrane Cemetery NW of Mount Forest with his wife's parents but when Mary Ann died of heart disease 13 Jun 1917 she was buried in Zion Cemetery in Amabel just west of Hepworth.

GEORGE SOCKETT b 29 Nov 1842, d 30 Jan 1917 | marr 19 Oct 1865 in Guelph to Ellen Jane Duffield b 29 Oct 1846 in Eramosa, daughter of Henry Duffield & Mary Ann Parkinson | after the birth of their second child in Eramosa in 1868 they moved up to Lot 62, Concession 3, Normanby Township. to farm the lot left to him by his father | here were born 5 more children | acquired his brother's Lot 61 in 1892 | retired into Mount Forest in 1916 where he died of a stroke only 1 week after his brother John & 3 weeks after his sister Caroline | Ellen died also of a stroke 7 July 1917 at her sons farm in Egremont Township | both are buried in Mount Forest Cemetery.

HENRY SOCKETT b 16 May 1844, d 6 Sept 1901 | marr 30 Dec 1869 in Eramosa to Mary Louisa Moore b 25 Nov 1850 in York Township. daughter of William J. Moore & Harriet Sophia Dew | they had 5 sons & 7 daughters | following his marriage he settled on Lot 63, Con 3, Normanby beside his brother George where he farmed and also worked as a blacksmith but he stayed only a short while, selling the farm in 1876 and moving to Clifford where he worked as a butcher for a few years | by 1880 he had relocated to Guelph Township. (4 miles NE of Guelph) where he resumed his blacksmithing trade, also shown as a wagon maker in a directory for 1888/89 | about 1889 he moved to Lot 1, Concession 3, Louth Township. Lincoln Co. just outside of St. Catharines where he worked at the Welland Vale Manufacturing Co. & farmed on his small 12 acre lot | he died at home from stomach cancer & was buried in Victoria Lawn Old Cemetery in St. Catharines | Mary then moved with 7 of her children to Toronto in 1904, living 4 years on Grove Ave only a couple of doors away from her sister in law Caroline Goold, then at 148 Wright Ave where she would spend the rest of her life | one married daughter together with her husband, and 3 unmarried sons would also spend the rest of their lives here and another single daughter lived here until 1952 | Mary died 14 Apr 1932 & was buried in Toronto's Prospect Cemetery in a plot where she had already placed two of her children.

FANNY RUTH SOCKETT b 2 July 1846, d 25 Nov 1905 in Guelph | marr 4 Oct 1864 in Guelph to Richard George McWilliams b 6 June 1838 in Ireland, son of Robert & Margaret Eleanor McWilliams who had immigrated to Eramosa in 1839 | Richard farmed on the W 1/2, Lot 17, Con 1 of Erin Township until retiring into Guelph abt 1904 where they lived on Durham St | their 10 children were all born in Erin Township | Fanny died of cancer as did also Richard on 4 June 1919 in Guelph | both are buried in Everton Cemetery in Eramosa.

CAROLINE ELIZABETH SOCKETT b 9 Oct 1848, d 10 Jan 1917 | marr 26 Mar 1874 in Eramosa to Jacob Leonard Goold b 2 Mar 1852 in Louth Township. son of Richard Alexander Goold & Maria Sophia Clement | Jacob's great grandfather John Goold Sr was a United Empire Loyalist who had fought with the famed Butler's Rangers during the American Revolution | Jacob gave up farming soon after they were married, moving to Guelph where he worked as a carriage maker, a traveling agent & an engine driver | moved to Toronto in 1898 where he worked as a sewing machine machinist | lived on Grove Ave, Grace St. & Cortleigh Blvd | Caroline died in Toronto of rheumatism & was buried in Toronto's Prospect Cemetery in the same plot as her husband's cousin Elizabeth Jane Goold who was the wife of her brother Charles Sockett | Jacob died of stomach cancer 5 Jun 1924 in Toronto & was buried in Prospect Cemetery but in a separate plot from his wife | they raised 3 sons & a daughter.

JOHN SOCKETT b 13 Dec 1850, d 24 Jan 1917 | marr 6 Apr 1875 in Eramosa to Lucy Sunley b 13 Nov 1856 in Eramosa, daughter of Henry Sunley & Eliza Benham | Lucy's grandfather James Benham was one of the 7 Eramosa settlers jailed at Hamilton on 16 Dec 1837 following MacKenzie's ill fated rebellion. Tried for treason at Hamilton in the spring of 1838, he was acquitted of the charge | John purchased Lot 8, Concession 4, Eramosa in 1872 just down the road from where he was born and farmed here the rest of his life | their 10 children were all born here | John died at home of heart disease 2 weeks after the death of his sister Caroline and only 1 week before the death of his brother George | Lucy died in Eramosa 14 Nov 1925 & was buried with her husband in the Stone Church Methodist Cemetery.

JAMES SOCKETT b 24 Oct 1852, d 10 July 1931 | marr 4 Nov 1875 in Guelph to Elizabeth Jane Forster b 23 Oct 1856 in Eramosa, daughter of James Forster & Louisa Morphy | inherited the east half of the west half of his father's Lot 12, Concession 4 where he farmed until abt 1904 when he moved to West Toronto Junction | worked here as a machinist until abt 1910, then moved to

Calgary where he ranched for several years | he died in Calgary & was buried in Burnsland Cemetery although there is no tombstone | abt 1937 Elizabeth moved to Toronto where she lived with her daughter Maria Louisa Harrison & following Louisa's death in 1942, she continued in Toronto for a year or two, then moved to Winnipeg where she spent her last year with her daughter Alice Lawrence | she died there 13 Nov 1945 & was buried in Winnipeg's Elmwood Cemetery | they had 3 sons & 8 daughters all born in Eramosa.

RUTH CATHERINE SOCKETT b 19 Nov 1854, d 19 Jan 1865 | was buried in the family plot across the road in the Stone Church Methodist Cemetery | nothing is known about the cause of her early death but it may have been somewhat unexpected for she died on the very same day that her brother Thomas was married.

CHARLES SOCKETT b 17 Aug 1856, d 8 June 1918 | marr 19 Sept 1878 in Guelph to Elizabeth Jane Goold b 1 Oct 1859 in Wainfleet Township. Welland Co. daughter of James Goold & Sarah Nunnemaker | Elizabeth was a 1st cousin of Jacob Leonard Goold who was married to Charles' sister Caroline | Charles farmed the homestead on Lot 13, Concession 4 as well as working as a sales agent for Massey Harris | upon his mother's death in 1906, he inherited the farm which he sold & moved to Toronto | Here he operated a real estate brokerage & also engaged in house construction | lived on 12 Northcliffe Blvd | their 4 sons & 4 daughters were all born in Eramosa | Elizabeth died 17 Jan 1913 in Toronto & Charles in Toronto from Bright's disease | both were buried in Prospect Cemetery.

MARY ELIZA SOCKETT b 24 June 1858, d 12 July 1938 | marr 14 Mar 1883 in Toronto to Robert E. Johnston b 24 June 1855 in Burford Township. Brant Co. son of Baptist Johnston & Sarah Rebecca McWilliams | Sarah's brother Richard was married to Mary's sister, Fanny Ruth Sockett | Robert worked as an agent or salesman & was known to have been in the Northwest in 1906 with his brother in law Charles Sockett who was a salesman with Massey Harris | moved to Toronto about 1907 and is believed to have died about 1912/13 | Mary died 12 July 1938 in Toronto and was buried with her daughter in the Tyrrell family plot but no burial has been located for Robert | they had 5 children, the first born in Burford Township & the rest in Guelph.

LUCY SOCKETT b 26 Feb 1860, d 18 Jan 1893 | marr 17 Jan 1888 in Eramosa to John Armes Newstead b 4 Aug 1851 in S. Waterloo Township. son of John Newstead & Martha Arms | John moved to Guelph Township. in 1877 where he farmed on the Eramosa Road until 1888 when he moved into Guelph | he founded the Guelph Biscuit Company but soon sold it | served many years on City Council & was Mayor of Guelph 1907–1908 & 1917–1918 | having suffered through 3 operations in the preceding 4 months, Lucy died aged only 32 in Guelph from a cyst on her kidneys & was buried in Guelph's Woodlawn Cemetery | John remarried in 1904 to Caroline Beatrice Smith b 1863 in Guelph & they had a son Jack | when John died 29 Apr 1920 in Guelph he was buried with his first wife Lucy in Woodlawn Cemetery.

Ruth Sockett's Will

THIS IS THE LAST WILL AND TESTAMENT of me RUTH SOCKETT of the City of Guelph, widow of the late George Sockett in his lifetime of the Township of Eramosa, deceased.

1) I hereby revoke any will by me heretofore made.

2) I devise to my executors hereinafter named all the estate real and personal of which I may die seized or possessed in my own right to and upon the trusts herein set out.

3) As to lot number seven hundred and ninety-four in the Canada Company's survey in the City of Guelph, to hold the same to the use of my daughter Mary E. Johnston during the term of her natural life.

4) I bequeath to my said daughter Mary E. Johnston one thousand one hundred and fifty dollars in cash; and also my extension table; my parlour hanging lamp; my parlour horse-hair furniture, comprising sofa, rocking chair and six chairs; window curtains, both red and white, and window blinds; tidies, center table and cloth; parlour carpet; stair carpet; my mangle; also my furnace and cooking stove and my coal that may be left here at my death; my brown shawl and waterproof cloak; my silk dress and gold watch; also two quilts which are marked; the photograph album given to me by her, with photographs therein; a pair of likenesses of her sister Lucy and myself to match; her father's likeness in crayon work; a pair of likenesses of my son George and myself to match; a likeness of Mr. Drinkwater; two pictures of Petworth Rectory and two small pictures.

5) I devise to Ruth S. Johnston, my granddaughter, one hundred and fifty dollars in cash; also the organ and stool which are now in the possession of Ruth Grace Poole; my second-best feather bed and bedstead; swing looking glass, wash stand and jug, two pillows and three quilts; a picture of a woman washing a boy and two small pictures; also the sea-chest of drawers.

[There was no clause 6.]

7) As to that part of lot number six on Kirkland Street described in the conveyance to me from James Hudson dated 18th August, 1877 registered No. 627 having on it a small brick house, and as to that parcel of land on the London Road in the City of Guelph, on which is erected a small brick house, as described in the deed thereof made by W. Cooper to James Hicks, dated 20th of December, 1876, registered No. 184 Guelph West, to hold the same to the use of my daughter Fanny McWilliams during her natural life, and after her death to sell and convey the same and divide the proceeds thereof among her daughters who may survive her.

8) I bequeath to my said daughter Fanny McWilliams the sum of eight hundred

dollars in cash; also my dog-skin coat and cap; picture of the south view of West Grinstead Rectory and head of our Saviour; a picture of a basket of flowers; likenesses of her Aunt Fanny and Sockett in cases; a crayon likeness of myself, and also my writing desk. (I have already given her some land)

9) To Ruth Rodgers, daughter of the said Fanny McWilliams, I bequeath the sum of one hundred and fifty dollars, and also a wreath of feather flowers in a case. To her other two daughters, Maggie and Lizzie, I bequeath fifty dollars each.

10) As to the northerly part of lot number twenty-seven in Palmer's survey, Canada Company's survey lots twenty-three and twenty four, having a frontage on Glasgow Street from the northerly corner of forty nine feet two inches and the depth of the whole lot, having on it a frame cottage and as to those parts of lots twenty-five, twenty-six and twenty-seven in Palmer's survey, Canada Company's survey park lots twenty-three and twenty-four in the City of Guelph, having a frontage on Glasgow Street of sixty-seven feet five inches from a point forty-nine feet two inches from the northeast corner of lot twenty-seven, and a depth of the whole lot, having on them a double plastered house, to hold the same upon trust during the life of my daughter Caroline E. Goold to permit and suffer her and her children during their minority and so long as they remain with her, to reside in any of the houses upon the same which she shall select. And upon trust to rent any of the said houses that may not be required for the purpose of such residence, and the rents to pay over to my said daughter personally upon her own receipt only. And I hereby declare that she shall not have power to charge, assign or anticipate the same during her coverture or otherwise, and that in case she shall anticipate or attempt to charge or assign any such moneys as aforesaid, or should the same be seized or attached for debt, the said trustees may discontinue such payments to her, and pay such sums as they may deem expedient for the benefit of her children during their minority. Should all of her children become of age, marry or leave her, the said rents shall be paid and applied by my said trustees as they deem best for her benefit.

11) I bequeath to my said daughter Caroline E. Goold the sum of one thousand one hundred and fifty dollars in cash; also the picture of the north view of West Grinstead; a picture of a spaniel dog; the motto "Absent but not forgotten"; the likeness of her Aunt Caroline and her grandmother Leslie in cases; my work table and striped shawl; the black dog which is marked for her, and one quilt which is also marked.

12) As to the southwest part of lot six according to survey and plan of park lots fifteen and sixteen in the said City of Guelph, made by T. W. Cooper P. L. S., and more particularly described in the deed thereof to me from Messrs Hall, McIntosh and Innes, bearing date the 15th of June A.D. 1883, and also

that part of the said lot six described in the conveyance thereof from Elizabeth Skinner and Clara V. Skinner to me dated 1st of May A.D. 1883 and registered as number 2976, to hold the same to my granddaughter Ruth Grace Poole in fee simple.

13) I also bequeath to the said Ruth Grace Poole the sum of three hundred dollars and the five shares I hold in the Guelph Skating Rink Company; also my piano, piano stool and cloth; the sewing machine which my daughter Lucy gave me; my best bedroom set and best feather bed; my gold watch chain; the locket which her father gave me; my plush album with all the photographs in it.

14) I direct that the interest taken by any of my daughters under this will shall be held by them free of the debts, obligations and control of any husband during their respective marriages, and without power of anticipation; and that their personal receipts shall discharge my executors. Except as otherwise specified I direct my trustees at the decease of any of my daughters aforesaid to sell the lands in which any daughter so deceased had a life estate hereunder, and the proceeds of such sale invest, and the income arising therefrom apply towards the support, maintenance and education of any child or children of any such daughter so deceased who may not have attained the age of twenty-one years; and after such child or children have attained the age of twenty-one years the proceeds of said sale to be divided amongst them equally share and share alike.

15) As to lot 19 on Surrey Street to hold the same to the use of my son Charles Sockett during the term of his natural life, and at his death to sell the same and the proceeds divide among his children when the youngest of them have attained the age of twenty-one years, the income arising from the investment of the proceeds of such sale to be applied in the meantime towards the maintenance, education and support of such child or children during their minority.

16) I also bequeath to the said Charles Sockett the sum of one thousand dollars; the gilt framed picture of his grandfather teaching a boy; picture of a woman with a basket; picture of Balmoral Castle; my bird organ* and whatnot.

17) To Ruth Sockett, daughter of the said Charles Sockett, I bequeath the sum of one hundred dollars and three quilts which are marked. To his other daughters Sarah and Lucy Newstead, I bequeath fifty dollars each. I also bequeath to the said Sarah Newstead one quilt which is marked.

18) I devise to my son Henry Sockett that part of lot number eleven in division "C" of the Township of Guelph known as the Blacksmith Shop in fee simple.

---

* A bird-organ, or serinette is a miniature, hand cranked barrel organ, which plays small wind pipes. They were supposed to teach caged birds to sing along with them.

46. A French bird-organ, by George C. Leighton.

19) I also bequeath to the said Henry Sockett eight hundred and fifty dollars in cash; picture of Petworth Church and two small pictures; picture of a school scene; a painting of a bridge, and his uncle Henry's likeness in a case.

20) To Ruth Rea Sockett, daughter of my son Henry Sockett, I bequeath one hundred dollars; one feather bed, three quilts which are marked; two pillows and the wooden rocking chair. To his daughter Caroline Haynes I bequeath the sum of one hundred dollars, my walnut leaf table; my sideboard and five dining room chairs. To his daughter Lucy I bequeath fifty dollars and one quilt which is marked.

21) To my son George Sockett I bequeath the sum of one thousand and fifty dollars; the bagatelle board and balls; the hanging lamp in my dining room; my gold spectacles, flesh brush and the horsehair rocking chair which is upstairs; a picture of Petworth House and also of Fanny's house, and Mr. Brydon's group.

22) To my granddaughter Bessie Sockett, daughter of my said son George Sockett, I bequeath the sum of one hundred dollars and one quilt which is marked.

23) To my son James Sockett I bequeath the sum of eleven hundred and fifty dollars; picture of a boy fishing and a girl spinning; washstand and things belonging to it; swing looking glass; carpets and mats upstairs; kitchen table

and chairs; my clock, paper rack and two small pictures.

24) To Ruth Sockett, daughter of my son James Sockett, I bequeath the sum of one hundred dollars, the chest of cherry drawers, and three quilts which are marked.

25) To my son Thomas Sockett I bequeath the sum of fourteen hundred dollars; a picture of the Duke of Wellington and one of Sir John MacDonald; picture of a shipwreck and of my son Charles' family; my dining room carpet and two mats which Ellen made and which I bought of her; also a picture of a child playing with a dog.

26) To Ruth Griffin, daughter of my said son Thomas Sockett, I bequeath one hundred dollars; also three quilts which are marked and my trunk.

27) To my son John Sockett I bequeath the sum of one thousand and fifty dollars; picture of a child playing with a lamb, pictures of the Crystal Palace, Crazy Janet and two small pictures; drawing of a woman with a dog, and my iron safe.

28) To my granddaughter Ruth Georgina, daughter of my son John Sockett, I bequeath the sum of one-hundred dollars and two quilts which are marked.

29) All the said legacies to my grandchildren or heirs not twenty-one years of age at the time of my death are to be deposited in the Post Office Savings Bank by my executors to the credit of my said grandchildren to accumulate until they are respectively of the age of twenty-one years.

30) I bequeath to the Methodist Church on the fourth line of the Township of Eramosa, in the County of Wellington where the remains of the deceased members of my family are interred, the sum of two hundred dollars. The said amount to be deposited in the bank and used for the purpose of fixing up and keeping the graveyard in repair. I direct that my son Charles Sockett be trustee of the same until it is exhausted.

31) I direct that the devises herein contained to my daughters and each of them shall be in the satisfaction of the last two hundred dollars mentioned in my late husband's will devised to them or any of them and to be paid at my death, as the assets of my said husband's estate will not provide funds to make such payments.

32) I desire it to be understood that the books in my house belong to my children whose names are written in them.

33) I desire my executors to keep all money, life insurance and proceeds, securities of every kind to include also the first months rent of all my real estate which accumulates after my death belonging to my estate in the bank, whether little or nothing until it is known that there is enough to carry out this will as regards the real estate devised to my daughters and granddaughters in my will that each of them shall receive the second month's rent thereof due after my death; the first months rent to go as aforementioned.

34) I direct that should any dispute arise between any of my devisees with regard to the division or identification of any of the property devised to them; that the same shall be settled by my executors herein after named, and that the decision of any such dispute by my executors shall be final and binding upon the devisees. And in case any devisee shall refuse to be bound or submit to the decision of my executors aforesaid, then I revoke the devise herein made to the devisee or devisees so objecting to be bound as aforesaid, and direct that the specific devise to such legatees or legatee which is the cause of dispute shall be sold and the proceeds equally divided among my children, excluding those so refusing to be bound.

35) And whereas I am trustee with my son Thomas Sockett of a certain sum amounting to nine thousand five hundred and twelve dollars and twenty-seven cents under settlement made by the late, the Reverend Thomas Sockett and Caroline Sockett, and several sums of the said moneys I have lent to different members of my family.

And whereas all securities and notes for the said moneys and other moneys invested in my own name but belonging to the said trust fund, I have marked with the words "Trust Money", and have made a list thereof, and delivered the same to my said co-trustee.

And whereas I am entitled to the interest arising from the said investments at the time of my death.

I devise to any of my sons or daughters who are indebted to me in respect of the said Trust Moneys, all the interest which would otherwise be part of my estate but which is not overdue and payable at the time of my death. But direct that all interest that is overdue and payable in respect of the same shall pass to my executors subject to agreements hereof.

I also devise to my executors, the notes, mortgages and other securities held by me for any of the said Trust Moneys, and which I have marked as aforesaid in order that they may be transferred to my co-trustee to carry out the objects of the said trust. And should there be any deficiency in the said sum for which my said co-trustee might in any respect be liable, I direct that the same be made good in the first place out of my estate as a personal debt, I having assumed the sole discharge of the said trust as between my said co-trustee and myself.

36) All the rents and interest which are past due from any of my children at the time of my death are to be paid to my trustees for the purpose of the trusts herein contained, but I direct that my executors remit to any of my said children the rents and interests which are not yet payable by them respectively at my death.

37) For the help and direction of my executors I have marked all my bed quilts with the names of the parties to which they are bequeathed, and some

of the ornaments I have also marked in the same way with the names of those who gave them to me, so that they may have them to enjoy. The rest of my ornaments and shells are to be divided by my daughters into nine parts, and one part to be given to each family of my children.

38) Since my daughter Lucy's death I have decided that too much haste was made in the division of her effects, so I now direct that after my death all my effects be brought into my house, and that the house be locked up for one month by my executors. I have also directed that my granddaughter who lives with me at my decease to give my safe keys and other keys to my son Charles in the presence of my son George Sockett, my son Charles to keep the keys during the said month. Then all my sons and daughters to meet and receive their respective shares bequeathed to them herein. All my effects are to be divided by my daughters and my executors only, no assistance or interference to be given either by my sons-in-law or my daughters-in-law.

39) My wearing apparel and jewelry of every kind that is not willed is to be divided between my daughters as they can agree among themselves.

40) My household linen which is not marked is to be divided by my daughters into nine parts, and one part given to each family of my children.

41) My executors will have time during the said month to settle up my money matters and also to settle with my co-trustee with regard to the Trust Moneys.

42) I also direct that after my decease all perishable food be given to my daughter Mary E. Johnston on the day of my funeral.

43) I direct that my name, age and date of death be inscribed on the monument before the said month expires and before the last division is made.

44) I direct that before payment of the legacies hereinbefore mentioned, my just debts, funeral and testamentary expenses be paid by my executors.

45) The residue of my estate real and Personal is to be realized by my executors, and divided equally among my children living at the time of my death.

46) I appoint my sons George Sockett and Charles Sockett to be executors of and trustees under this will.

Ruth Sockett

Signed, Published and Declared by the said testatrix as her last will and testament in the presence of us, who in her presence, at her request and in the presence of each other, have hereunto subscribed our names as witnesses, this 29th day of January A.D. 1900

Dunbar, Guelph, Barrister

David Wiggins

This is a Codicil to the last Will and Testament of me, Ruth Sockett, bearing date the 29th day of January, A.D. 1900.

1) I revoke all Codicils to the said will by me at any time heretofore made.

2) I reduce the legacy of One thousand dollars given to my son Charles Sockett by clause sixteen of my said will to One hundred dollars; and I hereby revoke the said bequest of One thousand dollars and bequeath to my said son Charles instead thereof the sum of One hundred dollars. I make this change because I think I gave Charles more than I ought to have done in my Will. The Surrey Street property devised to him and his family by Clause Fifteen was his own choice and he has had the use of the farm and will have until my death, so I hope he will be satisfied.

3) To my daughter Fanny McWilliams in addition to what I have given her by my will I bequeath the further sum of Three hundred dollars.

4) To my son Thomas Sockett in addition to what I have given him by my will I bequeath the further sum of Two hundred dollars.

5) To my daughter Mary E. Johnston in addition to what I have given her by my will I bequeath the further sum of Two hundred and fifty dollars.

6) I revoke clauses eighteen and nineteen of my said will, my son Henry having died.

7) I devise to Louisa Sockett, Widow of my son Henry that part of Lot number Eleven in Division "C" of the Township of Guelph, known as the Blacksmith Shop, in fee simple and I also bequeath to the said Louisa Sockett the sum of Eight hundred and fifty dollars in cash and the pictures which I gave to Henry by clause nineteen of said will.

8) I also devise and bequeath to the said Louisa Sockett the share in the residue of my estate which would have gone to my son Henry had he survived.

9) I appoint my son Thomas Sockett an Executor and Trustee of my said Will and of this Codicil in addition to my sons George and Charles.

10) In all other respects I confirm my said will.

Ruth Sockett

Signed, published and declared by the said Ruth Sockett, as a Codicil to her last Will and Testament in the presence of us, who at her request and in her presence, and in the presence of each other, have hereunto set our names as witnesses at the City of Guelph, this Eleventh day of March, A.D. 1902

Dunbar, Guelph, Solicitor

Edwin Joseph Lingwood

This is a second Codicil to the last Will and Testament of me, Ruth Sockett, which will bears date the 29th day of January, A.D. 1900.

As it is my desire that the amount owing to me by my daughter Mary E. Johnston at the time of my death be paid by her out of the devises and bequests made to her in my will and in the first codicil thereto, I direct that should the amount which my said daughter will receive under the Fourth and forty-fifth clauses of my will and under the Fifth clause of the first Codicil thereto, and from the trust funds which will be devisable at my death be insufficient to satisfy the amount owing to me at my death by the said Mary E. Johnston, then my executors and trustees are hereby empowered to sell that portion of Lot 794 in the Canada Company's Survey of the City of Guelph upon which is erected a double roughcast house and out of the proceeds thereof to apply an amount sufficient to make up such deficiency in payment thereof, and the balance of the said purchase money to hold upon the same trusts and subject to the same conditions as are attached to the devise of the said real estate by the terms of my said will.

Except in so far as its terms are modified by this Codicil I hereby confirm my said will and the first Codicil thereto bearing date the 11th day of March, A.D. 1902.

Ruth Sockett

Signed, published and declared by the said Testatrix Ruth Sockett as and for a second Codicil to her last will and testament, in the presence of us, who at her request, in her presence and in the presence of each other, have hereunto subscribed our names as witnesses, at the City of Guelph, this 10th day of December A.D. 1903

A. Dunbar, Guelph, Solicitor,

Maggie McPhail, Guelph, Stenographer

Ruth died on July 27, 1906 and the will was probated on September 7, 1906 (see Wellington County Surrogate Court file No. 5693, Archives of Ontario, RG 22/318)

Transcribed by Gary Wilson.

André William, 1743–1807, surgeon at Petworth House, possibly son of John André, MD, College of Physicians, London

Angouleme, Duc d', 1775–1844, son of Comte d'Artois; refugee in Great Britain; went to the Pyrenees to join Duke of Wellington's army, 1814

Arnold, Benjamin, music master at Petworth House

Arnold, George Benjamin, 1832–1902, Petworth. Organist Petworth and Winchester. Composer of oratorio 'Ahab', performed Exeter Hall, London 1864. See West Sussex Records Office PHA 13903

Arnold, George Frederick Handel, 1795, Petworth, son of Benjamin and Harriet, organist, vestry clerk, postmaster

Arnold, Reverend Frederick Henry, 1831– , Petworth, son of George and Mary; Sockett's godson; author of *History and Antiquities of Petworth*, Petworth, 1864

Artois, Charles-Philippe Comte d', 1757–1836, brother of exiled Louis XVIII, King of France; refugee in Great Britain 1795–1814; reigned as Charles X of France, 1824–30

Ayliffe, Thomas Hamilton, 1774–1852, sons George, 1802–44; Thomas 1814–; Henry 1819–90, sent to Australia 1839; brother of Elizabeth Ilive/Ayliffe, wife of third Earl of Egremont

Balfour, Clara Lucas, 1808–78, worker, writer and lecturer for women's emancipation and the temperance movement

Bampton, John, Oxford University, instigated eight lectures to be given each year by a lecturer in Holy Orders in defence of the Christian religion within the Church of England

Barbauld, Anna Laetitia, 1743–1825, poet, pamphleteer, author of children's lessons and hymns

Barcellon, Joseph, French; men's singles world champion at real tennis, 1785

Barneby, John, 1799–1846, Conservative MP for Worcester, member of Select Committee on Poor Law, 1837

Barry, Sir Charles, 1795–1869, renowned architect; built Royal Sussex Hospital in Brighton 1826–1828; rebuilt Houses of Parliament, 1836

Bartelott Smyth, George, 1788–1872, resumed spelling 'Bartellot' by 1837; married 1819 Emma Woodbridge

Barwell, Richard, 1741–1804, served with East India Company in India, wealthy owner of Stansted Estate, West Sussex, from 1781

Beath, Reverend P. B., Curate of Northchapel c1804–11; perpetual curate of Capel and vicar of St Margaret's, Bungay by 1842

Beauclerk, Reverend Lord Frederick, 1773–1850, renowned cricketer and tennis player, President of Marylebone Cricket Club; infrequent presence in his three parishes

Beche de la, Letitia Whyte, married 1818 Sir Henry Thomas de la Beche; legally separated 1828 after an 'acrimonius public controversy'; mistress of Henry Wyndham. See entry in DNB by J. A. Secord

Bell, Reverend Dr. Andrew, 1753–1832, published in 1797 *An Experiment in Education made at the Male Asylum at Madras*, the foundation of the Anglican monitorial system, first used in 1798 at the Charity School at St Botolph's, Aldgate

Berri, Charles, Duc de, 1778–1820; son of Comte d'Artois; refugee in Great Britain 1789–1815; assassinated in Paris

Biddulph, John, Burton Park, West Sussex; Roman Catholic

Bourbon, Louis-Antoine, Duc de, –1803; refugee in Great Britain from 1789

Bourke, Richard Southwell, 1822–72, MP for Cockermouth, 1847–52 and 1857–68; Earl of Mayo 1867; Viceroy of India 1868 until his assassination 1872; married 1848 Blanche Julia, daughter of George and Mary Wyndham

Boydell, John, alderman, Lord Mayor of London, publisher and founder of Shakespeare Gallery, Pall Mall; his niece married George Nicol

Brightman family — see family tree on page 10

Bromwich, Reverend Dr Bryan J'Anson, 1738–1815, rector of Duncton 1775–1815

Brown, Lancelot 'Capability', 1716–83, renowned landscape gardener and architect; worked at Petworth 1751–65

Brown, Reverend Thomas, rector of Barlavington, chaplain of Petworth Gaol; mourner at Sockett's funeral, 1859

Brunel, Isambard Kingdom, 1806–59, son of Marc, engineer, steamship and railway builder

Brunel, Marc Isambard, 1769–1849, b. France, came to Great Britain 1799, engineer

Brydone family — see family tree on page 88

Buckner, John, Right Reverend Lord Bishop of Chichester, 1798–1824

Bull, William, 1738–1814, minister of Independent Chapel at Newport Pagnell; founder of Congregational Academy for boys; friend of William Cowper; renowned preacher

Bulmer, William, 1757–1830, Newcastle and London, publisher and printer in Pall Mall; associate of the Nicols, William Nicol married Harriet Bulmer, Bulmer's niece

Burrell, Charles Merrik, 1774–1862, Conservative MP for Shoreham, Deputy Lieutenant of Sussex, married Frances Wyndham, eldest daughter of Earl of Egremont and Elizabeth Ilive

Canning, George, 1770–1827, Tory MP in Lord Liverpool's ministry; as Foreign Secretary responsible for sending 4,000 troops to Portugal in 1826 to intervene in civil war between two rivals for Portuguese throne; Prime Minister of Great Britain, April to September 1827

Carleton, William, alias Peacock, footman to the Earl of Egremont; Sockett's friend and tennis opponent

Chadwick, Sir Edwin, 1800–90, Whig, Benthamite reformer; secretary to the Poor Law Commission, 1834

Chichester, Henry Thomas Pelham, third Earl of, 1804–86, Stanmer Park, East Sussex; evangelical, social reformer; facilitator of 1834 Poor Law Unions in his area; sponsor of emigration

Chrippes, Thomas, 1783–1860s, Petworth, churchwarden, surveyor, and builder; one of three members of PEC

Clarke, Reverend L., rector of Iping 1840; mourner at Sockett's funeral, 1859

Clousley, Clara nee Ware, bap 1807 Northchapel; died in Canada, married David Clousley, March 1827; emigrated with Petworth Emigration Committee (hereafter, PEC), 1836

Clousley, David, alias Sharp, bap 1806 Fittleworth; husband of Clara; emigrated with PEC to Canada, 1836

Cobbett, William, 1763–1835, influential radical journalist and writer; his *Rural Rides* were collected in 1830, and include several visits to Sussex

Cockerell, Mary, 1749–1810, Walberton, housekeeper to William Hayley, mother of Thomas Alphonso Hayley

Cole, Reverend J. Francis, rural dean and vicar of Kirdford; mourner at Sockett's funeral, 1859

Colville, Charles Robert, 1815–86, Liberal MP; member of Select Committee on the Poor Law, 1837

Cowper, William, 1731–1800, essayist, poet, hymn and letter writer; neighbour of the Sockett family at Weston Underwood, 1788

Cox, Philip, 1779–1841, men's singles champion at real tennis 1819; Earl of Egremont bought racquets and balls from him

Creevey, Thomas, 1786–1838, politician, gossip; author of letters and journal giving descriptions of contemporary society

Crosbie, General J. Gustavus, Lord of the Manor of Donnington; Major-General by 1831

Darwin, Charles Robert, 1809–82, naturalist, geologist; his book, *On the Origin of Species by means of Natural Selection*, 1859, outlining theories of evolution, caused a storm in scientific and religious circles

Davy, Sir Humphrey, 1778–1829, philosopher; Professor of Chemistry at Royal Institution

Douglass, Andrew, living at Ponders End in 1788; 'natural son' of Andrew Gray, half-brother of Sarah Gray, Sockett's first wife

Dunster, Reverend Charles, 1750–1816, rector of Petworth, 1783–1816; scholar and antiquarian

Egremont, George O'Brien Wyndham, third Earl of, 1751–1837, Petworth House, and landlord of estates in Cumberland, Yorkshire, west of England, Ireland; farmer, sponsor of the arts, philanthropist; (and much more); see Wyndham family tree

Ellis, Captain John Lutman, 1783– Petworth, solicitor, churchwarden; vice-chairman of Petworth Board of Guardians; President of Petworth Friendly Society

Farington/Farringdon, Joseph, 1747–1821, Lancashire and London, artist; his diary is a valuable source of information and gossip about artists and contemporary society

Fitzclarence, Colonel George, 1794–1842, son of Duke of Clarence later William IV, and Dorothy Jordan, famous actress; created Lord Munster in 1831, married Mary Fox, 1819

Flaxman, John, 1755–1826, sculptor and designer; Thomas Alphonso Hayley was his apprentice; Flaxman designed the memorial plaque to Thomas in Eartham Church; first Professor of Sculpture, Royal Academy, 1810

Fox, Charles James, 1749–1806, Tory, Whig, Radical, aristocrat and statesman; friend of Prince of Wales

Fox/Crole, Elizabeth, daughter of Fox, proprietor of Theatre Royal, Brighton; mistress of third Earl of Egremont and of Prince Regent, by each of whom she had several children; 'some say she is youngish and pretty ... others that she is oldish, fat and looks like a good House-keeper'; see M. J. Levy, *The Mistresses of King George IV*, London, Peter Owen, 1996, 102

Fox, Mary, 1791–1842, daughter of Earl of Egremont and Elizabeth Fox; brought up at Petworth House with the children of Elizabeth Ilive, married first Lord Munster 1819

Galland, Reverend Thomas, 1791–1843, Sockett's curate at North Scarle, 1827–43

Gibbon, Edward, 1737–94, author of *The History of the Decline and Fall of the Roman Empire*, 1770–88; friend of Hayley and Lord Sheffield; Sockett worked on his memoirs

Godden, Reverend William Worcester, 1825–post 1881, curate of Petworth 1851–1860; conducted Sockett's funeral service, 1859

Godden, Evelyn Maria Campbell, 1860–1931, daughter of William Godden and Emma Godden, married 1 Henry Sockett, 2 Henry Louis Newman

Goldring, James, –1823, Petworth stationer and printer

Graham, Sir James Robert George, 1792–1861, Conservative/Liberal MP; member of Select Committee on the Poor Law, 1837

Gray family — see family tree on page 88

Greetham, Reverend John Knight, 1795–1865; Sockett's curate at Petworth 1820–31; rector of Kirdford 1831–38/9; chaplain to fourth Earl of Egremont

Griffin, Ruth, 1822–1906, emigrated from Shoreditch with mother and stepfather, J. T. Leslie, 1827; wife of George Sockett — see family tree of the Sockett family in Canada on page 236

Grose, Sir Nash, 1740–1814, judge 1766–1813; bought the eleventh century Cluniac Priory of St Helen's, Isle of Wight, 1799

Guy, William, –1825, Chichester, surgeon; pupil of John Hunter; fellow student of Edward Jenner

Habbin, John, 1815–, Petworth, labourer; imprisoned for poaching and theft

Hale, Captain J.C., surgeon, superintendent of the PEC ship *England*, 1833

Hale, Thomas Hampton, c1799–1846, Petworth, surgeon

Hawkins, John, 1761–1841, Bignor Park, West Sussex, and Trewithin Cornwall; traveller and naturalist; Fellow of Royal Society

Hawley, William Henry Toovey, 1793–1874, Hampshire, son of Catherine Jepson and 'presumed' father, W. H. T. Hawley; Assistant Poor Law Commissioner for East and West Sussex, 1834–39

Hawley, William, 1853–, Cumberland, son of William Hawley and Margaret Graham

Hayley, Elizabeth Ball, –1797, married William Hayley, 1769

Hayley, Thomas Alphonso, 1780–1800, Eartham, son of William Hayley and Mary Cockerell

Hayley, William, 1745–1820, Eartham, poet, writer; cultivated notable friends and needy protégés, including Thomas Sockett

Herington family — see family tree on page 104

Hislop — see Gray family tree on page 88

Holland, Reverend Charles, perpetual curate of Shipley; evangelical rector of Petworth 1859–97

Holroyd, Maria Josepha, 1771–1863, Sheffield Park, married John Thomas, first Lord Stanley of Alderley, 1796

Horace, Quintus Horatius Flaccus, 65–8 BC, poet; favourite of Sockett

Hurdis, Reverend James, 1763–1801, Bishopstone; friend of Cowper and Hayley; Professor of Poetry, Oxford, 1793

Hurst, Reverend John, 1797–1881, rector of Thakeham, 1834–81

Ilive, Elizabeth, c1770–1822, mother of eight children by third Earl of Egremont, whom she married in 1801 becoming Countess of Egremont; separated in 1803
Inman, Reverend Henry, rector of North Scarle in 1860

Jenner, Edward, 1749–1823, surgeon and pioneer of smallpox vaccination
Johnson, Reverend John, 1769–1833, Norfolk, writer; cousin of William Cowper
Johnson, Samuel, 1696–1742, renowned author and lexicographer

Kaye, Dr. John, 1783–1853; Right Reverend Lord Bishop of Lincoln 1846; had charge of North Scarle
Kemmish, John, b. c1827 Beaulieu, Hampshire; Superintendent of Police at Sockett's funeral, 1859; has house with wife and children in Prison Yard Petworth, 1861
King, Lady, and son, **John**, who married 1823 Charlotte Wyndham, daughter of Earl of Egremont and Elizabeth Ilive
Klanert, Reverend Charles, 1808–75, curate of Petworth 1831–51, rector of Iping with Chithurst 1851–1875, rural dean, 1861
Knight, William, 1785–1844, Petworth, surveyor, corn chandler; member of PEC

Ladbrooke, James Weller, 1773–1847, Petworth, chairman of Petworth Quarter Sessions
Lamb, Charles, 1775–1834, writer of prose, poetry and essays; clerk, East India Co. House, London
Lancaster, Joseph, 1778–1838, founder of monitorial system of education favoured by Nonconformists
Langshaw, Reverend Thomas Wall, 1807–89, rector of West Grinstead; his second wife was Frances Sockett
Lannaway, James, 1808–75, Petworth, groom and coachman to Earl of Egremont; emigrated with wife Sarah and children via the PEC to Canada, 1838
Leslie, John Thomas, stepfather of Ruth Griffin, father–in–law of George Sockett; emigrated to Canada in 1827; storekeeper in Guelph, Upper Canada
Leslie Mary, daughter of John Leslie, author; half–sister of Ruth Griffin

Maclean, Charles Hope, 1802–39, Assistant Poor Law Commissioner
Malthus, Reverend Thomas Robert, 1766–1834, author of seminal book, *An Essay on the Principle of Population*, 1798

Mance, John, 1793–1856, Keeper, Petworth House of Correction 1824–56; formerly Army NCO in Ireland, and police constable in Shoreditch

Mann, Ann, 1783–1845; emigrated with husband Samuel, and their children with the PEC from Wisborough Green to Canada, in stages between 1832 and 1836

Manning, Reverend Henry Edward, 1808–92, Anglican Rector of Graffham; converted to Roman Catholicism 1851; became Cardinal Manning, 1875

Maudslay, Henry, 1771–1831; renowned mechanical engineer, employed by Brunel

Meachen, James, 1818–, Petworth; poacher; journeyman tailor in 1841

Melbourne, 2nd Viscount formerly William Lamb, 1779-1848 Prime Minister of Great Britain 1834-41.

Mills, Hannah, 1796–, Northchapel, parish workhouse girl; 'put out' yearly from 1810; taken in 1812 by Sockett family

Milne, Reverend Colin, 1743–1815, rector of Deptford, and Northchapel where Sockett was his curate; popular preacher; author of sermons; botanist

Mitford, Charles, 1785–1831, member of the Mitford family of Pitshill, the re–built mansion finished in 1790s; friend and tennis opponent of Sockett

Montgomery, Alfred, Kingston House, Knightsbridge, son of Sir Henry Montgomery; married 1842 Fanny Charlotte, daughter of George and Mary Wyndham

Mucklow, Keeper of the St James's tennis court in London

Murray, Charles, 1768–1847, steward and lawyer to the Earl of Egremont and Col. George Wyndham 1835–47

New, Reverend John, curate of Duncton 1849, rector from 1859–91; married Henrietta Brydone, 1854

Newman, Reverend Henry Louis, 1870–1941, Sutton, married Henry Sockett's widow, Evelyn Godden

Nicol, George, 1740–1828, bookseller and publisher in Pall Mall; married Mary Boydell; guardian of Sarah Gray, Sockett's first wife, and witness at their marriage

Nicol, William, 1775–1834, son of George, printer and publisher; friend of Sockett; married Harriet Bulmer

Nicol, William Bulmer, 1812–86, son of William and Harriet; emigrated to Canada on the PEC ship of 1835; friend of George Sockett; became Professor of Materia Medica, University of Toronto

Nicholls, George, 1781–1865, Poor Law Commissioner, 1834–1847

O'Keeffe, Adelaide, 1776–1855? children's poet, daughter of John O'Keeffe, Irish dramatist; lived with her father in Chichester and later in Southampton; friend of Sockett

Park, Mungo, 1771–1806, explorer in West Africa seeking source of the Niger; relation of Elizabeth Hislop, Brydone's wife

Peacock, Catherine, housekeeper at the Egremont Brighton house; previously lady's maid in the Egremont London household

Peacock, Thomas Love, 1785–1866, satirist, novelist and poet; employed by East India Co. London

Penrose, Reverend John, 1779–1859, Bampton Lecturer, Oxford University, 1808

Perceval, Lord Spencer, 1762–1812, Prime Minister of Great Britain 1809–12 when he was shot in the House of Commons

Phillips, John, c1790s–1840s, Petworth, printer and stationer; printed material for the PEC

Pilkington, Henry, 1787–, barrister; Assistant Poor Law Commissioner for West Sussex, 1834–35

Pitt, William, the younger, 1759–1806, Prime Minister of Great Britain, 1783–1801 and 1804–06

Polignac, Probably Count Jules de Polignac, created Duc 1780, died 1817; his wife was a friend of Marie Antoinette; Jules and his wife came to Great Britain, 1789

Pullen/Hooker, Elizabeth, Northchapel; son Richard emigrated with wife and children to Canada with the PEC, 1837

Quiverful, Mr, rector of Puddingdale in Trollope's Barchester novels, has fourteen living children; 'Like as the arrows in the hand of the giant: even so are the young children. Happy is the man that hath his quiver full of them.' Psalm 127; Mr Quiverful is very poor

Raddish, Reverend Thomas, 1763–1819, vicar of Kirdford

Randall, Reverend R. W., rector of Woollavington with Graffham; mourner at Sockett's funeral, 1859

Richmond, Charles Gordon fifth Duke of, 1791–1860, Goodwood; member of the House of Lords, Lord–Lieutenant of Sussex; Colonel of Sussex Militia (and far more)

Ridsdale, Reverend Robert, rector of Tillington, 1834–76

Romney, George, 1734–1802, fashionable portrait painter; friend and protégé of Hayley

Roscoe, William, 1753–1831, Liverpool attorney; historian

Rose, Samuel, 1767–1804, lawyer, friend of Cowper, Hayley and Sheffield; successfully defended William Blake on a charge of treason at Chichester 1804

Rubidge, Charles, superintendent of the Waterloo, Irish emigrant ship sponsored by George Wyndham 1839

Russell, Lord John, first Earl, 1792–1878, Prime Minister of Great Britain, 1846–52

Sheffield, John Baker Holroyd, Lord, 1741–1821, Sheffield Park, author — with Sockett's help — of the *Memoirs* of Edward Gibbon

Shepherd, William, 1814–, labourer, poacher; emigrated with PEC in 1832; returned to England, 1833

Sinclair, Reverend Latham W, rector of Pulborough; mourner at Sockett's funeral, 1859

Smiles, Samuel, 1812–1904, author of popular *Self-Help*, 1853, and biographies of notable industrialists

Smith, Charlotte, 1749–1806, novelist and poet; protégée of Hayley

Smith, Reverend Sydney, 1771–1845, writer and wit

Sockett family — see family tree see page 4

Somersell, John, m. Ann Pullen, Northchapel; coffin bearer at Earl of Egremont's funeral

Somerset, Elizabeth, daughter of Lord Charles Somerset, married Henry Wyndham

Spencer, George John, second Earl, 1758–1834, politician, book collector

Strachan, John, Right Reverend Bishop of Toronto, born Aberdeen Scotland 1778, emigrated to Upper Canada 1799, died Toronto 1867; schoolmaster; ordained priest in Church of England 1804; advocate of the unity of church and state

Talbot, Mr, Olney, executor of Henry Brightman's will, 1805

Teedon, Samuel, Olney, impoverished schoolmaster; friend of Cowper

Thurlow, Edward, first Baron, 1731–1806, fellow law student with Cowper; Lord High Chancellor; friend of Earl of Egremont

Townsend, Reverend Thomas Jackson Milnes, 1820–, curate of North Scarle, 1844

Tierney, Sir Matthew, 1776–1845, physician at Brighton to Prince Regent, William IV, and third Earl of Egremont

Trollope, Anthony, 1815–82, prolific novelist; his Barchester series describes religious, political and social nuances within Church of England

Tyler, William, c1764–1835, Petworth, lawyer and steward to the third Earl of Egremont

Unwin, Mary Cawthorne, 1723–1796, Olney; Cowper, after a severe mental collapse, lived with the Unwins and continued to live with Mary after her husband died in 1767

Victoria, 1819–1901, became Queen of Great Britain and Ireland from 1837 and Empress of India from 1876; married Albert of Saxe-Coburg-Gotha 1840; nine children
Vinson, George, 1812–, Petworth, labourer and poacher

Wagner, Reverend Henry Michell, 1792–1870, vicar of St Nicholas's Church, Brighton; sent emigrants to Canada with PEC, 1834
Wake, Reverend W. R., curate at Petworth; by 1842 rector of Courteen Hall, Northampton
Walter, John, 1776–1847, second son of founder of *The Times*; innovator of the steam printing-press; friend of Sockett
Wanton, Reverend Joseph Brenton, 1777–1853, b. Rhode Island, North America; curate at Petworth, 1814–19; then in semi–retirement on the Isle of Man; his health was said to be always delicate from paralysis of the throat caused by entering his college rooms when newly painted, see J. A. Venn, comp., *Alumni Cantabrigienses* (Cambridge, 1954), 381
Wellington, Arthur Wellesley, first Duke of, 1769–1852, General in British army, hero of Waterloo; Prime Minister of Great Britain, 1828–30
Wesley, Reverend John, 1703–91, founder of Methodism
Wilberforce, William, 1759–1833, MP and evangelical philanthropist
Williamson, Thomas, Park St, London, steel-engraver; friend of Griffin and Leslie family
Willis, Captain, at Petworth 1805, possibly became Rear Admiral Willis died 29 Jan 1829, aged 74
Withereby, Reverend Robert, rector of Northchapel; mourner at Sockett's funeral, 1859
Wyndham family — see family tree on page 22
Wynne, Reverend John Welchman, c1769–1841, curate of Petworth –1814; impoverished

Yonge, Charlotte Mary, 1823–1901, Hampshire, prolific popular novelist; influenced by the High Church of England Oxford Movement
Young, Arthur, 1741–1820, agricultural reformer and journalist; friend of Earl of Egremont and Elizabeth Ilive

ENDNOTES

Abbreviations:
AO — Archives of Ontario; BL — British Library; BPP — British Parliamentary Papers; BRO — Buckinghamshire Record Office; CRO — Cornwall Record Office; DNB — Oxford Dictionary of National Biography; ESRO — East Sussex Record Office; HMSO — Her Majesty's Stationery Office; IGI — International Genealogical Index; LRO — Lincoln Record Office; PHA — Petworth House Archives; PRO — Public Record Office (now, National Archives); WSRO — West Sussex Record Office.

[1] CRO, Hawkins Papers, JS/19/2081 Sockett to Mrs Hawkins
[2] Sockett to James Brydone, [1835], letter in the possession of Barbara Brydone
[3] Information supplied from a family Bible given by Thomas Sockett to his son, George, in Canada, now in the possession of Clare Sockett
[4] William Hayley, *Memoirs of the Life and Writings of William Hayley*, ed. John Johnson, 2 vols, Colburn & Co., Simpkin & Marshall, 1823, *Memoir of Thomas Alphonso Hayley,* 54
[5] *The Girlhood of Maria Josepha Holroyd,* (Lady Stanley of Alderley), ed. J.A. Adeane (Longmans, 1896), 286
[6] William Hone, *The Every-Day Book and Table Book ...* (London), vol I, 1839, 1166–1250
[7] Charles Lamb, *Essays of Elia, first series, The Praise of Chimney-Sweepers,* 1822
[8] William Hone, *The Every-day Book*, I, 1839, 1160–1250; II, 1827, 1196–1197
[9] Andrew Fuller, *The Nature and Importance of Walking by Faith...* (Northampton: T. Dicey and Co, [1784])
[10] 'List of Dissenting Congregations in and near London' *The Gentleman's Magazine,* 1796, II, 723
[11] BL, Early Printed Collections, London, 4402 cc45(5), 1783
[12] WSRO, PHA 1679, Thomas Sockett, Journal, 13 April 1806
[13] PRO, PROB 11/1341, will of Elizabeth Brightman, 1800; PROB 11/1426, will of Henry Brightman, 1805
[14] BRO, PR 226/5/1, Weston Underwood Churchwardens' Book, 1752–1827
[15] BRO, QPR L/7/14, Land Tax records for Weston Underwood, 1793
[16] William Cowper, *The Letters and Prose Writing of William Cowper*, ed. James King and Charles Ryskamp, 5 vols. (Clarendon Press, 1979–86) III: 96
[17] Cowper, *Letters and Prose Writing,* III: 90
[18] Cowper, *Letters and Prose Writing*, III:109
[19] Cowper, *Letters and Prose Writing*, III: 535
[20] Cowper, *Letters and Prose Writing*, III: 271
[21] Cowper, *Letters and Prose Writing*, III: 511
[22] *Ibid*
[23] *Sussex Agricultural Express,* 26 March 1859
[24] John Wesley, *The Journal of John Wesley,* 9 November 1756
[25] WSRO, Add. MSS 2816, William Hayley and John Thornton, Letters, November 1777
[26] Cowper, *The Letters and Prose Writings*, IV: 92
[27] William Hayley, *Memoir of Thomas Alphonso Hayley,* 54
[28] William Hayley, *Memoir of Thomas Alphonso Hayley*, 55
[29] William Hayley, *The Life of George Romney Esq.* (Chichester, 1809), 72
[30] WSRO, Add MSS 2817, Thomas Alphonso Hayley, letters to his father, 16 November 1793
[31] Cowper, *Letters and Prose Writing*, IV, 189

[32] Cowper, *Letters and Prose Writing,* IV, 216

[33] Hayley, *Memoirs,* II: 200–01

[34] Mark Anthony Lower, 'William Hayley', *The Worthies of Sussex* (Lewes, 1865), 258

[35] WSRO, Add. MSS 2816, Thomas Alphonso Hayley, *Letters...*, 16 November 1793

[36] WSRO, Add MSS 4859

[37] James King, *William Cowper,* 247

[38] WSRO, Add MSS 2757, William Hayley, *A Singular History in a series of letters from a Father to his son*

[39] William Hayley, *Memoirs...,*11, 200

[40] Cowper, *Letters and Prose Writing,* IV: 216

[41] William Hayley, *Memoirs,* I: 441

[42] Cowper, *Letters and Prose Writing,* IV: 206

[43] Cowper, *Letters and Prose Writing,* IV: 103

[44] Cowper, *Letters and Prose Writing,* IV: 253

[45] Loraine Fletcher, *Charlotte Smith, A Critical Biography* (Basingstoke: Macmillan Press, 1998)

[46] Charlotte Smith, *The Old Manor House* (1793; Oxford University Press, 1969)

[47] Cowper, *Letters and Prose Writing,* IV: 324

[48] Sussex University Library, Special Collection, Sx Ms 50, Kenneth Povey, *Three Minor Sussex Poets,* 1/1 Notebook. Ms. 'William Hayley.'

[49] Cowper, *Letters and Prose Writing,* IV: 175; 206

[50] *BPP* 1837 (131), XVII, pt 1, *Select Committee on the Poor Law Amendment Act*, Thomas Sockett, Minutes of Evidence, 9 March 1837

[51] *New Monthly Magazine and Literary Journal* (London)*,* XI*,* British Galleries of Art, No VII, 'Lord Egremont's Gallery at Petworth'. The *New Monthly Magazine* began in 1814 and continued, with changes in its title, until 1884.

[52] Joseph Farington, *The Diary of Joseph Farington*, ed. Kenneth Garlick and Angus Macintyre, 16 vols. (New Haven: Yale University Press for the Paul Mellon Centre for Studies in British Art, 1978–1984), III: 1115, 2 December 1798

[53] William Hayley, *Memoir of Thomas Alphonso…*, 60

[54] WSRO, Add. MSS 2817

[55] *Ibid*

[56] Joseph Farington, *Diary,* II: 288

[57] WSRO PHA 731

[58] *Girlhood of Maria Josepha Holroyd*, 286

[59] *Ibid.* 122

[60] WSRO, PHA 55, Jenner to the Earl of Egremont, 10 November 1799

[61] William Hayley, *The Life and Letters of William Cowper*, 1803, Cowper to Lady Hesketh, 1 January 1788

[62] ESRO, Sheffield Park Papers , Book 24, Household Menu Book, 1799–1801

[63] *Girlhood of Maria Josepha Holroyd,* 287

[64] *Girlhood of Maria Josepha Holroyd*, 294

[65] William Eden, Baron Auckland, *The Journal and Correspondence of William, Lord Auckland*, 2 vols. (R. Bentley, 1861), II: 457, October 1792

[66] BL, MSS 61980, Sheffield Papers, William Hayley to Lord Sheffield, 24 December 1794

[67] *The Gentleman's Magazine,* LXV: 1

[68] BRO, D/A/We/91/63, will of Henry Brightman of Weston Underwood, Gent, 1761

[69] *Girlhood of Maria Josepha Holroyd*, 320 and 327

[70] See Lord Sheffield's advertisement to the first edition of *Gibbon's Miscellaneous Works*, Sheffield Place, 6 August 1795

[71] BL, MSS 61980, Sheffield Papers, William Hayley to Lord Sheffield, 3 April 1796

[72] WSRO, PHA 1679, Sockett's Journal, 22 January 1806

[73] See WSRO, 015/10R, letter from W Batting/Botting to Tyler, 18 February 1795, expressing anxiety about George and mentioning 'Midhurst fever'

[74] William Hayley, *Memoirs, 1795–1798*

[75] University of Sussex, Special Collections. Sx Ms.50, Kenneth Povey, *The Sussex Poets*, 1/10, Loose notes, Ms., ts, on eighteenth-century minor Sussex poets, William Hayley etc

[76] Thomas Alphonso Hayley, *Memoir*, 334

[77] Thomas Alphonso Hayley, *Memoir*, 480

[78] WSRO, PHA 2088

[79] WSRO, PHA 10490

[80] WSRO, PHA 8064

[81] *Ibid*

[82] WSRO, PHA 5952, presumably Anna Laetitia (Akin) Barbauld, *Lessons for Children of Three Years Old*, 2 pts, (Dublin: R Jackson, 1779 and 1788), or *A New Sequel to Mrs. Barbauld's Lessons, ... Embellished with a beautiful plate*, 3rd edition, enlarged' (G Sael, 1796); *Lilliput, Cabinet of Lilliput (Stories)*, 10 vols. (J Harris, 1802)

[83] WSRO, PHA 2228, 2230, 2233, 2238, 2240, 2242

[84] WSRO, PHA 8064

[85] *Ibid*

[86] Joseph Farington, *Diary*, III: 113–14.

[87] WSRO, PHA 8064

[88] James Woodforde, *The Diary of a Country Parson, 1758–1802* (OUP, 1978), 573

[89] F.H. Arnold, *The History and Antiquities of Petworth* (Petworth: A.H. Bryant, 1864)

[90] WSRO, PHA 8142

[91] WSRO, PHA 8082; the author of *Topsy-Turvy* was George Huddesford.

[92] WSRO, PHA 69

[93] WSRO, PHA 10621

[94] WSRO, PHA 69, and PHA 7547

[95] WSRO, PHA 11191

[96] WSRO, PHA 8060

[97] WSRO, MP 1505 , 28 letters from Arthur Young to the Earl of Egremont, 1793–1815, letter 2

[98] WSRO, MP 1505, letter 8

[99] WSRO, PHA 2242

[100] Alison McCann, 'A Private Laboratory at Petworth House, Sussex, in the late 18th Century', *Annals of Science,* 40 (1983): 635–55

[101] WSRO, PHA 2236, 2237, 2238, 2239

[102] WSRO, PHA 8025

[103] WSRO, PHA 1679, Sockett's Journal

[104] WSRO, PHA 1679, Sockett's Journal, 22 January 1806

[105] WSRO, PHA 1679, Sockett's Journal, 13 April 1806

[106] William Hickey, *Memoir*, ed Alfred Spencer (Hurst and Blackett, 1913), vol II: 1775–1782, 308

[107] Ron Brown, *The Pubs of Portsmouth* (Horndean, Hants: Milestone publications, 1984).

[108] *The Dispatches and Letters of Vice Admiral, Lord Viscount Nelson,* 7 vols. (Henry Colburn, 1845–46), VII: August–October 1805, 35

[109] WSRO, PHA 2088, Half yearly accounts of servants' wages and tradesmen's bills, vol. II, 1801–1809

[110] WSRO, PHA 10496

[111] WSRO, PHA 10490

[112] Samuel Smiles, *Industrial Biography: Iron Workers and Tool Makers*, Henry Maudslay (John

Murray, 1863)

[113] BRO, D/A/We/91/63

[114] PRO, PROB 11/ 1426, 371

[115] *The Gentleman's Magazine*, 12, 1, May 1816

[116] WSRO, PHA 8505

[117] *The Gentleman's Magazine*, Theatrical Register, September 1805

[118] DNB, William Roscoe.

[119] WSRO, PHA 2249

[120] WSRO, PHA 2238, PHA 2243

[121] WSRO, PHA 6318

[122] WSRO, PHA 8064

[123] WSRO, PHA 5951

[124] WSRO, PHA 8025

[125] WSRO, PHA 2242

[126] For some notes on Sockett as botanist, see T.C.G. Rich, B.C. Rich, and N.J. Sturt, 'Notes on some early Sussex botanical records by Thomas Sockett (1777–1859)', *Watsonia*, vol. 21, pt 3, February 1997

[127] *The Gentleman's Magazine,* 1838 ,1, 89

[128] For information on the Petworth Yeoman Cavalry, see WSRO, PHA 53; PHA 111; PHA 114; PHA 127

[129] WSRO, Mitford Archives, A catalogue, ed. Francis Steer (Chichester 1961)

[130] WSRO, Mitford MSS 1359

[131] James Boswell, *The Life of Samuel Johnson, LL.D.*, 2 vols. (Everyman,), I: 338

[132] WSRO, PHA 697, Sockett to the Rev. Hurst, 19 November 1839

[133] WSRO, PHA 690; *Brighton Guardian*, 20 May 1840, account of the toasts at a meeting of the Petworth Agricultural Association

[134] See Margery Weiner, *The French Exiles, 1789–1815* (John Murray, 1960)

[135] WSRO, PHA 5951

[136] *The A-Z of Regency London* (Lympne Castle, Kent: Harry Margary, in assoc. with Guildhall Library, London, 1985)

[137] See Mrs Basil Holmes, *The London Burial Grounds; Notes on Their History from the Earliest Times to the Present Day*, 1896, and extracts in the *East London Observer*, at the Whitechapel Family History Centre

[138] D. Foster, *Inns, Taverns, Alehouses, Coffee Houses, etc., in and around London,* c 1900, vol. 19

[139] WSRO, PHA 8060

[140] I am indebted to Brian C. Rich for information about tennis at Petworth and in London.

[141] Benjamin Disraeli, Earl of Beaconsfield, *Coningsby, or the New Generation, 3 vols.* (Henry Colburn, 1844), book VII, chap. 2

[142] WSRO, PHA 127

[143] Sussex University Library, Special Collections, Sx Ms. 50, Kenneth Povey, The Sussex Poets, 1/10, Loose notes, MS, ts, on eighteenth century minor Sussex poets, William Hayley

[144] *The Journal of Elizabeth, Lady Holland*, (1791–1811), ed. Earl of Ilchester, vol. 11 1799–1811, 16

[145] Elie Halevy, *A History of the English People in 1815*, vol.1, 114, Political Institutions, Privates and Officers. (Penguin 1937)

[146] WSRO, Goodwood Archives, MSS 1508, f.294

[147] Westminster City Archives, St Margaret's, Westminster, Marriages, vol. 59; *The Gentleman's Magazine*, 1810, vol. 11, Meteorological tables for July 1810

[148] Westminster City Archives, Sexton's Day book, St Martin-in-the-Fields, Baptisms, 1785 (at a charge of one guinea)

[149] Westminster City Archives, Marriages at St-Martin-in-the-Fields, vol. 36
[150] PRO, PROB 11/1162
[151] PRO, PROB 11/1518
[152] WSRO, STM4, MF 1028
[153] *The Gentleman's Magazine*, 1825, 94, 1,236
[154] William B Todd, comp., *A Directory of Printers and Others in Allied Trades, London and Vicinity*, 1800–1840 (Printing Historical Society, 1972)
[155] WSRO, PHA 8082
[156] Joseph Farington, *Diary*, III: 1057
[157] James Marr Brydone, OBE, *Mungo Park and the Brydones of Selkirk* (privately printed).
[158] Mungo Park, Surgeon, *Travels in the Interior districts of Africa: Performed under the Direction and Patronage of the African Association 1795, 1796 and 1797...* (Printed by W. Bulmer and Co for the author, and sold by G and W Nicol, book sellers to His Majesty, Pall Mall, 5 April 1799)
[159] John Dreyfus and Peter C.G. Isaac, *Studies in the Book Trade in Honour of Graham Pollard*, Oxford Biographical Society, new series, XVIII: 351, William Bulmer's will, PRO Prob. 11/1775
[160] John Wesley, *Journal*, 3 August 1758
[161] LRO, CORB 5/4/124/2
[162] LRO, Census of North Scarle, 25 September 1851
[163] LRO, CORB 5/4/124/2, Letter to the Bishop of Lincoln
[164] For the correspondence over this purchase, see WSRO, PHA 2682, Tyler's Letter book 1810–1814
[165] WSRO, PHA 8503 and MP 2963
[166] WSRO, PHA 12016, William Tyler's Letter Book, December 1809
[167] *The Gentleman's Magazine,* 1833, 11, 317
[168] WSRO, PHA 7878
[169] WSRO, Plan of Rectory of Northchapel, photographed by Dr Philip Brittan; Pamela Bruce, *Northchapel, a Parish History* (Northchapel: Northchapel Parish Council, 2000)
[170] WSRO, EPI/41/33
[171] WSRO, PAR 142/31/2, Northchapel Rate Book
[172] WSRO, PAR 142/20 September 1812
[173] Thomas Gray, *Elegy in a Country Churchyard*, 1751
[174] WSRO, PHA 8503
[175] WSRO, MO 2963
[176] WSRO, PAR 142/1/1/2
[177] Thomas Phillips's painting 'The Allied Sovereigns at Petworth', 24 June 1814
[178] WSRO, PHA 8503
[179] *Victoria History of the Counties of England, Sussex,* vol. 2, ed. William Page (A. Constable & Co., 1905–)
[180] WSRO, PHA 9350
[181] WSRO, PHA 12018
[182] WSRO, PHA 8770, *A Case of the Extreme Distress of the Revd Mr Wynne, Curate at Petworth*
[183] WSRO, 19-O- 1816
[184] Hertford Archives and Local Studies, DE/Z117/5/23
[185] WSRO, Ep 1/7/3
[186] WSRO, PHA 10547, Sockett to Tyler 1819
[187] Diocese of Chichester, *Calendar of Sussex Marriage Licences … January 1731 to December 1774,* Sussex Record Society, XXXII (Lewes, 1926), 26 May 1773
[188] PRO, PROB 11/1553, 11 March 1814; WSRO, PHA 5443

189 WSRO, PHA 1068, Sockett to George and Mary Wyndham, 23 August 1838
190 CRO, Hawkins Papers, J3/19/2081, Sockett to Mrs Hawkins, 24 June 1836
191 WSRO, PHA 1765
192 WSRO, EP 1/41/36
193 WSRO, PHA 10530
194 *BPP* 1835, XXII, *Report of the Commissioners to Inquire into the Ecclesiastical Revenues of England and Wales,* tab IV
195 WSRO, PHA 9029
196 William White, *History, Gazetteer & Directory of Lincolnshire* ... (Sheffield, 1842)
197 WSRO, PHA 10420
198 WSRO, MP 1505, Arthur Young, *Letters to the Third Earl of Egremont*, letter 17, 27 September 1800
199 WSRO, PHA 2200, 2201, 2202
200 WSRO, Ep 1/41/36
201 WSRO, PHA 684, Sockett to Wyndham
202 *BPP* 1844 (543), X, Report from the Select Committee on Poor Relief (Gilbert Unions), 28 June 1844
203 *An Account of the Augmentation of Small Livings by the Governors of the Bounty of Queen Anne* ... (Nichols & Son, 1826), 53–54
204 M.B. Dallaway, FSA, *The Parochial Topography of the Rape of Arundel in the Western Division of the County of Sussex*, new ed. Edmund Cartwright, MA FSA (1832), II: 334–35
205 WSRO, PHA 728
206 Sockett to J. M. Brydone, [March 1835], letter in the possession of Barbara Brydone
207 C.R.O. J/3, '*I am my dear Sir …*' *A selection of Letters written mainly to and by John Hawkins, FRS, FGS, 1761–1841, of Bignor Park, Sussex and Trewithen, Cornwall,* ed. with an intro. by Francis W. Steer, 1959
208 *Sussex Agricultural Express,* 28 September 1839
209 Thomas Sockett, Letter to the *Standard,* February 1837
210 WSRO, PHA 697, Adelaide O'Keeffe to Sockett, 16 June 1840
211 Sockett to Brydone, 5 November 1827, private paper in the possession of Gary Wilson
212 DNB, and *The Gentleman's Magazine*, VII, new series, May 1842, 549
213 *The Letters of Queen Victoria, A Selection from Her Majesty's Correspondence between the years 1837 and 1861*, ed. A.C. Benson et al., vol. I: 1837–1843 (John Murray, 1908), 21 March 1842
214 Charles Greville, *Memoirs, 1814–1860*, ed. Lytton Strachey and Roger Fulford, 8 vols. (Macmillan, 1938), I, 21 March 1842
215 WSR0, Goodwood MSS 1504, f.86, 12 January 1834
216 WSRO, Goodwood MSS 1505, f.29, 6 March 1834
217 Sockett to Brydone, 24 February 1834, letter in the possession of Barbara Brydone
218 WSRO, PHA 3277
219 WSRO, PHA 729
220 *BPP* 1837, *Select Committee on the Poor Law Amendment Act*, Minutes, March 1837
221 *BPP, Select Committee on Postage*, Minutes, 23 May 1838
222 BPP, Select Committee on Postage, 23 May 1838
223 BPP, Select Committee on Postage; [T. Sockett], *Emigration: A Letter to a Member of Parliament, Containing a Statement of the Method Pursued by the PETWORTH COMMITTEE in Sending Emigrants to UPPER CANADA in the Years 1832 and 1833* ... (Petworth: John Phillips, and London: Longman, 1833)
224 PRO, MH 12/13061
225 CRO, Hawkins Papers, J3/19/2081, Sockett to Mrs Hawkins of Bignor Park, 24 June 1836

226 Sockett to Brydone, November 1827, letter in the possession of Gary Wilson
227 WSRO, PHA 691
228 MSS in the possession of Gary Wilson
229 WSRO, PHA 2686, Tyler's Letter Book, May 1821
230 PRO, WO 25/792 M/BC 2822
231 WSRO, Goodwood MSS 1460, f.23
232 WSRO, Goodwood MSS 1463, f.434
233 WSRO, Goodwood MSS 1465, f.16a
234 CRO, Hawkins Papers, J/3/2/845, Sockett to Hawkins, 16 September 1833
235 *BPP, Select Committee on Postage*, 23 May 1838
236 William Cobbett, *Rural Rides*, Petworth, 1 August 1823, Penguin Classics, 1985
237 *English Immigrant Voices: Labourers' Letters from Upper Canada in the 1830s*, ed. W. Cameron, S. Haines, M. McDougall Maude (Montreal & Kingston: McGill-Queen's University Press, 2000), letter 106
238 Arthur Young, *General View of the Agriculture of the County of Sussex* (1813; reprint, Newton Abbott: David & Charles, 1970), 378
239 *BPP*, Select Committee on the Poor Law Amendment Act, 9 March 1837
240 William Cobbett, *Rural Rides*, Petworth, 1 August 1823, Penguin Classics, 1985
241 *BPP*, Select Committee on the Poor Law Amendment Act, 9 March 1837
242 A.C. Day, *Glimpses of Rural Life in Sussex.* (Oxford: The Countryman, 1927), 22
243 *BPP*, Select Committee on the Poor Law Amendment Act, Evidence of Mr Butt, 20 March; and James Slements, 17 March 1837
244 *Brighton Guardian,* 20 May 1840
245 *BPP*, Select Committee on the Poor Law Amendment Act, 9 March 1837
246 *Ibid*
247 T. Sockett, Emigration: Letter to a Member of Parliament
248 Peter Jerrome, *Petworth, from the Beginnings to 1660,* (Petworth: The Window Press, 2002)
249 K.H. Macdermott, *Sussex Church Music in the Past*, Sussex Archaeological Collections (SAC), LX, 1
250 WSRO, PHA 9123
251 WSRO, *Psalms and Hymns for the use of Petworth Church principally selected and adapted by the Late Rev. C. Dunster M.A., Rector of that Parish* (Petworth, James Goldring, 1820)
252 K. H. Macdermott, *Sussex Church Music in the Past*, SAC LX,1; WSRO, PHA 8766
253 WSRO, PHA 8639
254 WSRO, PAR 149/4/4
255 *Religious Census of Sussex, 1851*, ed. John A. Vickers (Lewes: Sussex Record Society, 1989), 75
256 *Sussex Agricultural Express*, 3 January 1846
257 *Sussex Agricultural Express*, 7 August 1841; W. Cowper, *Olney Hymns* XXII
258 *Sussex Agricultural Express*, 6 July 1844
259 William Cobbett, *Rural Rides*, 1 August 1822; and *New Monthly Magazine and Literary Journal* (London)*, XI (1824), 162–70, British Galleries of Art, No VII, 'Lord Egremont's Gallery at Petworth'
260 Abstract of the Answers and Returns Made in Pursuant to an Act Passed in the First Year of the Reign of His Majesty King George IV, Sussex, Petworth and Duncton.
261 Sydney Smith, *Letter to Sir James Mackintosh, Recorder, Bombay*, 1 October 1805
262 Sydney Smith, *Letter to Lord Holland,* 1 June 1820
263 *Brighton Gazette,* 12 May 1836
264 *BPP*, Select Committee on the Poor Law Amendment Act, 9 March 1837
265 WSRO, E 149/1/1, Minute book of the Petworth Sub-Committee of the Society for educating the infant poor, in the principles of the established church 1816–1824

[266] WSRO, PHA 8064

[267] WSRO, PHA 2088

[268] WSRO, PHA 9369; 'A catalogue of the entire remaining library of the Revd. Charles Dunster M.A. deceased ... 1816'

[269] William Hayley, 'Hymn for the Children of Petworth School', from C. Dunster, *Psalms and Hymns for the Use of Petworth Church* (Petworth: James Goldring, 1820)

[270] John Caffyn, *Sussex Schools in the Eighteenth Century: Schooling Provision, Schoolteachers and Scholars* (Lewes: Sussex Record Society, 1998)

[271] John M. Caffyn, 'Sunday Schools in the Late Eighteenth Century', SAC 132 (1994): 151–60

[272] WSRO, PHA 11571

[273] WSRO, PHA 1765

[274] WSRO, PHA 1066

[275] WSRO, PHA 10339

[276] *BPP*, Select Committee on Postage..., 23 May 1838

[277] Petworth Parish Register, Marriages, 1816, 1817, and 1844

[278] *BPP*, Select Committee on the Poor Law Amendment Act, 17 March 1837

[279] *BPP*, Select Committee on Postage, 23 May 1838

[280] *BPP*, Select Committee on Postage, 23 May 1838

[281] *Hampshire Telegraph*, 8 April 1820

[282] British and Foreign School Society, *Minutes of the Inspectors*, Committee, 1829–31

[283] Thomas Love Peacock, *Crotchet Castle* (London: T. Hookham, 1831), chap. V

[284] WSRO, PHA 12020

[285] WSRO, PHA 11097

[286] *BPP*, Select Committee on the Poor Law, 9 March 1837

[287] *BPP*, Select Committee on the Poor Law, Appendix No. 7, p. 59

[288] *BPP*, Select Committee on the Poor Law, 14 March 1837

[289] WSRO, PHA 8543; PHA 9029

[290] WSRO, PHA 8623

[291] WSRO, PHA 12020

[292] See Alison McCann, 'The Greatest Rascal I Ever Heard of ..'., *Petworth Society Magazine*, no 115, March 2004

[293] *English Immigrant Voices*, letter 67, James and William Goldring

[294] WSRO, PAR 86/31/1, Fittleworth Overseers Accounts 1815–1846

[295] *BPP*, Charles Hope Maclean, 'Report... on the Administration and Practical Operation of the Poor Laws', 1834, 8, 525A

[296] *BPP*, Select Committee on the Poor Law, 9 March 1837

[297] *BPP* 1834, Charles Hope Maclean, 'Report ... on the Administration and Practical Operation of the Poor Laws', 1834, 8, 582A

[298] *BPP*, Charles Hope Maclean, 'Report ... on the Administration and Practical Operation of the Poor Laws', 1834, 8, 559A

[299] *BPP*, Select Committee on the Poor Law, 9 March 1837

[300] See Mike Matthews, *Captain Swing in Sussex and Kent*. Hastings Press, 2006.

[301] WSRO, PHA 8618

[302] *BPP*, Charles Hope Maclean, 'Report ... on the Administration and Practical Operation of the Poor Laws', 1834, 8, 580A

[303] WSRO, Goodwood MSS, 1473, f.73

[304] *Hampshire Telegraph*, February 1822

[305] Thomas Sockett, Journal, 1 May 1806

[306] Thomas Creevey, *Creevey Papers*, ed by H Maxwell, John Murray, 1903, 18 August 1828

[307] *BPP*, Charles Hope Maclean, 'Report ... on the Administration and Practical

Operation of the Poor Laws', 1834, 8, 525A

[308] WSRO, PHA, 2684, Tyler's Letter Book no 3, 1818
[309] WSRO, PHA 2687
[310] WSRO, PHA 2686
[311] WSRO, 0.18 1814
[312] WSRO, PHA 2684, 13 September 1816
[313] WSRO, PHA 2684, 15 September 1816
[314] WSRO, PHA 2687, August 1823
[315] WSRO, PHA 2686
[316] Thomas Creevey, *Creevey Papers,* ed by H Maxwell, John Murray, 1903, 18 August 1828
[317] WSRO, PAR 149/4/4
[318] WSRO, PHA 110
[319] WSRO, PHA 6572
[320] *Hampshire Telegraph*, 6 December 1830
[321] WSRO, PHA 12009, PHA 10495
[322] WSRO, PHA 2687
[323] WSRO, PAR 69/7/5
[324] *Brighton Gazette*, 2 December 1830
[325] Sockett to Hawley, 17 May 1836; quoted in the *Standard*. Considerable research into the work of the PEC and the emigrants who went was published in 2000: see Wendy Cameron and Mary McDougll Maude, *Assisting Emigration to Upper Canada, The Petworth Project, 1832–1837* (Montreal & Kingston: McGill-Queen's University Press, 2000) and *English Immigrant Voices, Labourers' Letters from Upper Canada in the 1830s,* ed. Wendy Cameron, Sheila Haines, and Mary McDougall Maude (Montreal and Kingston: McGill-Queen's University Press, 2000)
[326] PRO MH 32/38, Sept. 1835
[327] William Cobbett, *Two-Penny Trash, or, Politics for the Poor,* no.10, vol 11, 1 May 1832
[328] *BPP*, Select Committee on the Poor Laws, 9 March 1837
[329] *The Times,* 9 April 1933
[330] Thomas Sockett, Emigration: A Letter to a Member of Parliament
[331] WSRO, PHA 697
[332] WSRO, PHA 4457
[333] CRO, Hawkins Papers, J/3/2/805
[334] PRO, CO 384/39, f.316
[335] WSRO, PHA 1068, Sockett to Wyndham, 10 October 1838
[336] *English Immigrant Voices*, letter 127 from Ann Mann
[337] WSRO, PHA 1068, Sockett to Wyndham, 10 October 1838
[338] Thomas Robert Malthus, *On Population*, chap. IV of *Emigration*
[339] WSRO, PHA 729, Sockett to George Wyndham, December 1838
[340] Thomas Sockett, Emigration: A Letter to a Member of Parliament, 12
[341] WSRO, PHA 1068
[342] *Brighton Gazette*, April 1834
[343] Society for Promoting Christian Knowledge (SPCK), *Annual Report*, 1838
[344] WSRO, PHA 138, Log of the *England*
[345] *English Immigrant Voices*, letter 139 from Elizabeth (Pullen) Hooker
[346] PRO MH 12/13198
[347] *BPP*, Select Committee on Poor Relief (Gilbert Unions), 28 June 1844
[348] *Ibid*
[349] PRO, MH 12/13028, May 1835
[350] Thomas Love Peacock, *Crotchet Castle* (1831), chap. VI
[351] *BPP*, Select Committee on Poor Relief (Gilbert Unions), 28 June 1844

[352] PRO, MH 32/38, September 1834

[353] PRO, MH 32/39, September 1837

[354] WSRO, PHA 1099, 29 April 1835

[355] *BPP*, Select Committee on the Poor Law Amendment Act, 1837, evidence of John Stapley, June 1837

[356] PRO, MH 32/38, April 1835

[357] PRO, MH 32/38, January 1835

[358] PRO, MH 32/38, May 1836

[359] PRO, MH 32/38, April 1835

[360] *The Letters of Queen Victoria*, vol 1, Melbourne to Queen Victoria, 21 March 1842

[361] DNB, quoting from R. Wright's *Life of Wolfe*, p 329

[362] IGI; St Marylebone marriage register, 3 November 1794; Her Majesty's Court Service, the will of William Henry Toovey Hawley, 1868

[363] PRO, MH 32/39, April 1837

[364] *BPP*, Select Committee on the Poor Law Amendment Act, 16 March 1837

[365] PRO, MH 32/38, October 1835

[366] *BPP*, Select Committee on Poor Relief (Gilbert Unions) 1844, 28 June 1844

[367] PRO, MH 32/38, June 1836

[368] *The Standard*, 22 February 1837

[369] PRO, MH 12/13061, January 1837

[370] PRO, MH 12/13060, December 1835

[371] *Brighton Gazette*, 21 July 1836

[372] PRO, MH 32/38, August 1836

[373] *Hansard Parliamentary Debates*, 3d ser., vol. 36, 24 February 1837

[374] *Sussex Agricultural Express*, 11 February 1837

[375] PRO, MH 32/39, January 1837

[376] PRO, MH 32/39, September 1837

[377] For a lively account of Hawley in East Hampshire, see Ian Anstruther, *The Scandal of the Andover Workhouse* (Geoffrey Bles, 1973)

[378] *Hampshire Telegraph*, 10 April 1837

[379] *BPP, Select Committee on the Poor Law*, 9 March 1837

[380] Probate Registry, Her Majesty's Court Service, Will of William Henry Toovey Hawley, Proved 18 May 1874

[381] PRO, MH 32/39, January 1838

[382] WSRO, PHA 730, November 1840

[383] *BPP*, Select Committee on Poor Relief (Gilbert Unions), 1844, 28 June 1844

384 WSRO, MP 2317

[385] *Sussex Agricultural Express*, 10 June 1854, a popular ballad attributed to Mr Neal.

[386] 6 & 7 William IV c. 85 and c. 86

[387] *BPP*, Marriage and Divorce, vol. 3, 1830–96, 115

[388] Burial Act, 1852, 15 & 16 Vict. c. 85

[389] *Sussex Agricultural Express*, 19 August 1843

[390] *Sussex Agricultural Express*, 11 September 1852

[391] 15 & 16 Vict. c. 81

[392] See SPCK, tract 1725, *Kennerby Church, The Font*, 1874; and BL, Gathermole Collection, British Museum 908c5

[393] Charlotte M. Yonge, *The Daisy Chain; or, Aspirations* (n.p.: Macmillan, 1888), chap. VIII, 1856

[394] Tithe Commutation Act, 1836 (6 & 7 Will IV, c. 71)

[395] *Sussex Agricultural Express*, November 1840

[396] 1 & 2 Vict., c.106

[397] *Sussex Agricultural Express*, November 1840

[398] LRO, CORB 5/4/124/2 December 1844

[399] LRO, CORB 5/4/124/9, February 1829

[400] LRO, CORB 5/4/124/2, 29 January 1850

[401] *Sussex Agricultural Express,* 23 November 1850

[402] *Brighton Patriot and Lewes Free Press,* August 1836

[403] *Brighton Patriot and South of England Free Press*, 28 November 1837

[404] *Brighton Patriot and South of England Free Press,* 12 December 1837

[405] WSRO, PHA 110, Petworth Friendly Society, Copy of the Resolutions of the meeting held 13 September 1832

[406] *Sussex Agricultural Express*, 20 May 1837

[407] Attributed to Henry Russell, 1812–1900. With thanks to the English Folk Dance and Song Society

[408] *English Immigrant Voices,* letter 132, Elizabeth (Pullen) Hooker, and Ann and John Summersell, Petworth, to Richard and Frances Pullen, Delaware, Upper Canada, 22 April 1838

[409] *The Gentleman's Magazine,* vol. IX, January 1838

[410] *Sussex Agricultural Express,* 5 August 1837

[411] WSRO, PHA 7381

[412] Thomas Sockett, Journal, 17 August 1806

[413] WSRO, Zouche Papers, Parham 17/61, Harriet, Lady Zouche, to her mother, Tuesday, 14 November 1837

[414] *Sussex Agricultural Express*, 18 November 1837

[415] The Order for the Burial of the Dead, *Book of Common Prayer*

[416] WSRO, PHA 684

[417] *English Immigrant Voices*, letter 132

[418] WSRO, PHA 11096

[419] WSRO, PHA 11097

[420] WSRO, PHA 728

[421] See Leigh Lawson, 'Post-1837 Petworth Emigrants' online: www.petworthemigrations.com (consulted July 2006)

[422] WSRO, PHA 734

[423] WSRO, PHA 740

[424] WSRO, PHA 1066

[425] WSRO, PHA 7917

[426] WSRO, PHA 728

[427] *Sussex Agricultural Express,* 23 June 1838

[428] WSRO, PHA 11082

[429] WSRO, PHA 734

[430] WSRO, PHA 5275

[431] *Sussex Agricultural Express,* 23 June 1838

[432] WSRO, PHA 729

[433] WSRO, PHA 729, WSRO PHA 730. For an account of Murray before he became land steward to the Earl, see Peter Jerrome, 'One of That Atrocious Crew …', *Petworth Society Magazine,* June 2003

[434] WSRO, PHA 735

[435] *The Letters of Queen Victoria*, vol. 1, 1837–1843, 1 February 1842

[436] *Sussex Agricultural Express,* 30 June 1838, 29 January 1842

[437] *Sussex Agricultural Express,* 6 December 1846

[438] *Sussex Agricultural Express,* 4 November 1848

[439] WSRO PHA 729

[440] *BPP* 1847 (737) (737-II), VI. I, *Select Committee of House of Lords on Colonization from Ireland*, Minutes of Evidence, James M. Brydone, 18 June 1847

[441] WSRO, PHA 733

[442] WSRO, PHA 733

[443] WSRO, PHA 734, *Supplement to copies of the statements of Col Wyndham and Gen Wyndham; and the correspondence relating thereto* (Petworth: John Phillips, August 1839). The bulk of the material for an account of this quarrel is to be found in PHA 734; other sources are footnoted where appropriate

[444] J.A. Secord, 'Sir Henry Thomas De la Beche', *DNB* (OUP, 2004–6); WSRO, PHA 696 J.K. Greetham to George Wyndham, 26 April 1839

[445] WSRO, PHA 697, George Wyndham to Sockett, 7 November 1839

[446] *Brighton Guardian*, 23, 30 October, 6 November 1839

[447] WSRO, PHA 694

[448] *Brighton Guardian*, October 1839

[449] *Brighton Herald*, 29 March 1840

[450] WSRO, PHA 697, George Wyndham to Sockett, 7 November 1839

[451] See WSRO, PHA 1664 and PHA 1105, for the correspondence over this affair.

[452] WSRO, PHA 1105

[453] AO, F 129, Canada Co. Papers A–G–11, vol 2, 358

[454] WSRO, PHA 5389

[455] WSRO, PHA 697, Adelaide O'Keeffe to Sockett, June 1840

[456] Sockett to Brydone, 5 Nov 1827 Letter in the possession of Gary Wilson; C.R.O., J3/19/2081, Hawkins Papers; WSRO PHA 729; PHA 7837

[457] Surrey Local History Centre, QS 5/5/10, Entry book of patients to Lea Pale House, 1832–1851

[458] Surrey Local History Centre, QS 5/5/6, Visitors' Minute Book, 1836-1862

[459] Charles Lamb, *Letters of Charles Lamb*, to Mr Hudson, The Legacy Office, Somerset House, 1 Feb 1826

[460] WSRO, PHA 1664

[461] AO, F675, MU 1717, J.T. Leslie copybook (1843–1851), Letter to Sockett, n.d. [1842/1843]

[462] WSRO, PHA 1664

[463] AO, F675, MU 1717, J.T. Leslie copybook (1843–1851), Letter to Williamson, November 1845

[464] AO, F983-2, Correspondence of Bishop Strachan, 26 June 1846

[465] AO, F675, MU 1717, J.T, Leslie copybook (1843–1851), Letter to Williamson, 1845

[466] AO, F675, MU 717, J.T.Leslie Copybook, (1843–1851), Letter to Williamson, Oct 1848

[467] AO, F675 MU 1717, J.T. Leslie Copybook (1843–1851), Letter to Williamson, 20 Oct 20 1850

[468] WSRO, QAP 5/W5

[469] WSRO, PHA1664, and *Sussex Agricultural Express,* Nov 1841

[470] 22nd George III, cap 74

[471] Sheila R. Haines, *A Good Read: The East Sussex Bookhawking Assocation, 1855-88*, SAC 124(1986),227–41

[472] Anonymous navvy from John Burnett ed, *Useful Toil...*,(Allen Lane, 1974), 60

[473] WSRO, QAP/5/8 Bundle 1, part 11

[474] 1851 census of West Grinstead Rectory

[475] General Register Office, death certificate, 29 September 1857

[476] *Sussex Agricultural Express...*, 18 April 1857

[477] General Register Office, death certificate, 11 August 1852

[478] see F.F, Cartwright, *A Social History of Medicine*, Longman, 1977, Chapter 7

[479] WSRO, QAP/5/W18

[480] St George's Church, West Grinstead, Memorial Inscriptions, Area 4, Row 2, Stone 12

[481] AO, F675, MU 1715, J.T. Leslie's copybook (1843–1851), letter from Thomas Williamson to Mary Leslie, 10 June 1857

[482] WSRO, PHA 5392

[483] *Sussex Agricultural Express*, 6 June 1857.

[484] General Register Office, death certificate 28 December 1876

[485] General Register Office, death certificate 13 March 1889

[486] F.F. Cartwright, *A Social History of Medicine*, Longman, 1977, Chapter 7

[487] WSRO, PHA 1066

[488] WSRO, PHA 1664

[489] *Brighton Guardian*, 12 June 1839

[490] *Sussex Agricultural Express*, 2 May 1840

[491] *Ibid*

[492] WSRO, PHA 1066; J. T. Howard Turner, *The London, Brighton and South Coast Railway*, 1977, vol.1, 41

[493] *Brighton Guardian,* 29 July 1840

[494] *Sussex Agricultural Express*, 2 May 1840

[495] *The Letters of Queen Victoria...* ed, A. C. Benson, Murray, 1908, Vol 1, 256

[496] *Sussex Agricultural Express*, 13 March 1858

[497] K. G. Doern, *Balfour, Clara Lucas*, DNB, OUP, 2004–6

[498] *West Sussex Gazette*, 24 March 1859

[499] General Register Office death certificate, 22 March 1859

[500] WSRO, PAR 149, Marriage Register, 31 December 1850

[501] WSRO, Census of Petworth, 1861

[502] WSRO, STM 4, MF 1028

[503] WSRO, PHA 1113

[504] General Register Office, death certificate, 13 May 1862; WSRO, STM 4, MF 1028

[505] AO, MU 1714, f.675

[506] AO, RG 22/318, Wellington County Surrogate Court file 5693

[507] *Religious Census of England and Wales,* GRO, Report and Tables, Eyre and Spottiswoode, for HMSO, 1853

[508] *Sussex Agricultural Express,* December 1850

[509] WSRO, PHA 1113

[510] James Marr Brydone, *Mungo Park and Brydones of Selkirk* (privately printed)

[511] WSRO, PHA 13903

[512] AO, F 675, MU 1717, J.T. Leslie copybook (1843–1851)

[513] General Register Office, Petworth sub-district, certificate of death, 13 May 1862

[514] AO, F 675, MU 1715, John Thomas Honeywood Leslie to his mother and father, 8 November 1860

[515] AO, Wellington County Surrogate Court, will 88, MF 23

[516] AO, F 675, MU 1717, J.T. Leslie copybook

[517] AO, RG 22/318,Wellington County Surrogate Court file 5693

[518] AO, F 675, MU 1714, Mary Leslie to her sister Elizabeth, 10 October 1864

[519] AO, RG 22/318, Wellington County Surrogate Court, file 5693

ILLUSTRATION CREDITS

1. Thomas Sockett, 1841 by Thomas Phillips, the Reverend Thomas Sockett, courtesy of Lord Egremont, photograph. Courtauld Institute of Art.

2. The Beautiful Dolphin, the Performing Pig and the Mermaid. William Hone, Every-Day Book, 5 September 1826–7.

3. West Smithfield, from Horwood's Plan of London, 1792–1799. Courtesy of Guildhall Library, London. Image created by Adrian Hancock from two images.

4. Weston Lodge, William Cowper's house at Weston Underwood, 1822. Engraving by J. & H.S. Storer, London.

5. The Electrostatic machine. Photograph courtesy of Cowper & Newton Museum, Olney.

6. Hayley's house at Eartham 1792. WSRO PD 1425.

7. William Hayley. Engraving, 1779, by Johann Jacobé, after George Romney. WSRO F/PD 519.

8. George Romney 1784. Self portrait engraved by Thomas Wright. From *Memoirs of the Life and Works of George Romney* by Rev. John Romney, BD 1830. Baldwin & Cradock, London. ND 497 R7 University of Sussex Library.

9. Sheffield Place. T. W. Horsfield, *The History, Antiquities and Topography of The County of Sussex* (1835) Vol I p378.

10. Maria Josepha Holroyd 1795. Portrait by Edridge with Sheffield Place in the background. J.H. Adeane (ed.) *The Girlhood of Maria Josepha Holroyd [Lady Stanley of Alderley] recorded in Letters of a Hundred Years Ago: From 1776–1796*, Longman, Green & Co, 1896.

11. Elizabeth Ilive, Countess of Egremont. Photograph courtesy of Elinor Gallant and Allan Sewell.

12. Payment to Ann Wild, wet nurse to Lady Elizabeth Wyndham. WSRO PHA 8025.

13. Thomas Sockett's Journal 1805–1808, with example of shorthand. WSRO PHA 1679.

14. Stansted House, 1820. WSRO PD 1122.

15. William Carleton's Account with the Earl of Egremont, including a trip to Portsmouth, 1805. WSRP PHA 10496.

16. Drury Lane Theatre, 1804. *Old and New London*, Cassell & Co. Ltd. 1891.

17. Richard Roberts's account with the Earl of Egremont, for boats 1801–02. WSRO PHA 5951.

18. East Lodge, by W. A. Delamotte, 1853. Courtesy of Royal Pavilion Libraries and Museums.

19. Pitshill. Image by Adrian Hancock from a photograph, WSRO PH 1580.

20. The heading from an invoice for billiards, 1801. WSRO PHA 5951.

21. Charles Mitford, 1785–1831 as an Eton boy, with his college in background. From a miniature by J. Downman, 1800. WSRO Mitford Archives, LIB 5603.

22. Portrait of Charles of France (1757–1836) Count of Artois, future Charles X, King of France and Navarre (oil on canvas) by Danoux, Henri-Pierre (1753–1809) Chateau de Versailles, France / Lauros / Giraudon / The Bridgman Art Library.

23. Charles Ferdinand de France, Duc de Berri (1778–1820), 1814 (litho) by Delpech, Francois Seraphin (1778–1825) Private Collection / The Bridgman Art Library.

24. Cross Keys, St John's Street, Smithfield. John Tallis, 'London Street Views'. Peter Jackson, Nattali & Maurice, London Topographical Society. Courtesy of Guildhall Library.

25. The Royal Institution of Great Britain. From *Old and New London by* Edward Walford. Cassell & Co. 1891.

26. The Old Tennis Court, James Street. *Old and New London*, Cassell & Co. Ltd. 1891.

27. Thomas Sockett's Journal 1805–1808. Entry for baptism blacked out, 24 August 1806. WSRO PHA 1679.

28. North Scarle, Lincolnshire. Photograph by Leigh Lawson, 2002.

29. Northchapel church and rectory, from a drawing by Grimm, late-eighteenth century. *Gentleman's Magazine*, October 1833.

30. Plan of Northchapel Rectory; repairs, 1825. WSRO EPI/41/33.

31. Duncton Church, 1795. WSRO PD 2586 118.

32. Auction of Sockett's household goods on 12 May 1859 and following days. *West Sussex Gazette* 14 April 1859 p2, col 2.

33. Plan of Petworth parsonage 1819, Plan by Thomas Chrippes showing proposed repairs. WSRO EPI/ 41/36.

34. Thomas Chrippes's handritten estimate for repairs to the parsonage. WSRO Ep1/41/36.

35. Plan of Petworth Rectory by Thomas Chrippes, showing proposed repairs. WSRO EPI/ 41/36.

36. 'Reading Sentimental Novels'. Engraving by George Cruikshank (1792–1878).

37. Petworth House and Park. Engraving by J. Harwood from a work by A. Willmore. WSRO M/PD 273.

38. Emigration poster, by courtesy of the Trustees of the Goodwood Collections and with acknowledgements to the West Sussex Record Office and the County Archivist. ref: Goodwood Ms 1473 f185.

39. 'The Fine Old English Gentleman', melody and text by Henry Russell (1812–1900). With thanks to the English Folk Dance and Song Society.

40. Funeral procession of the 3rd Earl of Egremont, 21 November 1837. *Gentleman's Magazine*, January 1838.

41. Eramosa. The home of George and Ruth Sockett near Guelph, Ontario, Canada. Photograph by Sheila Haines, 1991.

42. Petworth House of Correction, 1860. WSRO PD 1471.

43. Reverend Henry Sockett 1818–1900 [n.d]. Archives of Ontario, F675, B1265, Mary Leslie fonds.

44. George Sockett, his wife Ellen Jane Duffield and their four children circa Christmas 1880. Archives of Ontario, F675, B1265, Mary Leslie fonds.

45. Thomas Sockett and his wife Mary Ann Clare, married 19 January 1865. Archives of Ontario, F675, B12665, Mary Leslie fonds.

46. The French bird-organ. Engraving by George C. Leighton, *Illustrated London News*, Volume 56, 1870.

Front cover: WSRO Mitford MS M/PD 273 detail.

Illustrations 6–10, 13, 21, 27, 30, 32–3, 35 and 43 photographed by Philip J. Brittan.

Family trees drawn by Adrian Hancock, who also repaired most of the illustrations in the book.

Index

House of Correction, 195, 219-221, 263
Literary and Scientific Institution, 225, 227
National School, 116, 136-138, 140, 145, 147
philosophic group, 37
Poor House, 128, 147, 175
Providence Chapel, 103, 232
rectory repairs, 107-113
Savings Bank, 105
Petworth House,
laboratory, 37-38
lake, 36, 38, 42, 226
library, 36, 38, 116
Lunar Globe, 37
managery [menagerie], 35
toys in the nursery, 35
Phillips, John (printer and stationer), 80, 158, 213, 264
pigs, 5, 6, 9, 28, 127-129, 143, 239
Pilkington, Henry (Asst. Poor Law Commissioner), 169-71, 264
Pitt, William, 23, 264
Pitshill / Pits Hill (house, West Sussex), 58, 61, 63, 115, 263
bills for food, 61
poaching, 143-144, 146, 231
Poor Law Commissioners, 115, 128, 149,156-7, 167, 169-182, 185
Poor Law Guardians, 147-148, 170-173,177, 181
Portsmouth, Hampshire, 41, 44-51, 117, 156, 160, 163, 166
dockyard, 41, 50-51, 117
George Hotel, 44-45
printers and stationers, 25, 31, 35, 89, 137, 158
Pott's disease, 33
Pulborough, West Sussex, 57, 83, 265
Pullen, Elizabeth, mother of Petworth emigrant, 164, 193, 197, 264
puppets, 6

Queen Anne's Bounty, 108, 186
quoits/Coits, 21

races,
Ascot, 116
Brighton, 65, 82
Cheltenham, 216
Epsom, 116
Lewes, 65, 152
Raddish, Thomas, Revd., 91-92, 264
railways, 3, 51, 156, 200, 227
Ratcliffe Highway (London), 9, 18, 31
Registrar of Births, Marriages and Deaths, 183
Religious Census 1851, 232
Religious Tract Society, 7
Reynolds, Mary Ann Maria, *see Langshaw*
Richmond, 5th Duke, 118, 121-122, 124, 135, 149, 160, 188, 264
Ridsdale, Robert, Revd., 139, 229, 264
Robertson, William (historian), 56-57, 70
Rogate Lodge, West Sussex, 196, 211
Roman Catholic Church, 7, 103, 187, 233
Romney, George (artist), 15-21, 89, 264
Roscoe, William (writer), 54-56, 265
Rose, Samuel (lawyer), 24-25, 265
Royal Institution, 76-77, 79, 226, 259

St Bartholomew's Fair (London), 6, 9
St Bartholomew's Hospital (London), 6
St John's Street (London), 5, 11, 76-78
Scott, Elizabeth Ann, *see Wyndham, Elizabeth Ann*
Select Committees,
Education of the Poor (1818), 138
Poor Law Amendment Act (1837), 83
Poor Relief (Gilbert Unions, 1844), 108
Postage (1838), 121
sermons, 121, 133, 135, 139, 164, 195, 220, 223
Shakespeare Press, 89